Social Work and the City

Charlotte Williams
Editor

Social Work and the City

Urban Themes in 21st-Century Social Work

palgrave
macmillan

Editor
Charlotte Williams
School of Global, Urban and Social Studies
RMIT University
Melbourne, Victoria, Australia

ISBN 978-1-137-51622-0   ISBN 978-1-137-51623-7   (eBook)
DOI 10.1057/978-1-137-51623-7

Library of Congress Control Number: 2016940593

Cover illustration: © Zoonar GmbH / Alamy Stock Photo

Printed on acid-free paper

This Palgrave Macmillan imprint is published by Springer Nature
The registered company is Macmillan Publishers Ltd. London

Contents

Part I **Making Sense of the City** 1
Charlotte Williams

1 **Social Work and *The Urban Age*** 15
Charlotte Williams

2 **Beyond the Soup Kitchen** 43
Charlotte Williams

3 **Reconstructing Urban Social Work** 71
Charlotte Williams

4 **Social Work Research and the City** 97
Charlotte Williams

Part II   Social Issues and the City: New Directions in Practice   121
Charlotte Williams

5   **Superdiversity and the City**   127
Dirk Geldof

6   **Ageing in Urban Environments: Challenges and Opportunities for a Critical Social Work Practice**   151
Chris Phillipson and Mo Ray

7   **Disabling Cities and Repositioning Social Work**   173
Michael J. Prince

8   **Care, Austerity and Resistance**   193
Donna Baines

9   **Homelessness in Western Cities**   215
Carole Zufferey

10   **Living on the Edge: New Forms of Poverty and Disadvantage on the Urban Fringe**   235
Sonia Martin and Robin Goodman

11   **Educating for Urban Social Work**   259
Susie Costello and Julian Raxworthy

Conclusion: Urban Themes in Twenty-First Century Social Work   281
Charlotte Williams

Index   289

Notes on Contributors

Editor's Biography

Charlotte Williams, OBE is Professor and Deputy Dean Social Work at RMIT University, Melbourne, Australia. She is a qualified social worker and has over 25 years of experience in social work education. Her research is underpinned by an interdisciplinary body of theory drawing largely on comparative social policy, critical race theory, social geography, social development, and theories of migration and multiculturalism. She has extensively theorised issues of place, locality and nationhood as they impact on welfare practices, particularly in relation to the racialisation or exclusion of minoritised groups. Her most recent publications include: *Social Work in a Diverse Society: Transformatory Practice with Ethnic Minority Individuals and Communities* (with M. Graham) (Policy Press, 2016); the Special Issue of the *British Journal of Social Work* entitled 'A World on the Move': Migration, Mobilities and Social Work (2014) (co-edited with M. Graham); and *Race and Ethnicity in a Welfare Society* (2010) (with M. Johnson), Open University Press.

Contributors' Biographies

Donna Baines is Professor of Social Work and Social Policy at the University of Sydney. Professor Baines has published extensively on managerialism and restructuring social service work under neo-liberalism, and now under austerity. She also publishes in the area of anti-oppressive and critical approaches to social work practice. Professor Baines has published recently on care work in the *Journal of Social Work*, *Critical Social Policy* and the *Journal of Industrial Relations*, and is working on the third edition of her best-selling (in Canada) edited collection *Doing Anti-Oppressive Practice, Social Justice Social Work* (Fernwood, 2017).

Susie Costello is a Senior Lecturer in Social Work in the School of Global Urban and Social Studies at RMIT University in Melbourne, Australia. Her practice background was in family social work in child protection, family support, disability and psychiatry in health and institutional settings. Her last role as a social work practitioner was with the City of Yarra in Victoria, where alongside where responding to the welfare needs of families, council social workers contributed to the planning and infrastructure of the city, for example, participating in the implementation of the Disability Discrimination Action Plan to upgrade streets and services across the city and advocating for safety for vulnerable residents as part of the city's Community Safety Strategy. Susie's publication and research interests include violence against women, indigenous homelessness, cross-cultural education and international social work. She leads RMIT's initiatives in contributing to urban planning in cities in Myanmar.

Dirk Geldof is Professor at the Faculty of Design Sciences of the University of Antwerp (Belgium), lecturer and researcher at the Higher Institute for Family Sciences (Odisee University College, Brussels) and lecturer in Social Work at the Karel de Grote-University College (Antwerp). He holds a PhD in Political and Social Sciences from the University of Antwerp. In 2013, he published *Superdiversiteit. Hoe migratie onze samenleving verandert* (Acco, 5th edn, 2015). The English edition *Superdiversity in the Heart of Europe: The Belgian Case* will be published in January 2016 (Acco).

Robin Goodman is Professor of Sustainability and Urban Planning and Deputy Dean in the School of Global Urban and Social Studies at RMIT University in Melbourne, Australia. Robin holds a BA (Hons) from La Trobe University, and a Masters of Urban Planning and a PhD from the University of Melbourne. She was the Director of RMIT's Australian Housing and Urban Research Institute (AHURI) Research Centre for three years from 2010, and subsequently the inaugural Director of the Centre for Urban Research. Robin has published widely on issues around planning, public policy, sustainability and housing. She is co-author of a forthcoming book entitled *Growing Pains: Planning Melbourne in the 21st Century*.

Sonia Martin is a Lecturer and Programme Manager in Social Work at RMIT University, where she teaches in the fields of social policy and social research. Sonia has previously worked at the Universities of South Australia, Adelaide and Melbourne and the Brotherhood of St Laurence in the Research and Policy Centre. Her work on a large three-year ARC Linkage grant at the University of Melbourne contributed to the award-winning publication *Half a Citizen: Life on Welfare in Australia*.

Grounded in the discipline of sociology, her research interests include quantitative and qualitative analyses of poverty, inequality and social exclusion; theoretical issues to do with agency, structure and 'choice', and contemporary social policy arrangements and welfare reform.

Chris Phillipson is Professor of Sociology and Director of the Manchester Interdisciplinary Collaboration for Research on Ageing (MICRA), based at the University of Manchester, UK. Before moving to Manchester, Phillipson held a variety of posts at Keele University, including Dean of Research for the Social Sciences and Director of the Social Science Research Institutes. He was also a Pro-Vice Chancellor for the University and founded (in 1987) the Centre for Social Gerontology. He has published extensively on a range of topics in the field of ageing, including work in the field of family and community studies, transnational migration, social inclusion/exclusion, urban sociology and social theory. He is the co-author of the *Sage Handbook of Social Gerontology* (Sage Books, 2010), *Work, Health and Wellbeing* (co-authored, Policy Press, 2012), and

Ageing (Polity Press, 2013). His present research involves work around the theme of developing 'age-friendly cities' where he co-ordinates a research project based in a number of neighbourhoods in Manchester. He is a Fellow of the Gerontological Society of America and a Past-President of the British Society of Gerontology.

Michael J. Prince is a Professor and holds the Lansdowne Chair in Social Policy in the Faculty of Human and Social Development, University of Victoria, Canada. Among his books are *Changing Politics of Canadian Social Policy* (with J. J. Rice, University of Toronto Press, 2nd edn, 2013), *Rules and Unruliness: Canadian Regulatory Democracy, Governance, Capitalism, and Welfarism*, (with G. G. Doern and R. J. Schultz, McGill-Queen's University Press, 2014), and *Struggling for Social Citizenship: Disabled Canadians, Income Security, and Prime Ministerial Eras* (McGill-Queen's University Press, 2016).

Julian Raxworthy is a Landscape Architect. He has an Honours Bachelor degree and research Master's degree (by design) in landscape architecture from RMIT, Australia, where he was also a Senior Lecturer until 2004. He was a Senior Lecturer at the Queensland University of Technology (QUT) from 2005 until 2011. He has been a registered landscape architect in Australia and is now registered as a Professional Landscape Architect in South Africa, where he is a Lecturer in the Master of Landscape Architecture programme at the University of Cape Town. Raxworthy completed his PhD with the University of Queensland, Australia, in 2013, concerning the relationship between gardening and landscape architecture, which he is currently adapting into a book to be published by MIT Press in 2017: *Overgrowing Landscape Architecture*. A co-founder of *Kerb*, the student landscape architecture journal from RMIT in 2004, he co-edited *The MESH Book: Landscape & Infrastructure*, RMIT Press, and, in 2011, Sun Publishers in Amsterdam published *Sunburnt: Landscape Architecture in Australia*, co-authored with Professor Sue-Anne Ware.

Mo Ray is Professor of Gerontological Social Work and Programme Director for Social Work in the School of Social Science and Public

Policy at the University of Keele, Staffordshire. She holds a PhD in Social Gerontology from the University of Keele. She spent many years as a social worker and manager specialising in practice with older people, and remains a registered social worker with an active interest in practice. Her research and writing include social relationships in later life and social work practice with older people. She has developed and delivered a range of inter-disciplinary, continuous professional development courses to support the development of Age Friendly Cities and environments.

Carole Zufferey is a Senior Lecturer at the School of Psychology, Social Work and Social Policy. She completed her PhD on social work and homelessness in 2008 at the University of South Australia. Her research interests include social work, social policy and social work education responses to housing, home, homelessness, children and domestic violence.

List of Abbreviations and Acronyms

ACGA	Australian Common Ground Alliance
CBD	Central business district
COS	Charity Organisation Society
CRPD	United Nations Convention on the Rights of Persons with Disabilities
EU	European Union
GIS	Geographical Information Systems
GNAFC	Global Network of Age Friendly Cities
IFSW	International Federation of Social Work
NGO	Non-governmental organisation
OECD	Organisation for Economic Co-operation and Development
OoH	Office of Housing
PIE	Person in environment
QGIS	Qualitative Geographical Information Systems
RCT	Randomised control trial
WHO	World Health Organization

List of Figures

Fig. 10.1   Housing stress across Melbourne   242

Part I

Making Sense of the City

Charlotte Williams

Introduction and Overview

Social work is a creation of city life. The profession was born and grew up in the city, and has evolved a particular symbiotic connectedness to matters of the city. Its defining methodologies and approaches emerged as a response to the impacts of nineteenth-century industrialisation, urban growth and development. In many ways, the city has shaped the profession and professional identity. This process is far from over. In the contemporary era, social work is being reconceptualised in response to the modern city. It is being reshaped by technological developments, by the speed and scale of demographic diversity, by new sources of distress and disadvantage and, significantly, by new forms of politics and governance.

C. Williams (✉)
School of Global, Urban and Social Studies,
GPO Box 2476, Melbourne, VIC 3001, Australia

© The Editor(s) (if applicable) and The Author(s) 2016
C. Williams (ed.), *Social Work and the City*,
DOI 10.1057/978-1-137-51623-7

1

Today's city is changing rapidly and, in tandem, social work is in the process of reworking its role, approaches, thinking and identity alongside these developments.

An urban revolution is happening under our noses. Cities across the world are being radically transformed, both growing and shrinking within the flux and turbulence of global processes. All around us, places are changing in ways that are both exciting and threatening—and nowhere is the impact of change more keenly felt than in the metropolis (Glaeser 2011). It is possible to be simultaneously fascinated and troubled by what we witness: spectres of deepening impoverishment appear alongside advances that produce emancipation and empowerment. Urbanisation is identified as one of the most significant social trends of the twenty-first century. By the turn of the twenty-first century, more than 50% of the world's population were city-dwellers (50+ %) and this figure is set to grow to some 75% by 2050 (UN-Habitat 2012). Now, more than at any point in history, people are resident in urbanised areas. The scale and pace of this change is unprecedented—particularly so in the developing world, where nine out of ten people are living in cities in Africa and Asia. We are experiencing the so-called 'Urban Age' (Gleeson 2012), the century of the city, and we cannot ignore it.

Amidst profound political, economic, environmental and technological upheavals—which are the result of global economic restructuring—vulnerabilities are exaccerbated, inequalities are growing and new forms of need are emerging. These impacts coincide with a deepening crisis in welfare provisioning as Western democracies have restructured and residualised provision under neo-liberal politics. The reconfiguration of welfare states is by no means an even process. Different states will reflect different manifestations of this political trend. However, notable similarities are apparent in neo-liberal tendencies cross-nationally. The creation of a mixed economy of welfare, the retraction of certain forms of welfare spending and the residualisation of services are noted characteristics of this trend, as are the reconfiguration of the relationship between the state and the individual, and increasing reliance on self-help and on decentralised forms of service delivery (Harris 2014). Our professional positioning demands both an examination and a response to the complex configurations of need produced by these effects.

As a profession, we have set our sights high in relation to addressing these global impacts on human wellbeing. The Global Agenda for Social Work (IFSW 2012), for example, commits the profession to promoting economic and social equality, to promoting the dignity and worth of individuals, to strengthening human relationships and to working towards environmental sustainability. The reach and the breadth of these ambitions is constantly growing as social work seeks to engage with the causes of social distress whilst, at the same time, working on its manifestations in everyday life. Such a manifesto can be overwhelming and produce a sense of ineffectualness, given the magnitude of what is at stake. Social workers are frequently berated—both for having limited horizons and for their 'heroic agency' in aspiring to effect social change (Marston and McDonald 2012). We require analytical scales in order to make sense of this, parameters against which to calibrate the effectiveness of interventions and, I would argue, a sphere in which to assert claims for recognition. Cities mediate scale. They are socio-cultural, economic and physical environments that give context to welfare relations. They are the spaces in which global processes are realised and encountered, and the locale in which social work can lay claim to being a key stakeholder.

It is perhaps more useful to assert that social work is, of necessity, *glocal*, as it operates at the intersection of local, national and global scales (Hong and Han Song 2010). Global events and processes are lived and shaped in everyday lives, and most acutely influenced within arenas that are proximate and immediate. In the contemporary moment, we stand between two countervailing trends. On the one hand, governments and private businesses seek greater levels of globalisation; on the other, across the world a localisation movement is emerging generated by local lives. In this respect, the social work task is multi-layered, embedded in national policy contexts but, at the same time, transcending them in recognising interdependencies that are transnational. The argument of this text is that the city provides an appropriate parameter for action for social work energies, a context within which concerns with the everyday micro-experiences and the wider social structural processes shaping those experiences can be mediated—a context within which our compelling stories can come to bear.

Yet, as a profession, we have neglected to reconsider and re-theorise our relationship to this twenty-first-century phenomenon. For a number of reasons, not least the very symbiotic connectedness of the profession to matters urban, the city has been largely assumed, rather than interrogated. As social workers, we have been seen as so much *of* the place that a critical revisiting of our positioning, role, strategies and identity within urban contexts has eluded us. The city itself has been subsumed by a focus on responding to its impacts; to issues such as homelessness, migration, sex trafficking, street children, poverty and more. It has, perhaps, been too familiar, too known, as academics and commentators have looked outward to other compelling concerns: the nature of rural social work (Pugh and Cheers 2010), environmental and 'green' social work (Dominelli 2012), globalisation (Dominelli 2010) and internationalism (Gray 2005, Gray and Webb 2010), all of which have more recently captured our attention within the profession. Yet, cities lie at the heart of these political, economic and social processes that define and shape the contemporary world. As such, the city readily maps onto wider perspectives that have emerged in social work, such as concern with environmental ecologies and sustainability, with migration and diversity; yet, examination of the processes of urbanisation itself has been neglected.

Cities matter to people, they place and shape (if not determine) what people can do and how they relate. They generate forms of distress, distrust and disadvantage, producing what has been called *the urban condition* (Meyer 1976) and simultaneously they generate opportunities for the resolution of contemporary issues. Putting people back into the picture as agents of change, valorising their investments in identity and place, opens up the city as a creative space for social work practice and for the co-production of social work knowledge. These matters deserve our attention, for evaluation of the strategies that are being deployed, for a consideration of how social work is responding to new demands and for a consideration of social work itself.

The insights of this text are no less relevant to understanding the issues of rural areas. Depopulation, out-migration, environmental sustainability, social reciprocities and exchange, and other forms of interdependency between town and country can be revealed via an examination of cities. Urban sprawl affects rural ecologies and economies, and urban policies; for example, transport, waste disposal and water supply impact on rural dwellers. Cities form a focal point for rural inhabitants in terms of access to critical services and cultural opportunities, and act as sites for the expression of protest and making the public's voice heard over political issues that affect them. Hence, it is argued cities act as hubs of human development as a whole (UN-Habitat 2012).

This book takes as its starting point the view that social work practice is a product of its milieu. It argues that the rapid transformation of cities presents new challenges and opportunities for the profession in terms of its methodologies, skills and identity. Accordingly, it is timely to revisit social work's relationship to the city. This revisiting will require looking back and looking forward, drawing on social work histories to consider continuities and departures as social work mutates in context. It will require interrogating those antecedants in setting the course forward. There are spatial visionings and social work scripts of the city to inquire into, new methodologies being proposed, new forms of collaboration in addressing social issues and innovative interventions to foreground. Above all, this exploration will make disciplinary departures in order to engage with insights emerging from urban studies, social geography and cultural sociology.

Orientation, Themes and Approaches: Some Useful Starting Points

Despite the catchy title of the book, it is more accurate to speak about cities than 'the city'. Cities are extremely diverse: they differ in their demographic profile, economic infrastructure, institutional arrangements, transport and other aspects of the built environment; they also vary in terms of their global location and connectedness. However, in critically exploring the concept of *the urban age*, I construct the city as an entity (here, there or anywhere) that requires theoretical and conceptual examination in order to unravel key themes, issues and debates about twenty-first-century transformations and their significance for social work. Indeed, as will become clear, the city is a social construction, an idiom of our making, to which we apply our disciplinary orientation. The question I pose is: What are the specificities of the city for social work consideration and in what ways is the profession responding to this urban dynamic?

There are, of course, a number of theoretical orientations applicable to the analysis of the city as explored in the opening chapter, which draw on a rich tradition in the social sciences. With various emphasis these insights enable us to probe aspects of the social relations of the city at multi-level, accommodating the relationship between the everyday micro-experience and the wider structural processes shaping that very experience. These are not simply analytical abstractions. As a profession, we are concerned with applications, with making change for the better, with interventions and the evaluation of our interventions, with constructing and articulating visions of socially just futures. Cities as an arena of governance provide proximate spaces of influence and opportunity for social work. Thus, I contend that city-making is a process in which we are deeply implicated and in which we have a role to play.

Social work is also a construction characterised by competing claims as to its nature, role, focus of intervention and visionings of the future. It is an activity that is highly contextual, reflecting cultural norms and orientations, and organisational and policy contexts. Yet, at the same time, there are master narratives of origins and destinations; dominant discourses that mark out the professional remit, claims and aspirations, values and knowledges. I don't seek here to reduce that contestation and diversity. This book works with the construction of social work in its broadest sense, combining multiple roles and actors engaged in practice interventions directly and indirectly, group and community work, those running non-governmental organisations (NGOs), and those working in policy, advocacy work and research. Lavalette (2013) has recently used the term 'popular social work' to embrace a wide range of roles and responsibilities undertaken by human service workers, social support and care workers alongside those working in professional and statutory roles. It is the nature of the alliances, the values orientation and the goals that cohere this broad set of activities that comprises social work in the city.

This text seeks to reinsert urban themes in contemporary social work. A clear departure is made from those writers who argue for the individualisation of response as a counter to the forces of alienation, anonymisation and anomie produced by the alien city and 'the urban crisis' (for example, Meyer 1976), and also from those who favour analysis of interventions based on the city as a system (Kolko Phillips and Lala Ashenberg Straussner 2002), or other extensions of functionalist analysis. Neither does this text fall foul of the logjam afforded by purely structural analyses of capitalist accumulation alone. This book eschews such approaches and seeks to explore, elucidate and illustrate how cities are complex *relational* entitites that are experienced and negotiated by multiple stakeholders in multiple ways. It is this shifting, fluid and dynamic propensity that should capture the imagination of social work and extend practice in useful and effective ways.

In establishing a normative basis to orient this book, I propose three central and inter-related concepts fundamental to social work practice: *social justice*, *care* and *sustainability*. These concepts speak to social work legacies in the city and provide a shorthand to encapsulate its contemporary aspirations.

As a profession, we aspire to contribute to extending social justice in terms of issues of recognition, promoting and enhancing rights, and enabling redistribution (Fraser 2009). These considerations raise questions about the nature of urban citizenship for some groups: why they live where they live; how they exert presence and power over place; how they participate and gain access to services, and create and mobilise well-being in place; and how they collectively organise resistance and voice their wishes and wants. Such social justice considerations will require an understanding of cities and their power relations—both the ways in which cities produce inequalities and the ways in which these are experienced and countered.

Cities also inspire us to consider the ways in which we relate to the immediacies of the contemporary moment, and the opportunties and deficits in how we relate to each other. Matters of cohesion, integration, reciprocities and care giving, conviviality and exchange that have emerged in social science literature are core social work concerns. Putting people into places and spaces in the context of care relationships that can be enabled or hindered are important dimensions of practice and signal our added value in these uncertain times. These critical elements of social work practice can be brought into view and mobilised under the broad concept of caring and care work, both as individual and collective practice. The concept of care in this sense can be extended in a variety of ways, not simply to consider the materialities of physical places and spaces of care, and the nature of care work, but also to track, enable and promote the plethora of exchange and reciprocities encumbent on the crafting of a *caring and inclusive city*.

None of this will have impact unless it can be maintained and sustained. The concept of sustainability—interpreted here as the ability to produce and reproduce those elements that maintain beneficial change—is gradually entering social work discourse, most particularly in relation to environmental sustainability (Coates 2003). That is not its specific usage here. Much has been written in social work about environmental sustainability that can be drawn on in relation to urbanisation and the city (McKinnon 2008; Bay 2010; Borrell et al. 2010; Zapf 2010).Here, the concern is to highlight the concept of *social* sustainability, which provides a way of thinking about empowerment of individual and community capacity and strengths, and the promotion of quality of life via a holistic integration of economic, social and environmental wellbeing (Coates 2003; Mary 2008). Human wellbeing, equity and democratic participation in governance are central constituents of social sustainability.

Much of this conceptual framework is reflected in what van Ewijk (2009) has recently labelled 'citizenship-based social work', which must be extended to capture those placed somehow beyond the nation-state yet within the realm of infra-political activity of any city. In reconstructing an urban social work, this book draws on this conceptual apparatus and the argument is made for social workers mobilised by an ethic of care to be framed as innovators, fixers, creators and entrepreneurs in the urban space, crafting and seizing opportunities in an effort to generate collaborative change. It returns to considerations of place and locates social work within a network of key social actors, as buffers and negotiators in localised welfare regimes, foregrounding co-production, co-operation, support and care, and facilitating participation in the making and shaping of the city. It extrapolates social work's capacity-enhancing roles, its roles in nurturing social solidarities, its social advocacy roles and its contribution to what Gleeson ultimately calls 'the good city' (2014).

It is important not to decontextualise the potentials of a reconstructed social work for the city from the powerful orchestrating force of neo-liberal politics dominating social work. In an era of economic austerity sweeping major Western cities, the residualisation of service delivery is apparent everywhere. It is a time when the euphemism of welfare consumerism and choice are overused to disguise reliance on self-help and self-sufficiency as government assistance is withdrawn. There are, of course, a number of cautions to be signalled in any celebratory call to cities and the resurgence of place-based localised initiatives. This is not a recipe for state withdrawal, or for patching and stitching the fabric of a worn-out version of social work's compensatory roles. Far from it. The contemporary stand-off from neo-liberal politics suggests the mobilisation of counter-narratives, the search for and demonstration of robust alternative interventions and their evaluation, and demonstrating a significant handing over of power in co-operatively designing the way forward. To do this will require a repositioning for social work. The effectiveness of the profession will be encumbent on the forging of new connections and collaborations, and seizing on the available spaces for action, both formal and informal. We have to understand the processes of urbanisation, city life and city living if we are to respond effectively to the scenario presented by *the urban age.*

The Structure of the Book

This text explores ways of thinking about the city and their relevance for the profession, and provides a foundation for these considerations. It invites the reader to give critical consideration to notions of urban crisis and to engage with the challenges and opportunities of the contemporary city. It aims to delineate the social work role with regard to other critical stakeholders—including service users themselves, welfare and community workers, planners and policy-makers, academics and activists. It considers how the profession is adapting to transformations in the city and what this means for social work identities and those invested in making and shaping the city.

The book is conceived in two parts. In Part I, I focus in Chap. 1 on the nature of the contemporary challenge and how we can make sense of it, drawing on a body of theory. In Chap. 2, I explore social work's historic relationship to the city and, in so doing, begin the work of re-theorising the relationship between social work and the city via a selection of key areas of focus: place and space, scale, sustainability and new civic governance. The book argues for a reconstructed approach and draws on the descriptive accounts of social workers in one city to complement messages from the literature, discussed in Chap. 3. This chapter draws out some principles for urban practice. Finally, in Chap. 4, which concludes Part I, I look at existing social work research in the field and suggest new lines of enquiry for social work investigation.

In Part II of the book, I introduce seven case studies which have been selected for the way in which they illustrate a new angle or perspective for social work in the context of urban dynamics. I refer to them as case studies in the sense that they explore a social issue of significance in modern city life by outlining the ways in which this issue is manifest in the debates it raises for consideration and by pointing to innovations and techniques being developed and anticipated for practice. There are invited contributions from the UK, continental Europe, Canada and Australia. I introduce these more fully in the Introduction to Part II. The selective areas are by no means exhaustive. There could have been any number of these but there are, as yet, few scholars in the field substantively engaging with urban perspectives. My collaborations in this endeavour arose serendipitously. I sought out those who are experts in their field, in the sense that they are with working at the frontier of some of the key issues pertinent to this debate: poverty, diversity, disability and ageing, homelessness and care work, or seeking out interesting cross-disciplinary collaborations in pursing city work, in this case co-learning.

About the Author

This book represents a collaborative project in forging connections between social work and urban theorising and planning. It is not a book about social work *in* the city but, rather, about social work *and* the city in efforts to urbanise social work thinking and action more deeply. I began my social work career as a housing welfare officer working in the local council offices in semi-rural Wales. I was, at that time, co-located in the town hall with environmental and urban planners, those working in accounting and finance, and those working on the built environment of the local authority. I wasn't located with the professional social workers working in social services and I had to work hard to assert social work perspectives with my colleagues in the town hall day-by-day. They were more interested in managing houses and estates than the people in them, and my colleagues down the road were more interested in responding to the crisis of individuals within the houses, rather than setting their sights on neighbourhoods, environments and the power of people in place. My core responsibilities were to attend to those presenting as homeless, to assess those seeking a place on the housing waiting lists and to make home visits to problematic families who could have just been messing up property owned by the local authority. I got used to tramping the housing estates on foot. I got used to talking to people in the street and getting to understand their problems. I got used to taking local councillors on walkabouts to demonstrate this point or that; I got used to lobbying and I quickly learned where the points of leverage were—and how to use them and with whom. There's a long story here which includes parochialism, territorialism, siloed thinking and professional enmities, financial cycles and institutional priorities. But what I did learn fast was that the inter-relationship between these sets of concerns is a matter of fact. The physical and material world is not irrelevant to doing social work. How people live, how people can live, the sense they make of their everyday lived experiences and their power over place is crucial to welfare delivery and welfare receipt.

My interest in the perspectives and politics of place, boundaries and border crossings has never left me, whether rural or urban, thinking across scales of governance—international, national, regional and devolved, or, indeed, the crossing of disciplinary borders to adventure into the new terrain of other disciplinary spaces. All have been part of my academic enterprise. I began with the rural and the locality, later devolution in the UK provided a spur to my thinking, in particular the social policy of Wales that foregrounds place-based welfare delivery. This current project of revisiting the city is inspired by my experience of Melbourne and the co-location of social work with sustainability and urban planning at RMIT University. Herein lies one of the caveats of this text. The issues confronting Western cities outlined in this book draw on my experiential and research base. That is not to discount the insights gleaned from cities in the global south or to ignore their inter-relationships—inter alia issues such as migration, global care chains, and immense global inequalities and exploitations. My 'note to self' here is to acknowledge that the paths of my reading and research are Western and that there are some important distinctions to be flagged between city concerns in the global north and those of the global south.

This venture is tentative and I hope others will be inspired to explore the refreshed urban practice.

References

Bay, U. (2010). Social work and the environment: Understanding people and place. *Australian Social Work, 63*(3), 366–367.

Borrell, J., Lane, S., & Fraser, S. (2010). Integrating environmental issues into social work practice: Lessons learned from domestic energy auditing. *Australian Social Work, 63*(3), 315–328.

Coates, J. (2003). *Ecology and social work: Toward a new paradigm.* Halifax/Nova Scotia: Fernwood Publishing.

Dominelli, L. (2010). Globalisation, contemporary challenges and social work practice. *International Social Work, 53*(5), 599–612.

Dominelli, L. (2012). *Green social work: From environmental crisis to environmental justice.* Cambridge: Polity Press.

Fraser, N. (2009). *Scales of justice: Reimagining political space in a globalizing world.* New York: Columbia University Press.

Glaeser, E. (2011). *The triumph of the city: How urban spaces make us human.* London: Pan Macmillan.

Gleeson, B. (2012). The urban age: Paradox and prospect. *Urban Studies, 49*(5), 931–943.

Gleeson, B. (2014). Coming through Slaughter. MSSI Issues Paper No. 3, Melbourne Sustainable Society Institute, University of Melbourne. http://www.sustainable.unimelb.edu.au/files/mssi/MSSI-IssuesPaper-3_Gleeson_2014_0.pdf. Accessed 10 July 2015.

Gray, M. (2005) Dilemmas of international social work: paradoxical processes in indigenisation, universalism and imperialism. *International Journal of Social WelfareVolume*, 14(3), 231–238.

Gray, M., & Webb, S. (2010). *International social work*. London: Sage.

Harris, J. (2014). (Against) neoliberal social work. *Critical and Radical Social Work, 2*(1), 7–22.

Hong, Y. P., & Han Song, I. (2010). Glocalization of social work practice: Global and local responses to globalization. *International Social Work, 53*(5), 656–670.

IFSW (International Federation of Social Work). (2012). A global agenda for social work and social development. http://ifsw.org/get-involved/agenda-for-social-work/. Accessed 5 Sept 2015.

Kolko Phillips, N., & Lala Ashenberg Straussner, S. (2002). *Urban social work: An introduction to policy and practice in the cities*. Boston: Allyn and Bacon.

Lavalette, M. (2013). The hidden history of popular social work (Inaugural lecture). https://www.youtube.com/watch?v=v5lXClLDo_c. Accessed 5 Sept 2015.

Marston, G. and McDonald C. (2012) Getting beyond 'Heroic Agency' in Conceptualising Social Workers as Policy Actors in the Twenty-First Century, British Journal of Social Work, 2012, Vol. 42(6), pp.1022-1038

Mary, N. L. (2008). *Social work in a sustainable world*. Chicago: Lyceum.

McKinnon, J. (2008). Exploring the nexus between social work and the environment. *Australian Social Work, 61*(3), 256–268.

Meyer, C. (1976 [1970]). *Social work practice: A response to the urban crisis*. New York: Free Press.

Pugh, R., & Cheers, B. (2010). *Rural social work: An international perspective*. Bristol: Policy Press.

UN-Habitat (United Nations Habitat). (2012). State of the worlds cities 2012/2013. http://unhabitat.org/books/prosperity-of-cities-state-of-the-worlds-cities-20122013/. Accessed 10 July 2015.

van Ewijk, H. (2009). Citizenship-based social work. *International Social Work, 52*(2), 167–179.

Zapf, M. K. (2010). Social work and the environment: Understanding people and place. *Critical Social Work, 11*(3), 30–46.

1

Social Work and *The Urban Age*

Charlotte Williams

Introduction

Cities are back on the map. They are being talked about and talked up in terms of large-scale initiatives capable of changing how we live and as being vibrant hubs of social change and development (UN-Habitat 2012, 2014). Cities are the focus of a wealth of interventions on a global scale aimed at measuring factors such as the liveability and wellbeing in place, or at tackling particular challenges such as human rights, tolerance and social cohesion, ageing, disability, environmental sustainability and more. Strap lines such as 'The Social City', 'Child Friendly Cities', 'Ageing Cities', 'The Human Rights City' and 'Divercities' are not exclusive to advertising; they feature in both political and academic debates, often as indicators of how people experience their city and how governments

C. Williams (✉)
School of Global, Urban and Social Studies, RMIT University, GPO Box 2476, Melbourne, VIC 3001, Australia

© The Editor(s) (if applicable) and The Author(s) 2016
C. Williams (ed.), *Social Work and the City*,
DOI 10.1057/978-1-137-51623-7_1

15

should respond. This labelling has more recently included grassroots mobilisation as activists coordinated across cities to declare themselves 'refugee cities' in response to the 2015 European migrant crisis, and the Spanish *indignado* movement appealed to the notion of 'safe cities'. Cities are in focus on a world stage (Sassen 2012).

Beyond all the hype, cities should hold our attention for a number of reasons. They present an exciting set of challenges in terms of diversity, density and the nature of populations; the range and frequency of social problems that arise; and the scope of assets and resources available for practice. Yet, paradoxically, the urban context is both familiar to social workers and yet eludes us; we know it and we don't. In some respects, the profession is so immersed in the history and the development of city that it is difficult to explicate the ways in which the city itself and city-thinking has changed and developed.

Today, more than ever before, cities deserve our attention. The processes of industrialisation which began in the 1800s ushered in unparalleled rates of urban growth that continue to this day. The nature of the city and the way we live now have, however, undergone far-reaching change—particularly so in the last quarter of the twentieth century. We are experiencing a revolution in how we live; a complex multi-faceted phenomenon characterised by economic, political and social restructuring, dubbed '*the Urban Age*' (Gleeson 2012).

The demographics tell one story. Now, more than at any other point in history, people are likely to dwell in urbanised areas and, if they don't, they are directly serviced by the reach of urban economies in patterns of interaction and dependence (Tonkiss 2013a). The growth of cities matters to both urban and rural contexts alike. Urban sprawl, rural depopulation, migration flows, the development of and access to critical services and resources, and issues of environmental degradation—all reflect the intimate inter-relationships between town and country. Cities are the coordinating hub for rural and remote policy-making. At the same time, city dwellers are reliant on food, produce and water from surrounding environs.

Recent decades have witnessed rapid growth in cities but also apparent is the rapid decline of cities worldwide, as global economic shifts produce the waning of centres once economically buoyant. These shifts, of both growth and decline, have human consequences. They produce growing inequality and poverty, visible immiseration, segregation and division, rampant crime and compromised security, urban sprawl and slum development (UN-Habitat 2012). Cities also destroy natural environments, depleting water supplies and generating pollution (UN-Habitat 2012). These factors are now indisputably linked to the generation of risk—natural risk and human induced risk—producing hazards, endangerment and disasters (Beck 1992). As trends they impact differentially across the world, producing global inequity and inequalities that prompts the mass movement of peoples fleeing poverty. The social costs of these global shifts fall disproportionately on the most vulnerable sections of society. The human impacts are apparent on city streets, in city quarters and slums, in the dislocation of peoples within cityscapes, in the diversity of peoples coming and going through forced or elective migrations, and in the emergence of new and more complex forms of need.

The upheavals of the era are accompanied by the wave of neo-liberal responses to *the crisis of welfare*. The downward pressure of austerity measures sweeping across many Western states forms a critical interface with these processes of urban change as the search for alternatives to state provisioning obliges those with complex social problems to become more reliant on their own resources and on market-based solutions (Clarke and Newman 2012; Oosterlynck et al. 2013). Individuals and communities everywhere are being co-opted into the change effort, sometimes for the good —at times, for the worst.

The city is the hub of these turbulent economic changes and social disruptions but it is also the hub of innovation and change. It is both the problem and the solution, the '*triumph and crisis*' (Glaeser 2011). The city has long been framed in these dualistic terms, heralded in academic and popular literature alike as both the apocalypse and the new dawn, as a source of emancipation and freedom and, at the same time, a source of endangerment, containment and control. This ambivalence is deeply embedded in the professional psyche of social work but it is an ambivalence characterised by a particular skew. The social work city is most typically negatively framed as being in '*urban crisis*' and is depicted in terms of the damaging effects of capitalist industrialisation (Meyer 1976) and, more latterly, neo-liberal politics (Harris 2014). The resistance positioning of social work is wholly justified but it is also true that this crisis notion has served to cloud attention to the opportunities of the city and to the redesign of a convincing role for social work in the light of these contemporary shifts. Social work is in retreat.

The transformation of urban areas presents a distinct challenge for social work futures. The profession has a role ripe for exploitation in influencing the shape of things to come, and the shape of responses and interventions that will make a difference to people's lives. In grappling with the significance and impacts of contemporary urban trends, it is necessary to engage with the ways in which the city has been understood and explained. This opening chapter begins with a critical exploration of trends in the modern city—more accurately, with the nature of urbanisation, its implications and impacts. It explores some of the evidence on contemporary city living and, in moving beyond the descriptive facts of the *urban age*, turns to a consideration of the ways in which the city has been theoretically understood.

The New Urban Ascendancy: Trends and Developments

It is worth considering the reasons why most people choose to live in cities. The powerful pull of the city has long been recognised in terms of employment opportunities and economic security, for the concentration of services and expertise, and as a cultural, convivial and creative environment in which to extend or express identities. The city is the 'home of prosperity' for those escaping rural poverty and pushed towards opportunity, and it provides a place of refuge for those fleeing economic adversity, war and political oppression (UN-Habitat 2012). Yet, contrary to popular perception, contemporary urban growth is more a product of growth within cities than of migration into them (UN-Habitat 2012).

Urban growth brings with it hazards and risks. Cities produce deepening poverty and inequalities, increased segregation and criminalisation of the poor; the crisis of affordable housing, homelessness, gentrification, displacement and the breakdown of social support (UN-Habitat 2012). The city, in Tonkiss' terms, '*embeds injustice*' in spatial scale, with marked geographies of income disparity, security, mobility, overall access to life chances, consumption, and levels of power and privilege (2013a: 20). The depth, chronic nature and racialised dimensions of poverty have virulent expression in city space (Wacquant 2014). Large social housing estates, high rise housing, overcrowding, decay and slums form a visible reference point associated with a range of social problems such as unemployment, crime and violence, truancy, addictions and more. The high risks of such concentrated poverty are known to be associated with the incidence of child abuse and behavioural problems in children, with disability and with mental illness (Frederick and Goddard 2007; Bai et al. 2012). Poor neighbourhoods are not simply materially impoverished; impacts are felt in terms of hopelessness, demoralisation and despair (Atkinson and Kintrea 2004). In addition, suburbanisation has become prevalent and is growing, generating new forms of poverty. In areas where the infrastructure of social support is poor, people experience transport difficulties in accessing services and inevitably face a poverty of participation (see Chap. 10). This exacerbation of poverty and inequality is a key trend and one to which, ironically, social work has paid so little attention in recent times (Jack and Gill 2013).

Movement to and within cities incurs major social upheavals in terms of the loss of kinship and friendship groups; loss of intimacy and connection, and the concomitant isolation affecting individual wellbeing, security and comfort. Older people may find themselves imprisoned in isolated spaces in the city as communities they have known change around them (Phillipson 2010). Displaced migrants may struggle to adapt to the encounter with strangers and the strangeness of the city, and those discharged from mental institutions are locked into service-dependent enclaves rubbing shoulders with others who are deeply vulnerable (Curtis 2010). These are issues not only of individual wellbeing, but also of collective transitions for vulnerable groups. Cities are accordingly often depicted as inimical to community and association yet, in as much as they can be alienating for some, the anonymity of the city can also be protective and desired. In an examination of what she calls the '*ethic of indifference*', Tonkiss (2003: 302) provocatively proposes a more nuanced look at the impulse towards community, pointing to the freedoms of solitude, lack of visibility and privacy, and the right to be anonymous and to be left alone that makes the city attractive for some. In this way, Tonkiss problematises predominant ideas of community—whether based on place, association or interest—and invites us to think about different ways of being in and imagining the city, which recognises diversity and difference.

It is worth noting that cities are also undoubtedly good for people and for their welfare. They provide access to a range of economic opportunities and services, and provide stimulating convivial ecologies conducive to wellbeing. There is evidence, for example, to suggest that older people in cities experience lower morbidity rates (OECD 2015) and that disabled people benefit from technological innovations and service density (Prince 2008). Those who are gay benefit from city-living in terms of their wellbeing (Wienke and Hill 2013) and there are noted health benefits—mental and physical, as well as health costs (Curtis 2010). By far, the majority of city dwellers benefit from public health advances (Bai et al. 2013).

Diversity is often cited as one of the most appealing features of city-living. Cities are extremely ethnically diverse places, but the nature of that diversity is rapidly changing (Vertovec 2007). Poor ethno-suburbs that have emerged in segregated patterns over time are now being transformed by new migrations and are subject to the flux and churn of movements in and out (Wacquant 2014). These new and diverse groups dwelling in particular quarters or suburbs of the city are highly associated with poverty and cities are struggling to cope with this transition, in terms of both settlement and cohesion. At one end of the continuum of a range of integration strategies that are required lies reducing the risk of riots and uprisings. New migrations of asylum seekers and refugees, and of economic migrants—documented and undocumented— produce complex settlement needs given social, religious and linguistic diversity, varying legal status and circumstance (see Chap. 5, Schrooten et. al 2015). What can be called the 'new transnational urbanism' raises issues of the responsiveness of service delivery and places new demands on service professionals.

Growth, density, diversity and a changing age profile are markedly contemporary trends affecting cities across the world with profound implications for service delivery (UN-Habitat 2012). Cities are rapidly ageing as a result of low fertility rates, improved health and longevity, and the phenomenon of affluent baby boomers downsizing into urban living (Phillipson 2010). These demographic shifts, including new ways of conceptualizing diversity and ageing, are reshaping the practice front (see Chap. 6). Old universal 'one size fits all' models are seen as unsustainable and a search for alternatives is afoot.

Cities reveal the range of social problems and human needs, costs and benefits, but many of these social issues are not specific to cities. The distinctiveness of the urban lies in the *size, density* and *diversity of populations*, coupled with proximity. Heterogeneity and closeness in geographical space characterises city-living, making social issues highly visible. In addition, whilst cities have readily been stereotyped as fraught with social problems, it is more the *scale* and *frequency* of these problems within a geographical area that mark out something specific to the urban context, and their exposure and *framing* as social issues. Migrant homelessness, child slavery, sex trafficking, reliance on welfare payments, youth gun crime, obesity, mass disaster—all become apparent by virtue of scale. Social workers are key framers and narrators of debates on emerging social issues. They are involved in and responsive to moral panics about behaviour on the streets, or the rates of incidence of particular social issues (Clapton et al. 2013). The social issues that arise, together with the complexity and inter-relationships of need, produce so-called 'wicked issues' (Rittel and Webber 1973) that suggest much for the nature of the social work response in urban contexts.

These demographic shifts and associated social issues are undisputed. Their deployment in levering up debates on *the urban age* is, however, contested. The phenomenon of the *urban age* deserves critical interrogation—in particular, given its various articulations. The selection and framing of evidence is acutely political. Dystopian imaginings furbish the critique from the left of politics that point to the deep social divisions and inequalities of the neo-liberal capitalist city and argue for an expansionist state. The triumphalist perspective, by contrast, can feed into right-wing neo-liberal justifications of welfare inequality and calls for increased reliance on self-help and the withdrawal of the state, with a focus on managing risk via surveillance and interventions that are reactive—even punitive—and stereotypical (Dee 2015). Social work will need a strong critical lens on these framing devices.

Brenner and Schmid (2014) contest the narrow focus on demographic change and argue against the territorial focus of much of the analysis. They point out that the urban is not an easily delineated and bounded cityscape but disturbed by reference to terms such as the *suburban*, *peri-urban*, *municipality*, *urban community* or even *boroughs* within cities and not least in the delineation from rural contexts. A more expansive under-standing of the inter-relationship between city and country than the terms suggest is required. Urban and rural boundaries are increasingly blurred by the effect of city sprawl; by the interdependencies of rural/urban living in terms of goods and services, and the trans-locality and transnational nature of virtual networks and virtual community exchange that defy place-based considerations. These considerations conspire to befuddle any simple notion of the *urban age* or, indeed, an urban social work. Thus a number of processes characteristic to city-living—more accurately referred to as *urbanisation*—reveal the complexities of the *urban age*.

Social work is yet to engage significantly with the debates on the *urban age*. Dominelli's recent assessment of urbanisation in the book *Green Social Work* (2012) is, for example, wholly dark in linking growth to environmental degradation. She describes the untrammelled growth of cities as producing: 'slums that are characterised by overcrowding; unem-ployment, the spread of infectious diseases like tuberculosis, diphtheria, cholera, typhoid and bilharzia; and crime' (2012: 45). Dominelli (2012) critiques urban growth as a product of neo-capitalist development which, she argues, reproduces structural inequalities on a global scale and cre-ates deleterious effects in their wake. She is not alone as a social work commentator in her concerns for the social and environmental impacts of urbanisation. In recent years, social work has begun to consider the environmental impacts on health and wellbeing (Zapf 2010: 30) and on environmental sustainability (Coates 2003). The management of mass disasters—such as the flooding of New Orleans, the earthquake in Christchurch, or the tsunami following the Fukushima nuclear power plant disaster—have also been the focus of debate and research (Mathbor 2007; Pyles 2007). There is little doubt that rapid urbanisation and unregulated growth are producing unsustainable and environmentally insecure cities, but this is far from the whole story.

Cities across the world are highly diverse and reflect differential devel-opment. In particular, distinctions can be made between the Western cities of the global north—such as Chicago, Melbourne or Toronto—and those of the global south—for example, Delhi, Lagos or Karachi. In addition, a very particular group of cities, known as mega-cities—such as Tokyo, Seoul, Shanghai, Mumbai, Mexico City, Beijing, New York and London—are distinctive not only by virtue of the size of their populations, but also by the fact that they hold a particular place in the world economy as conduits of connectivity (Sassen 2012). Cities are large and small, growing and shrinking at different rates. They are also differentiated internally in terms of population density and diversity by neighbourhood, the available infrastructure and transport, histories, traditions, networks and community cohesion. In acknowledging this differentiation, urbanists prefer to refer to *urban forms* depicting the variety of ways in which infrastructure, systems and populations combine (Tonkiss 2013). Cities, in effect, present a complex of interacting dimensions and processes of urbanisation and, above all, they are peopled.

People make cities in *relational* ways; they are not simply determined by them. Urban space is not just a matter of the physical infrastructure and spatial patterning; it can be expressed via critical inter-relations of people and place, movements, processes and practices. Cities are places in which childhoods are made, experienced and shaped (Horschelmann and van Blerk 2012); spaces that disabled people encounter and navigate (Curtis 2010, Prince, Chap. 7, in this volume); those who are homeless become conspicuous and visible (Zufferey, Chap. 9, in this volume); or those from particular migrant groups experience local and global geographies of race (Neely and Samura 2011). Cities evoke spaces of intimate encounter and care (Baines, Chap. 8, in this volume), they prompt emotions of belonging and attachment, both individual and collective, and they forge identities. In essence, people experience cities in a myriad of different ways.

These critical urban trends signal the need for planned interventions. They imply concerted and co-ordinated effort on the part of a range of partners in the public and private sectors, and in civil society.

The Opportunities of the City

There are undoubtedly cautions to be signalled in interpreting the contemporary trends. Nevertheless, the demands of global and national change are being lived and experienced by the majority within cities and they necessitate significant shifts in social work practice. Under the pressure of such rapid changes, social work stances have become more assertive in expressing the fundamental values of the profession and stressing commitments to social justice and ethical practice. This restatement of the intrinsic value of social work is critical but will dissipate in the ether of rhetoric if it cannot be accompanied by a swift, convincing and pragmatic engagement with the opportunities presented by the modern city. Van Ewijk (2009: 167) has argued for the need for the profession to look for 'new or re-invented basic concepts and designs' in an era of profound policy change.

Cities provide a critical arena in working for change. The United Nations suggests: 'a fresh future is taking shape, with urban areas around the world becoming not just the dominant form of habitat for human-kind, but also the engine-rooms of human development as a whole' (UN-Habitat 2012: v). The opportunities presented by virtue of cities as proximate political environments—in both the sense of the large P of formal Politics and the small p of infra-political activity—are immense. Cities are the object of policy interventions, investment decisions, planning and ordering mechanisms that serve to empower or disempower various groups and stakeholders. A vast political machinery drives the engine of the city: the city mayor, local government and nested layers of governance peopled by policy-makers and shapers, civil servants, the electorate, the activists, the lobbyists—a complex set of cogs and hubs. In this respect, social workers are poised as key stakeholders in the process of this city-making and shaping. If urban forms are shaped by the designs of social actors, then this is an arena in which we have a critical stake. Cities provide opportunities to engage with big themes such as de-growth, sustainability, wellbeing and redistribution but, at the same time, provide the best place to deal pragmatically with crisis challenges.

Increasingly, social workers are expected to act on both global and local scales on issues that have transnational determinants but localised impacts. The *UN 2012: Better Urban Future* report describes the city as 'a flexible, operational and creative platform for the development of collaborative agendas and strategies for local responses to global issues' (2012: 11). The turn towards localisms and the localisation of social policy is a noted trend in contemporary welfare state transitions (van Ewijk 2009). The literature evidences the significance of urban neighbourhoods in innovative design to meet needs via, for example, the co-production of localised welfare solutions, the development of social enterprises and care networks—all with beneficial effects not only for the individual, but also for the development of welfare systems and infrastructure (Oosterlynck et al. 2013). Forms of social innovation are emerging everywhere, both spontaneously and by design, as centralised bureaucratic models are increasingly acknowledged to have failed. Social workers' presence in localities offers opportunities for them to act as crucial mediators and, at the same time, as supra-local actors connecting localised knowledges to grand-scale initiatives at city level and beyond.

Cities are the crucible of economic development but it is increasingly recognised that they are not simply about their economic dimensions. Other dimensions, such as quality of life and wellbeing, are now being captured within new theoretical trajectories (Sen 1992; Nussbaum 2011). Contemporary shifts look away from the idea that the good life and wellbeing are only associated with material prosperity and towards measures of wellbeing that incorporate wider issues of participation and engagement; having a voice and say over one's destiny is central to psychological wellbeing. More tailored and personalised services with consumers having a greater say in things that affect them are becoming the norm. The *urban age* signals the importance of extending these dimensions of urban citizenship. Responsiveness to voice and choice in local policy, accountability, and the engagement of people in place-making and place-shaping, together with attention to cities as relational spaces that enhance trust, cooperation, social cohesion and community are all on the agenda (UN-Habitat 2014). Articulations of urban citizenship can be bolstered by social work interventions, particularly in relation to those most vulnerable and excluded.

The complex and contextual nature of social issues suggests not only more localised, but also more integrated approaches. New partnerships in working for change are implied. The cities of the future will see health/social security and welfare services working more closely together, with forums that promote inter-professional, inter-disciplinary and cross-sector exchange. Greater emphasis will be placed on effective professional coordination and cooperation, and the infrastructures and processes that can support this. The challenge will be to make these robust and effective.

Technological advancement has a longstanding relationship to the city. Cities are set to become 'smarter' as hubs of creativity where ideas, innovation, and a mix of skills and knowledges converge (Batty et al. 2012). Digital technology is critical not only to facilitating higher levels of collaboration, and creating productive networks via the sharing of data and analytics to enable the design and delivery of services, but also to the sharing of client information. The secure sharing of information is now the bedrock of service delivery. But these are not the only ways in which new technologies are transforming what we do. They are also transforming the client interface and reformulating the encounter between social worker and service user.

Recent attention to social work's engagement with new technologies has tended to focus on the impact of informatics on the work of social work practice, or the empowering potentials of care technologies for the service user (Reamer 2013). Jeyasingham, however, notes how the routine use of mobile phones, laptops and tablets, together with the introduction of more secure sites to allow for uploading of material remotely by both social workers and service users, is rapidly opening up opportunities for 'agile working' arrangements (2014: 189). These developments, he notes, reconfigure the spatial relations between workers and client group, creating new forms of surveillance, monitoring, simultaneity of communication, contact and connectedness; transforming not only the nature of work, but also power relations between service user and provider. It is not difficult to imagine a scenario where the work of social work is variously located, dispersed, flexible, mobile and organic, and performed closer to the point of need.

Being close to the centre of the action may become more significant to practice. Cities present opportunities to engage with and mobilise resources for activism and change. Across the world, we are experiencing the rise of hundreds of transition initiatives. Rooted in protest against gentrification, unaffordable housing prices, too many cars, a lack of place for people cycling or walking, or a lack of green space in neighbourhoods; as part of the protest against the crisis in financial markets after 2008, as part of the ecological movement of grassroots initiatives, more and more people reclaim the streets and reclaim the city. In the transition towns movement (Connors and McDonald 2011), people are not only protesting, they are acting and trying to change the city, starting from small, sometimes symbolic but concrete initiatives that bring citizens together. The range is wide, from squatting to urban gardening and urban farming; from sharing goods and services to local production or alternative currency systems and credit unions; from minority ethnic self-help organisations to local development initiatives and social enterprises. Sometimes, neighbourhood workers are involved, but often the transition initiatives start as informal grassroots projects, and can flourish with the assistance of an engaged social work (Delgado 1999). Social workers are part of these wider citizenship projects by virtue of their dual role as inhabitants and actors in city space.

A plethora of opportunities exists to effect change. Solutions to social problems and interventions formulated need to be grounded in the social, political and ecological realities of each city. We need, as Meyer suggests in her classic text, to understand the *context* in which we work in order to define the *contours* and *content* of what we do (Meyer 1976). Meyer argued way back in 1976 (x1v), 'without a map that will shape this knowledge to the purpose and function of social work, application of skills will be a scattershot affair'. I turn now to contextualise these trends in asking how we have come to know the city and how we gain insights into its processes, complexities and contradictions in making sense of the descriptive facts.

Theorising the City

Cross-disciplinary borrowings from urban studies, social geography and the cultural sociology offer interesting points of analysis and trajectories for social work practice, and provide theoretical grounding for social work research. In making sense of the city, we must take a disciplinary leap, engaging with the insights produced in the broad multi-disciplinary field that is urban studies.

The field of urban studies has a long scholarly tradition of describing and delineating the city, capturing focal points of concern and analysis, building concepts, offering a terminology and, in doing so, developing a strong body of theory (Eade and Mele 2002). What is evident from the paradigmatic shifts in thinking that have occurred over time is that no unified, all-encompassing theory can explain the city. There can be no single epistemology but, rather, engagement with a fascinating trans-disciplinary field of study. These various ways of thinking about the city are not value free; each contains beliefs and ideas about 'causes, consequences and cures', ways things ought to be, utopias and dystopias in their visioning and perspective. They are deeply ideological and inevitably partial. They provide a range of theory that is full of contestation, augmentation and departures. An appreciation of these contributions equips us to understand the contemporary city, locate significant trends and influences; it enables us to explore how these concepts, methods, frames and theories shape professional perspectives and interventions.

Knowledge of the city has significantly developed through the methods used to research it; the cartographers, the maps, charts, statistics and ethnographic explorations are discussed in Chap. 4. For now, we consider the underpinning theories that shape these endeavours.

The development of cities has a long history but the transformations brought on by nineteenth-century industrialisation and urbanisation evoked the city as a focus of study. The developing infrastructure of the industrial age, the impact of new technologies and new ways of working, the loosening of kinship ties as labour moved to industrial centres, and the encounter with the stranger were all worthy of the new sociological attention. Key sociologists such as Freidrich Engels (1820–1895), Emile Durkheim (1858–1917), Max Weber (1864–1920), Karl Marx (1818–1883) and Georg Simmel (1858–1918) would lay down the foundations for thinking about industrial life, the city and its impacts. Collectively, these classical theorists were concerned with the consequences of the rapid transformations of the time and the nature of modern life, and sought to respond to the question of order. Engels' study of Manchester, which informed his text *The Conditions of the Working Class in England* (1845), provided the foundation for seminal studies of the city based on a Marxist analysis that would fall into attrition and not return to ascendancy until the 1970s. The impact of city life as a pivotal concern of these theorists led to the emergence of enduring sociological concepts such as 'alienation' (Marx) and 'anomie' (Durkheim), which described the social estrangement and isolation of individuals forged by the loosening of social ties and the norms and rules governing behaviour. Suicide, crime and deviance and other aspects of social life considered highly individual were now divested of individual motivations and explained as collective social facts. For Weber, the rise of capitalism and its forms of rationalisation was associated with a particular form of Protestant Christianity and he focused his interest on the role of legal institutions and emerging forms of political and moral organisation. He developed his ideal-type bureaucracy as a distinct rule-bound form of social organisation capable of responding equitably and impartially to the impersonal formal transactions of city life.

Others sought to capture the emotional dimensions of city living. For Georg Simmel (1858-1918) and later writers like Louis Wirth (1897–1952), cities were capable of having deep psychological effects on individuals. The city, with its rapidly changing images, sights, sounds and demands, created an 'intensification of emotional life', a form of inner conflict and sensory overload that required adjustments to the individual's personality. Simmel's work is foundational for social work in linking urban life with psychological conditions such as psychic insecurity, psychic overload, agoraphobia, vertigo and other forms of mental distress. He spoke about the damage to man's individuality and development as a result of the economic organisation and techniques of industrial life.

Louis Wirth's writings emulate and extend these themes of urban stress based on the sheer density and diversity of city life, and the confluence of differing lifestyles, values and beliefs which he argued led to a fragmented and impersonal social life. Wirth proposed that the informalities of communal life had been forsaken and replaced by new forms of life called *urbanism* in which bonds of solidarity which formed the glue of communally oriented society had to be replaced with formal social control mechanisms.

What characterises these theorists is the search for an all-encompassing explanation and seeking out of a transferable theory of urban processes to explain human behaviour. As such, these theories were highly determinist and laid down particular ways of thinking about the city and its effects. In the search for comprehensive answers to the issues of contemporary life, cities were negatively framed, determining, bounded and material.

In the same era, forms of social work knowledge of the city were emerging from the practices and interventions aimed at countering the effects of capitalist development (Chap. 2). These were driven pragmatically by the same modernist concerns to respond to the problem of order and control but eschewed theoretical analysis of the development of capitalism and its causalities and casualties, in favour of evolving new and sustainable forms of intervention and administration aimed at their amelioration.

It was not until the emergence of the Chicago School of Urban Sociology (1915–45), most notably associated with the work of Robert Park and Ernest Burgess, that a fresh departure from the sociological studies of the late nineteenth century appeared and generated a distinctive strand of sociology known as 'urban studies'. Drawing on detailed urban ethnographies and mapping a diversity of cities in North America, they developed a conceptual framework that could explain *processes* within cities—such as segregation, change and development, and the human adaptations to re-organisation within cities. For them, the city was not simply a physical space or a collection of institutions but, rather, involved processes and particular forms of social life that shape the nature of the urban space. They viewed the city as an organism, an ecological system made up of interdependent components that reacted and adapted in uniform ways to changes in population, changes in the physical environment and wider external changes. These functional adaptations within the ecology of the city were seen as highly predictable, following predetermined patterns in the way they distributed peoples across place and with predetermined effects. Their analysis accordingly suggested the city as zoned. This zoning of the city enabled the mapping of the social characteristics of an area—by divorce rates, deviancy, drug use, mental illness and so on. For example, certain neighbourhoods or zones were seen to *cause* or amplify criminal and deviant activity. The Chicago theorists argued that this type of analysis would benefit the planning of the location of social agencies (Shaw 2011). Park and Burgess utilised detailed survey methods but are perhaps most well-known for the deployment of rich ethnographies of gang behaviour and for their studies of delinquent youth. They were interested in revealing the logics of the lives of those on the margins of society—the transients, the gangs, life in the ghettos and the slums—in the diversity of cultures within a complex urbanism.

The Chicago School framework of thinking held sway in urban studies well into the 1970s, when its explanatory power could not easily be extended to accommodate the so-called urban crisis of the late 1960s. Phenomena such as student riots, trade union revolt, persistent urban poverty and decay, and racialised housing policies (Rex and Moore 1967) revealed the Chicago School's silence on the role of state and its inability to explain conflict. In its focus on locality, it was criticised for neglecting the grand themes of class and inequality. Urban sociology required rethinking. Theorists now returned to the grand themes of Marxist analysis and sought to configure the built environment as a product of dominant power relations, exploitation and conflict.

The 1970s saw the development of a radical critique, arguing for a focus on social justice concerns and pointing to the structural processes that produce uneven development within and across cities with far-reaching effects in terms of unequal employment opportunities, poor housing conditions, poverty and distress. These themes implied the affirmation of an activist and politicised urban theory which would appear in the writings of the French sociologist Manuel Castells' *The Urban Question* (1972) and the urban geographer David Harvey's *Social Justice and the City* (1973) in the United States, and later Henri Lefebvre, *The Urban Revolution* (2003). Drawing on a Marxist analysis, these writers pointed to the role of the state in managing and supporting capitalist development. For them, the processes of urbanisation and advanced capitalism are deeply entwined and contain necessary contradictions in terms of the interests of the proletariat and the bourgeoisie. The city brings opportunities for capitalist accumulation for the bourgeoisie but it also brings together a working class better able to meet, organise and become aware of their oppressed position. This inherently antagonistic relationship underpins all forms of social relations in the city. It becomes the logic that structures all aspects of social life and, indeed, shapes the built environment. Harvey was significant in revealing the forces at work in producing the built environment. He noted how, of necessity, capitalist society had to create a physical environment conducive to its development, producing a struggle over space and conflict over land as the capitalists need space to drive accumulation and the workers need space to live decently and reasonably. In this way, an urban geography driven by a Marxist analysis could explain processes such as gentrification and displacement in inner cities, lack of investment in housing stock, ghettoisation, and urban policies driven by business interests.

Castells' interest lay in social movements and the nature of the urban unrest of the late 1960s. His belief was that lack of provision of collective services such as health, education and welfare and lack of access to resources explained urban conflict as cities united a working class in their revolutionary potential. His conceptualisation pointed to the failure of the local state and the failures of urban governance which produced these tensions and urban struggles. Whilst these big themes of the role of the state in capitalist accumulation and structural inequality entered the social work lexicon during the 1970s in the form of radical social work (Corrigan and Leonard 1978), these writers were less cognisant of the dimensions of place, space and geography in the mobilisation and manifestation of collective power, or the role these issues play in contestation over space that marks out the work of the urban Marxist writers. Indeed, whilst radical social work assumed the urban, it barely addressed it in its considerations—most notably in terms of the growing ethnic and racial segregation in cities.

Henri Lefebvre (1991 [1974]) provides an interesting inflection on the Marxist analysis and one that has barely featured in social work analysis despite its considerable potential application (Jeyasingham 2014). Lefebvre, in line with Marxist thought, saw the survival of capitalism as dependent on complete urbanisation, but his contribution through a series of works gives attention to the symbolic and cultural dimensions of life in the city. The urban, for Lefebvre, is the intermediary realm between the macro-level of global markets and institutions and the micro-world of everyday social reality. His framework includes attention to the global, the urban and the everyday in a non-determinist interplay that allows for a view of both the bigger structural processes and, at the same time, viewing agency in the everyday aspects of urban life. Lefebvre does not ignore structural determinants but, rather, allows for the interpretive meanings of different social groups and individuals as they make sense of and experience city space, both shaping it and being shaped by it.

Lefebvre was interested in space - how people use space and make claims on it in their everyday lives in processes of political struggle towards exerting their '*right to the city*'. This struggle over the resources of the city illuminates the tensions and conflicts at the heart of city life. He argued: 'One of the consistent ways to limit the economic and political rights of groups has been to constrain social reproduction by limiting access to space' (1991: 22).

Lefebvre proposed a tripartite conceptualisation of space as *material, imagined* and '*lived*'. Spaces, for Lefebvre, are *perceived* in terms of material social practices, they are *conceived* in as much as they are represented in language and in thought, and they are '*lived*' in as much as they are experienced subjectively on a day-to-day basis (1991). His analysis of each of these dimensions separately and as mutually interacting dimensions is full of serendipity and simultaneity; they are relational, but not causally implicated. Lefebvre provides a focus on spaces as created, imbued with historical resonance, relations of power, and linked into dominant relations of production and reproduction in the Marxist sense. For him, all social practices continue to express capitalist modes of accumulation as they are played out at local level. Lefebvre accordingly invites us to consider the built environment as structuring and embedding power relations; that is, space is not reducible to a mere setting but, rather, plays a key role in the construction and organisation of social relationships.

A central concept proposed by Lefebvre is 'rhythms of city life' (Lefebvre 1992). The rhythm of the day (time) and its localisation (space) provide the matrix on which we can map movements and interactions but also pauses, moments and stasis. This type of analysis opens up the possibility of a consideration of movements, mobilities, tracking, time and distance in city space. Stevenson (2013), for example, shows how this schema accommodates shifts in time: the daytime city; the city at night, dusk, or dawn; as well as changes in season: summer, winter—and the combination of the two; for example, *summer nights*. Consider what this type of analysis provides for an examination of homelessness, sex work, the night shifts of carers, gypsy life, therapeutic effects of graffiti on youth behaviour, or the workings of a city hospital.

This notion of rhythms provides an important departure for analysis of the city. Everyday rhythms are lived and experienced on city streets. These insights provide a language and a conceptual framework within which to consider concerns such as gentrification and displacement, globalisation and migration, individualisation, alienation, home and homelessness. Lefebvre introduces us to the multiplicity of cities and, importantly, to the multi-dimensionality of cities.

His analysis is particularly pertinent to social work in its engagement with notions of structural inequality and with lived experiences but, significantly, in a consideration of his core notion: the *right to the city*. As Harvey explains, Lefebvre's concept demands far more than freedom to access urban resources but speaks to the transformative potential of the city to express identity, to exert collective power to control and reshape the processes of urbanisation—to change the city. These dimensions of urban citizenship can be seen, as Harvey (2008: 28) suggests, as 'one of the most precious yet most neglected of our human rights'.

The critique of this broad repertoire of Marxist analysis points to the limitations of a focus on territoriality and settlement based understanding of city-ness. The urban is neither as bounded or enclosed a site of social relations as the Marxists would suggest, nor as uniform. Urbanisation came to be seen as a highly differentiated process which would see the collapse of the unitary political narratives of modernity. The urban/non-urban distinction and the national focus of much of this analysis became somewhat dated in the light of the digital age and a networked society, and more sophisticated accounts of the inter-dependence of urban and rural economies and of global interconnectedness came to the fore. The feminists also challenged Marxist analysis in its omission of the gendered aspects of city life (Deutsche 1991). In turn, other subjectivities—such as childhood, sexualities and disabilities— pointed to omissions in the analysis, as did emergent social identities underpinned by post-colonial thought that highlighted the transnational and global connectedness of place and space (Sassen 1991). These *relational* ways of viewing the city all transcended the class-based analysis of Marxist writings.

Developments in sociological thinking and the new critical geography proffered a sea change away from the grand explanation towards post-modern concerns with choice, behaviours, political strategies and identities as the 'cultural turn' emerged in social science. The post-modern city would be peopled with difference and diversity, with taste groups, lifestyles, ethnic diversity, stories, experiences, and competing visualisations and constructions. Signs, symbols and meanings were foregrounded for attention. City space would become complex, messy, variously constructed and unbounded in any quantifiable geography (Massey 1994). Post-modernism proposed a move beyond the essentialising tendencies of the materialist-oriented approaches to disentangle a variety of experiences underpinned by relationships of power and the associated narratives. It focused on subjugated knowledges, the marginalised perspective and varying viewpoints. It sought to examine how global processes are locally expressed; the meaning and experiences producing the complexities of social relations in forming identities and to detail notions of community, home, mobilities, resistance, and the tactics and negotiations deployed in everyday life (Massey 1994).

Thus, the maps, models, plans and statistics of city-thinking became displaced by attention to the semiotic, the iconography of the city, its text and their readings from a kaleidoscope of perspectives. Urban studies now turned to cultural anthropology to explore the city. Theories of culture and identity informed discussions of the ways in which space is infused with power relations. A spatial appreciation emerged that allowed for a consideration of positionality, diversity and power. City spaces could now be conceived in terms of attachments to place, place loss and displacements, relations of domination and subordination, of conflict and cooperation, subversion and resistance, cohesion and solidarity—as spaces that reverberate with local and global social relations. Critical spatial thinking would illustrate the ways in which space is contested, fluid and historical, relational and interactional, and imbued with difference and inequality. (Neely and Samura 2011).

A range of social science contributions has opened up the theoretical lens on place and space. It is possible to analyse city spaces as emotionally imbued, tense and fear laden, which allows us to tap into how the city is experienced in gendered ways, or by older people, children, the vulnerable or shift workers. We can consider the spatial and emotional dimensions of de-institutionalisation, containment and surveillance (Dee 2015). We can look at the city in terms of the therapeutic function of public meeting places, cafes, bars and other places of association in what Koch and Latham (2011) call the 'convivial ecology' of the city which opens up spaces for belonging, attachment and new socialities; or, indeed, we can consider the city as mapped out by spaces of care and support (Milligan et al. 2007). The applications are endless.

These are not dispassionate abstractions. Urban studies has been concerned with making sense of and acting on the world in an applied sense, and has not been slow in embracing advocacy and activism in generating ideas aimed at making things better. Urban theory informs a range of disciplines including landscape architects, urban and social planners and policy-makers, and others involved in the design of the built environment and with shaping better futures. Fincher and Iveson (2008) as an example, explore the *redistributive* potential of urban planning in redress for disadvantage. They consider the planner's potential to promote *recognition* in the design for the built environment that engages with groups such as migrants, working mothers, gay people or other marginalised groups; and they argue for designs that foster *encounter* through creating opportunities for sociality and interaction, such as drop-in centres and libraries. Fincher and Iveson refer to the 'crafting' role of planners in facilitating participation of different groups of citizens in matters of urban policy.

In this vein, Tonkiss (2013a: 1) also sees city-making as a social process engaging many stakeholders in both planned and serendipitous activity. Accordingly, urban studies, in pointing to the future of cities, reflects the 'communicative turn' in social science and the concerns with key issues of democratic consultation, participation and representation. In an extension to describing and explaining the processes at play in the variety of urban forms, urban studies casts an eye to the future and commentators speculate on the ways interventions today will shape the city of the future. The literature raises questions about how we can collectively shape 'the good city' (Gleeson 2014) or speculates on 'the possible city' (Tonkiss 2013a), considering ways in which the city can be re-made and designed through participation and engagement of citizens.

Conclusion: Engaging with the Urban— Theoretical Trajectories for Social Work

From this broad body of cross-disciplinary theorising, contemporary writing eschews the search for any totalising explanation of the city in favour of themes, multi-layered accounts and perceptual cuts through the city that illuminate some aspect or other of urban life (inter alia Stevenson 2013; Hall et al. 2008). The ways in which we draw on this body of literature however, reflects particular disciplinary concerns.

The new *urbanology* provides rich pickings to underpin social work action and intervention. If there can be no definitive answer to the question 'What is the city?', we certainly have a strong conceptual framework within which to consider social work intersections. From this body of knowledge, we come to understand the urban question and the varying ways in which it has been answered. From our disciplinary perspective, we are concerned with the urban geography of inequality, how it is structured and experienced, and ways in which it can be addressed. Issues of social justice and care ethics lie at the heart of this analysis. We are concerned with those who are disenfranchised, displaced, alienated and marginalised and, at the same time, seek alignment with them within the urban space as a creative place of struggle, conflict and change.

In moving beyond the impasse of the sinful or the saintly dichotomy of the city, or notions of perpetual crisis, it is worth delineating a few key considerations relevant to a theoretically informed social work practice from the foregoing discussion.

- The city is not a fixed and defined built or territorial object to be acted on but a social construction, produced, experienced and contested.
- Cities don't determine people but are lived and experienced as complex *relational* spaces and processes.
- Cities are necessarily diverse and highly differentiated internally. They are more usefully considered as complex urban forms.
- Cities reflect sets of social relations infused with power, privilege and advantage, inequality and insecurity. They reverberate with injustice in place and space scale.
- Cities mediate scale—they are the arenas in which we experience and can affect those macro-processes of globalisation and the micro-politics of exchange and reciprocity.
- Urbanisation, cities and their growth are significantly connected to rural issues.

The urban context is the critical arena for the development of viable responses to the issues of the day as outlined in this chapter: primarily those of inequality and social injustice, environmental sustainability, cohesion and solidarity, the impacts of human movement and the experiential impacts of the pace and nature of city living on the vulnerable and marginalised. It is also pivotal to the reassertion of social work identity. The city, its space, place and time is much more than a simple backdrop to social work practice. We cannot afford to ignore the implications of the urban age.

References

Atkinson, R., & Kintrea, K. (2004). 'Opportunities and despair: It's all in there'. Practitioner experiences and explanations of area effects and life chances. *Sociology, 38*(3), 437–455.

Bai, X., Nath, I., Capon, A., Hasan, N., & Jaron, D. (2012). Health and wellbeing in the changing urban environment: Complex challenges, scientific responses and the way forward. *Environmental Sustainability, 4*, 485–472.

Batty, M., Axhausen, K. W., Giannotti, F., Pozdnoukhov, A., Bazzani, A., Wachowicz, M., et al. (2012). Smart cities of the future. *European Physical Journal of Special Topics, 214*, 481–518. http://link.springer.com/journal/11734. Accessed 24 Jan 2016.

Beck, U. (1992). *Risk society: Towards a new modernity*. New Delhi: Sage.

Brenner, N., & Schmid, C. (2014). The 'urban age' in question. *International Journal of Urban and Regional Research, 38*(3), 731–755.

Clapton, G., Cree, V., & Smith, M. (2013). Moral panics and social work: Towards a sceptical view of UK child protection. *Critical Social Policy, 33*(2), 197–217.

Clarke, J., & Newman, J. (2012). The alchemy of austerity. *Critical Social Policy, 32*(3), 299–319.

Coates, J. (2003). *Ecology and social work: Toward a new paradigm*. Halifax/Nova Scotia: Fernwood Publishing.

Connors, P., & McDonald, P. (2011). Transitioning communities: Community, participation and the Transition Town movement. *Community Development Journal, 46*(4), 558–572.

Corrigan, P., & Leonard, P. (1978). *Social work practice under capitalism: A Marxist approach*. London: Macmillan Press.

Curtis, S. (2010). *Space, place and mental health*. London: Ashgate.

Dee, M. (2015). Young people and urban public space in Australia-creating pathways to community, belonging and inclusion. *International Journal of Social Science Research, 3*(2), 138–151.

Delgado, M. (1999). *Social work practice in non-traditional urban settings.* New York: Oxford University Press.

Deutsche, R. (1991). Boys town. *Environment and Planning: Society and Space, 9*(1), 5–30.

Dominelli, L. (2012). *Green social work: From environmental crisis to environmental justice.* Cambridge: Polity Press.

Eade, J., & Mele, C. (Eds.). (2002). *Understanding the city: Contemporary and future perspectives.* Oxford: Blackwell Publishing.

Fincher, R., & Iveson, K. (2008). *Planning and diversity in the city: Redistribution, recognition and encounter.* Basingstoke: Palgrave Macmillan.

Frederick, J., & Goddard, C. (2007). Exploring the relationship between poverty, childhood adversity and child abuse from the perspective of adulthood. *Child Abuse Review, 16*(5), 323–341.

Glaeser, E. (2011). *The triumph of the city: How urban spaces make us human.* London: PanMacmillan.

Gleeson, B. (2012). The urban age: Paradox and prospect. *Urban Studies, 49*(5), 931–943.

Gleeson, B. (2014). *Coming through slaughter* (MSSI issues paper No. 3) Melbourne Sustainable Society Institute, University of Melbourne. http:// www.sustainable.unimelb.edu.au/files/mssi/MSSI-IssuesPaper-3_ Gleeson_2014_0.pdf. Accessed 5 Sept 2015.

Hall, T., Hubbard, P., & Rennie Short, J. (2008). *The SAGE companion to the city.* London: Sage.

Harris, J. (2014). (Against) Neoliberal social work. *Critical and Radical Social Work, 2*(1), 7–22.

Harvey, D. (2008). The right to the city. *New Left Review, 53*, 23–40. http:// newleftreview.org/II/53/david-harvey-the-right-to-the-city. Accessed 9 Nov 2015.

Horschelmann, K., & van Blerk, L. (2012). *Children, youth and the city.* London: Routledge.

Jack, G., & Gill, O. (2013). Developing cultural competence for social work with families living in poverty. *European Journal of Social Work, 16*(2), 220–234.

Jeyasingham, D. (2014). The production of space in children's social work: Insights from Henri Lefebvre's spatial dialectics. *British Journal of Social Work, 44*(x), 1879–1894.

Koch, R., & Latham, A. (2011). Rethinking urban public space: Accounts from a junction in West London. *Transactions of the Institute of British Geographers, 37*(4), 515–529.

Lefebvre, H. (1991). *The production of space*. Oxford: Blackwell.

Lefebvre, H. (1992). *Rhythmanalysis: Space, time and everyday life*. London: Continuum.

Massey, D. (1994). *Space, place and gender*. Cambridge: Polity Press.

Mathbor, G. M. (2007). Enhancement of community preparedness for natural disasters: The role of social work in building social capital for sustainable disaster relief and management. *International Social Work, 50*(3), 357–369.

Meyer, C. (1976 [1970]). *Social work practice: A response to the urban crisis*. Revised 2nd ed. New York: Free Press.

Milligan, C., Atkinson, S., Skinner, M., & Wiles, J. (2007). Geographies of care: A commentary. *New Zealand Geographer, 63*, 135–140. http://www.researchgate.net/publication/249470500_Geographies_of_care_A_commentary. Accessed 14 July 2015.

Neely, B., & Samura, M. (2011). Social geographies of race: Connecting race and space. *Ethnic and Racial Studies, 34*(11), 1933–1952.

Nussbaum, M. (2011). *Creating capabilities: The human development approach*. Cambridge, MA: Belknap Press of Harvard University Press.

OECD (Organisation for Economic Cooperation and Development) (2015). *Ageing in cities*. http://www.oecd.org/regional/ageing-in-cities-9789264231160-en.htm. Accessed 14 July 2015.

Oosterlynck, S., Kazepov, Y., Novy, A., Cools, P., Barberis, E., Wukovitsch, F., Sarius, T. & Leubolt, B. (2013, April). *The butterfly and the elephant: Local social innovation, the welfare state and new poverty dynamics* (IMPROVE working papers, discussion paper No.13/03). http://improve-research.eu. Accessed 14 July 2015.

Phillipson, C. (2010). Growing old in the century of the city. D. Dannefer & C. Phillipson (Eds.), *The Sage handbook of social gerontology* (pp. 597–606). London: Sage.

Prince, M. (2008). Inclusive city life: Persons with disabilities and the politics of difference. *Disability Studies Quarterly, 28*(1). http://dsq-sds.org/article/view/65/65. Accessed 14 July 2015.

Pyles, L. (2007). Community organizing for post-disaster social development: Locating social work. *International Social Work, 50*(3), 321–333.

Reamer, F. (2013). Social work in a digital age: Ethical and risk management challenges. *Social Work, 58*(2), 163–172.

Rex, J., & Moore, R. (1967). *Race, community and conflict: A study of Sparkbrook.* London: Institute of Race Relations.

Rittel, H. W. J., & Webber, M. M. (1973). Dilemmas in a general theory of planning. *Policy Sciences, 4*(2), 155–169.

Sassen, S. (1991). *The global city.* New York/London/Tokyo/Princeton: Princeton University Press.

Sassen, S. (2012). *Cities in a world economy* (4th ed.). Newbury Park: Pine Forge Press.

Schrooten, M., Geldof, D., & Withaeckx, S. (2015). Transmigration and urban social work: Towards a research agenda. *European Journal of Social Work, 19*(1), 18–30.

Sen, A. (1992). *Inequality reexamined.* Cambridge: Clarendon Press.

Shaw, I. (2011). Social work research: An urban desert? *European Journal of Social Work, 14*(1), 11–26.

Stevenson, D. (2013). *The city.* Cambridge: Polity Press.

Tonkiss, F. (2013a). *Cities by design: The social life of urban form.* Cambridge: Polity Press.

Tonkiss, F. (2003). The ethics of indifference: Community and solitude in the city. *International Journal of Cultural studies, 6*(3), 297–311.

UN-Habitat (United Nations Habitat). (2012). *State of the worlds cities 2012/2013.* http://unhabitat.org/books/prosperity-of-cities-state-of-the-worlds-cities-20122013/. Accessed 10 July 2015.

UN-Habitat (United Nations Habitat). (2014). *The future we want, the city we need.* http://unhabitat.org/the-future-we-want-the-city-we-need/. Accessed 11 Jan 2016.

van Ewijk, H. (2009). Citizenship-based social work. *International Social Work, 52*(2), 167–179.

Vertovec, S. (2007). Superdiversity and its implications. *Ethnic and Racial Studies, 29*(6), 1024–1054.

Wacquant, L. (2014). Marginality, ethnicity and penality in the neoliberal city: An analytic cartography. *Ethnic and Racial Studies, 37*(10), 1687–1711.

Wienke, C., & Hill, G. J. (2013). Does place of residence matter? Rural–urban differences and the wellbeing of gay men and lesbians. *Journal of Homosexuality, 60*(9), 1256–1279.

Zapf, M. K. (2010). Social work and the environment: Understanding people and place. *Critical Social Work, 11*(3), 30–46.

2

Beyond the Soup Kitchen

Charlotte Williams

Introduction

The evolution and development of social work form a mutualistic relationship with the city. The history of social work is a history of adaptation and change to socio-economic and political circumstances of the time—more specifically, to particular forms of the organisation of capital. But social work is also a shaper of histories; a site of resistance, of innovation and change, much of which has become apparent within urban spaces. The morphology of social work is not complete. Social work is characterised by a fluid and changeable role that can be defined by those who practice it and by those who require the service, as well as by the forces of state engineering.

A number of contemporary tensions and dilemmas confront the profession which are crystallised within any discussion of urban change and

C. Williams (✉)
School of Global, Urban and Social Studies, RMIT University, GPO Box 2476, Melbourne, VIC 3001, Australia

© The Editor(s) (if applicable) and The Author(s) 2016
C. Williams (ed.), *Social Work and the City,*
DOI 10.1057/978-1-137-51623-7_2

development. The impact of the neo-liberal restructuring of welfare and associated neo-residualism on social work practice is hotly debated (Jani and Reisch 2011; Ferguson I. 2008). In most Western countries, social services have been targeted for residualisation, contracted out to a mixed economy of providers, and renewed emphasis has been placed on self-help and self-provisioning. In the so-called 'era of austerity', social workers are engaging with increasingly vulnerable and immiserated publics at the same time as public sources of support shrink. The space for community oriented preventative work has diminished alongside an evident loss of professional autonomy in designing futures. Public services have become reactive and risk averse as the crisis in welfare deepens. Rogowski (2010: 21) suggests 'What remains of social work is a limited version of what the possibilities once were'.

Everywhere apparent is something of a crisis of the political mandate of social work with the profession pilloried for working within the neo-liberal frame and its assumptions rather than recrafting or maintaining its critical distance (Reisch 2013). The critique points to an over-emphasis on the ascendancy of professional norms such as objectivity and rationality which, it is argued, works against the pursuit of social justice (Olson 2008; Stoesz et al. 2010).

At the same time, the remit of social work is stretched exponentially in responding to issues on a global scale. Its claims-making has become ever more grandiose as the scales of attention expand (IFSW Global Agenda 2012). Having a role in responding to the fallout of economic globalisation, dramatic demographic change, environmental impacts and technological development is part and parcel of contemporary practice. In this endeavour, however, the arena in which these issues become manifest is strangely quiet in the literature, assumed and un-interrogated. By and large, social work debate has neglected a reconsideration of the significance of place, locality and the urban space in the shift of attention to macro-processes of globalisation. Issues of migration, environmental disaster, global poverty and sustainability have demanded attention on an international level with less attention given to the socio-spatial contexts in which they are experienced, realised and negotiated. This disappearance of the local under the weight of attention to global processes is inhibitive. The city and its urban forms require a much more complex consideration of people, place and space. Social work needs to be cognisant of its limitations, its scope and political efficacy, and focus on the ways it knows best to lever up change.

A re-examination and a re-positioning of social work in urban space is suggested. Relocating social work in its milieu allows us to glimpse the ways in which the city has been framed in the past and is being constructed in the present. The historic evolution of social work has determined a particular assumptive base for the profession, underpinned by a set of institutional and ideological imperatives the goals of which are in direct opposition to the stated social justice ambitions of the profession (Reisch 2013). The profession has deeply conservatising tendencies which preserve established ways of working and sustain systems of power and privilege. Reisch, amongst others, argues 'the status quo must be challenged and destabilised for any desired changes to occur' (2013: 75). Social work is out of step with the new urban realities, voiceless and lacking in recognition in major debates on the urban age and increasingly envisioned only in terms of its compensatory and surveillance roles, for which it receives a bad press. Times beckon new wisdoms (Gleeson 2014).

The transformation of urban areas is profound and configures with the impacts of welfare reform to produce a complex set of issues and contradictions that suggest a new role for social work. The moment is critical. The contemporary city demands a reconstruction of the nature of social work if social workers are to be legitimate and recognised actors within the new social welfare paradigm. Social work will need to reposition itself in relation to the state, to service users and to other key actors in welfare delivery, including the private market. It will need to assert an authentic articulation of its core values and it will need to engage with these processes of change in positive and informed ways, to deliberate and to advance with others an alternative vision of change.

This chapter considers the historical and contemporary intersections between social work and the city. It looks at the ways in which the city has come into view for the discipline and practice of social work. It argues that both the city and social work are social constructions in constant interplay. In arguing for a repositioning of social work in the city, this chapter considers what is implied in terms of the assumptive base of practice and new ways of working. It sets out to redefine the place of 'urban social work' drawing on three core concepts: *social justice*, *care* and *sustainability* that have permeable and enduring significance for the profession.

Historical Intersections: Social Work and the City

Fran Tonkiss argues that 'The disciplinary lens through which urban forms are viewed is an important basis for how "the city" comes to be defined' (2013: 3). As such, it is useful to consider our disciplinary preoccupations and how these have been shaped, and to explore those viewings of urban space that define social work's key focus of intervention. These historical cuts at the intersection of social work and the city evidence the nature of the inter-relationship and how it is discursively framed. They reveal the evolution of the dualism forged between client (casework) and a place-based (community work) focus; between category and geography, a tension that lies at the heart of contemporary practice. They also suggest gaps and omissions, silences and departures in social work thinking—for example, in relation to gender and space, race and place—and they illustrate the ways in which particular discourses of change shape social work action.

Social work is both a highly diverse set of activities and highly contested, and there is no settled argument as to its nature. Its relationship to the state, to capital and to the service user are framed normatively from a number of perspectives reflecting competing wishes and wants, purpose and function, role and remit. If its origins as a profession are rooted in Western capitalism, this story of its evolution has come to form the master narrative of social work. However, it should not be forgotten that this role and cluster of activities, even if not state orchestrated, have been evident in some form in all countries beyond the West. There are, indeed, a variety of social work histories which can be traced in particular regions of the world.

That said, social work as a profession was born and grew up in the Western city. It is a phenomenon of nineteenth-century industrialisation, urban growth and development. As cities formed and developed, so did the increase in social problems which required organised intervention. Unemployment, work place injury, child labour, poverty, vagrancy, prostitution, squalor and disease, theft and social disorder, and, indeed, the emerging visibilities of ageing and disability, all required managing as the contemporary city emerged. The problems of city life needed solutions and interventions foregrounding a deliberate shift from the laisser faire thinking of classic liberalism to organised state commitments. The nineteenth-century upheavals may not have been the first urban revolution: cities had been emerging since 6000 BC but the processes of rapid industrialisation meant social issues were apparent on an unprecedented scale and magnified in the microcosm of the city.

The nineteenth-century city was a squalid place. Consider, for example, the London viewed via the writings of Karl Marx, Robert Mayhew, through the literature of Charles Dickens and via Hogarth's paintings. This London was both a miserable and fascinating place as Pearson describes:

> a place where glittering wealth lived cheek by jowl against alarming poverty. A fog bound sprawling city in which crime and violence lurked in every shadow. A place where homeless beggars littered the streets and where the working poor lived in maggot numbers in their squalid dwellings (1995: 85).

Pearson (1995) describes how sanitary metaphors were frequently used to describe the poor and their living conditions. They were 'human vermin', 'foul wretches', a form of lesser human life who inhabited 'cess pits', 'plague spots' and 'sinks of inquiry' (Pearson 1995: 85). The threat of encounter with this spectre of ramshackle city life and its occupants and their vices—vagrants, prostitutes, paupers, and street children—fuelled a climate of danger, fear and anxiety amongst the Victorian middle classes.

We can view this encounter via the perspective of social workers, philanthropists and social activists of the time who were increasingly guided by a philosophy that spoke of order, regulation, surveillance and control, and the belief that the state had a moral responsibility towards its citizens. The notion of systemised intervention to create a better society would ultimately lead to organised state intervention in the form of the Charity Organisation Society (COS) with its pioneering scientific approach to orchestrating philanthropic effort. The COS logic of empirical investigation, together with rigorous and documented procedures for the investigation of relief and assistance, established the core methodology of social work and the enduring primacy of social casework.

Alongside this approach to the urban uncertainties, the Settlement movement, with its 'soup kitchen' and place-based focus, offered an alternative methodology. The infrastructural development of settlement houses, refuges, mission houses, asylums, model homes and other institutional forms aimed at remoralising the poor and regenerating city slums—such as Octavia Hill's (1838–1912) housing experiments—reconstructed spatial relations of the city. Practioners found themselves venturing beyond the known sureties of house, home and neighbourhood to work and live amongst the poor. New proximities and exposures evolved via the immersing of practioners in poor neighbourhoods, quarters and areas of the city.

From Toynbee Hall in London to Hull House in Chicago, the Settlement philosophy and its methods spread, consolidating the development of the emergent profession and its methodologies. These institutional forms criss-crossed the Atlantic via the connectivity of cities.

The spread of ideas and infrastructural frameworks was also apparent in the development of philanthropic effort across cities. Philanthropy is linked to the historical growth of wealth in cities. The nature of philanthropic development in major cities—such as London in the nineteenth century, for example—had a direct effect on the development of charitable institutions and the directions of social policy in the rest of England. Organisations such as the NSPCC and Barnardos spread nationally in response to child welfare, as did organisations such as The League of Coloured Peoples, aimed at supporting particular disenfranchised groups. Thus, the emergence of organizational infrastructures, both philanthropic and state coordinated, was replicated across cities, within nations and transnationally.

However, it is the socio-spatial dimensions of this development within the city that were so formative in shaping social work practice. Webb's analysis (2007a, b) is particularly insightful in bringing the socio-spatial dimensions of the city to bear on an understanding of the genealogy of social work. In two essays on the evolution of social work in the late Victorian period, Webb considers the ways in which the dominant ideas of modernism and its associated discursive formations, *coupled with* the physical, visual and material factors of place, shaped social work in fundamental and enduring ways. *Place* (the city) formed the organising concept for social work activity. The COS was principally concerned with organising the district, and established locality offices with the emphasis on knowing the community and establishing patch-based intervention. Accordingly, the COS required that its practitioners had a detailed grounding in their local milieu. Webb argues this conferred on early social work not only the 'power *of* place' via local knowledges and experiences but also the 'power *over* place' via opportunities for surveillance, regulation and control of the poor (2007b: 52). Webb convincingly illustrates how particular, what he calls 'regimes of practice', developed under these conditions. The *home visit* and the technique of the *friendly visit* enabled domestic regulation of the poor via access to, influence over and monitoring of their private lives. This priviledged access to domestic space and its associated careful documentation back at the office enabled what Webb notes as 'regulation at a distance' as the surveillance power of the practitioner was extended through space (2007b: 52). The friendly visit, in turn, functioned to enable the neutralising of stranger-to-stranger encounter and to appease many of the uncertainties and discomforts of these imposed stranger relations in the newly enforced intimacies of the city (2007b: 203).

What is interesting about Webb's account is that he demonstrates the territorial dimensions of this new encounter between benefactor and beneficiary: an encounter which provided experiential new mobilities for social work, both material and spatial, in the achievement of charity work. This work exposed progressive professionals to localised experiences of poverty in a physical and material sense and, indeed, carried with it embodied sensory and affective dimensions in the movement across city space (Ferguson H. 2008). This incursion into the territorial and domestic space of the poor by largely middle-class women, with all its encumbent anxiety and exilaration, in many respects mirrored the broader colonial encounter of the time foreshadowing an encounter that would later be replicated on home ground as colonial migrants made their way to the motherland. It also had specific gendered dimensions, largely overlooked in documenting the practice trajectory of the new profession (Webb 2007b: 203).

Whilst Webb's focus is on England—more specifically, Victorian London—he extends his claim to suggest that these processes form part of a common European heritage of such modernising ideas amidst relatively common conditions and considerations impacting across Europe. Similar developments are also apparent in the USA (Kolko Phillips and Lala Ashenberg Straussner 2002). In the context of the USA, however, the encounter was always more overtly racialised. Black populations migrating to urban centres from places elsewhere across the USA found themselves ghettoised and segregated in areas of the inner city, a particular spatial dynamic that would become an enduring feature of urban living. The growing issue of racial segregation in cities in the USA at the turn of the century was also present in the port towns such as Liverpool, Bristol and Cardiff in the UK, if considered much more localized in the discursive framing of social issues of the city at the time.

An analysis of race and place in social work and welfare intervention of this period attests to the mechanisms of containment, control and oppression by the colonial power, even in post-slavery America. Freed Blacks were denied public assistance under Colonial Poor Laws and relied on mutual aid, self-provisioning and the emergence of Black-led organisations for social support (Kolko Phillips and Lala Ashenberg Straussner 2002). Settlement houses in the USA were largely White until well after World War I, when some separate houses for Black people emerged in cities such as New York, Tuskegee, Atlanta and Virginia (ibid 2002).

Analysis by race and place remains underworked in social work histories (Bryan et al. 1985). It is not simply the physical placement of racialised communities that warrants illustration, but restrictions on their movement within cities, places and spaces they are 'permitted' to inhabit and claim, and the discourses attributed to their lifestyle in place, largely under the auspices of social workers. Issues of racial segregation and discrimination have a long history in the city. The literature points to the ways in which the city space not only reflects physical segregation and attendant inequality, but also the ways in which urban life itself has become imagined and inscribed as racialised and accordingly as damaged, dangerous and unclean by contrast with imaginings of rural space as purified and clean (Neal and Agyeman 2006).

The city can also be mapped historically as the site for contestation over rights. In bringing people together in a geographical space, cities created a common experience, a politics of the common good, in which the obligations and responsibilities of citizenship were extended and in which those excluded became aware of their common predicament. Social work histories reveal social workers deeply involved in collectively organising for social action and resistance over issues such as child and maternal welfare, income maintenance, racial discrimination and more, in extending and enhancing the rights of citizenship (Reisch and Andrews 2001). The reformist urge manifests itself in alignments with social movements for change—campaigns, street marches, protest, riots and other forms of resistance.

These historical intersections between city and social work demonstrate the discursive framing of problems of urban living (in both political and popular imaginaries), the agency of individuals and groups *and* the ways in which the built environment of the city become determinants shaping methodologies of practice. Concepts of distance, proximity, movement, place and space all appear in this type of analysis and attest to the significance of the material and visual in shaping social work practice. They afford perspectives on movement through the physical landscape of the built environment and illustrate the significance of place in defining social work identity (Ferguson H. 2008).

Connections across cities on an international level enabled the sharing of intellectual ideas critical to the development of the profession, ideas that would ultimately lead to a turning away from locally based solutions towards international solutions based on client category, thus ensuring the ascendancy of individual casework.

What Is Urban Social Work?

What this little snapshot shows is that the nineteenth-century city, coupled with the articulation of key ideas of the time, was instrumental in shaping particular forms of social work practice. Such discursive framing of the city remains highly significant in delineating practice and social work identity: its *context*, *content* and *contours*, to use Meyer's framework (1976). Here, I suggest it is possible to elucidate four competing but overlapping constructions of the city which, in turn, propose different emphasis for urban social work. I label them: city as machine, city as system, city as community and city as environment.

City as Machine

This construction depicts the city as a piece of industrial machinery, a technological megalith driven by a relentless engine of capitalist economic productivity. This is perhaps best typified by Fritz Lang's futuristic film of the urban dystopia *Metropolis* (1927). Lang's city is, at one and the same time, a spectacle of wonderment and technological advancement, and a dehumanizing death trap. The relentless grind and toil of the huge machinery of the city is one in which workers get caught up, injured or perhaps collapse with exhaustion. This city is demanding of the individual both physically and psychologically, and socially damaging to the entire underclass. It is a machine that has dysfunctional effects, man-made risks and, to use Titmuss' term, generates '*diswelfares*' (Titmuss 1968). The function of social work is, accordingly, to ameliorate these potential impacts, to oil the cogs through enhancing the coping, resilience and adaptation of the individual to rapid social change, and to clean up the waste that the machinery discards. For Titmuss, the role of social welfare as *handmaiden* to this capitalist mechanism defined social work in compensatory terms, or what I call here a *street cleaner model*.

In this vein, Meyer (1976), for example, suggested the social work role is to enhance the social and psychological functioning of the individual in the face of perpetual *urban crisis*. Meyer's adopts Erikson's psycho-social model to argue for the individualisation of practice to confront an alienating and confusing city life world. Social workers have the knowledge and skill set to personalise and individualise the city that has become impersonal and based on institutionalised rather than kinship relationships, and to smooth out its alienating tendencies. Meyer argues for a casework focused on alleviating interpersonal estrangement,

> to include ways of connecting people with goods and services, possibly by arranging pathways, promoting accessible organisations, advocating and strengthening individuals to cope with the confusing array of urban structures and diffuse relationships that are symptomatic of the modern world (1976: 166).

The alternative response—but one that that equally evokes this economic determinist construct of the city—comprises the radical and Marxist approaches (Corrigan and Leonard 1978). The city of industrial capitalism is determining: it shapes and oppresses, and structures inequality between groups; it can only ultimately be overcome by the 'down tools' strategies of a revolution of the means of production.

City as System

The city as system suggests viewing the city as made up of a series of interconnected subsets or subcultures. This perspective eschews the primacy of economic determinism, underpinning the *city as machine* in favour of a biological or ecological analogy of interdependent elements which constitute the whole. The city is viewed as an organism where the function of the whole is greater than each of its parts. This type of understanding of the city is borrowed from the Chicago School human ecology of the city in which cultures and subcultures emerge for consideration. Links between the physical place and its social and economic dimensions are made in as much as they emerge in intricate patterns which can be analysed and subject to intervention. The city as system engages with the propensities of communities to survive, develop and shape their realities, and to claim resources and place in conflict with other. But it is a zero sum competition for scarce resources in which there are winners and losers. In *city as system*, deprived or disadvantaged areas, ghettos and slums are formed, and associated concepts such as the 'cycle of deprivation' and 'culture of poverty' enter the social work lexicon. The social work intervention becomes to break this cycle of identifications in family systems and the dysfunctional social networks of place. There are various ways to achieve this; via the communication of bourgeois values and ways of life, the removal of the vulnerable, or via more structural place-based interventions aimed at forging moral adaptation and change. The recognisable social work method that follows from this type of visioning is the systems approaches adopted by Kolko Phillips and Lala Shulamith Straussner's (2002) as the basis for urban social work. The critique of systems approaches in social work is well-rehearsed (Jani and Reisch 2011), principally on the basis of the fact that the search for stasis and equilibrium in the system is a recipe for maintenance of the status quo. Systems approaches are inherently conservative methods, embracing incremental rather than radical change, largely deficit-oriented and often silent on issues of power.

City as Community

The compositional elements of community are the focus of the work of early communitarians such as Jane Addams (1860–1935), with their interest in invigorating local neighbourhoods towards sustainable change. For them, the built environment is seen as prohibitive and determining, and the salve for such communitarians is empowering people themselves towards ownership and control of their environments. Octavia Hill's housing projects in city slums were underpinned by such ideas, coupling the shaping of the moral economy with an instrumental pragmatism. The settlement house, the soup kitchen, the model village, the community garden, the tenants association, the milieu of community—these become the place of intervention in this model. The city is composed of a community of communities, bounded and defined by place, patch, estate, quarter, postcode (see Henderson and Thomas 2015). The social work task is preventative, flexible to local needs, strengths-based and immersed. The work includes conscientisation, activism and co-production with communities founded on a place-based assets approach. Delgado's (2000) text advances an urban social work in this vein, focusing on community work and community empowerment, community assets in self-provisioning and forms of informal mutual aid (see also Smith et al. 2009). The notion is that, if the right resources are available to a community, it will manage its own relations and responsibilities. Thus, urban social work is community work with all the attendant issues incumbent on the critique of community and localism. How to define, determine and measure community? (Coulton 2005) How to avoid parochialism and the neglect of social structural impacts? How to garner and evaluate community effort such that it doesn't go into attrition and fragment into disparate localisms that constantly reinvent the wheel? (Brueggermann 2014). And ultimately, city as community is challenged by its neglect to analyse the role of the state in local affairs (Mowbray 2011).

City as Environment

More recently, social work attention has focused on resurrecting the missing dimension of *person in environment* (PIE) approaches—that of the natural ecology. Zapf's (2010) argument, for example, is that although PIE is deeply embedded in social work thinking, the environment in this formulation is the social environment of family, kinship and network, rather than the natural ecology of place. The movement for environmental sustainability in social work encapsulates the risks cities pose to natural environments, the risks that ensue from waste, over-consumption and growth for human wellbeing and the risks from climate change. The city as a construct is damaging to the environment and urbanisation has deleterious consequences (Dominelli 2012). Responses include approaches focused on the promotion of environmental sustainability, such as international advocacy and activism and eco-systems. These perspectives have brought green issues to the fore, including the role of green spaces in wellbeing. Rather less attention has been given to other aspects of the physical environment—most particularly, the built environment. The literature also has a tendency towards determinist interpretations of environment, neglecting to consider city environments as highly *relational* spaces and places in which people exert agency.

As will be evident, these visionings are not mutually exclusive; neither do they suggest a unified urban social work. But they are instructive in illustrating the relative emphasis of social work approaches and the ways in which the city becomes defined within the discursive field of social work. They are, however, partial and don't attest to the complexities of work in the modern city. It is of note that the late 1990s marked a watershed in the focus on something distinctively named 'urban social work'. The city, place, neighbourhood, urban or its referents, now scarcely appear in the social work literature. Ask a practitioner today 'What is urban social work?' and you'll be lucky to get a coherent answer (see Chap. 3). This, in itself, is interesting as it begs the question why the urban should have fallen into attrition at the very moment the explosive import of the *urban age* (itself a discursive mechanism) has come into academic and popular parlance. We appear to have lost our place in one of the most critical debates of our times.

Finding Our Place: Revisiting Urban Themes, Repositioning Social Work

A new paradigm for action attuned to these twenty-first-century realities is under development, if not as yet coherently articulated. In an era of economic globalisation and neo-liberal ideologies, creative solutions and strategies are implied and, as social work is being reconfigured, so its transformative potential is being released. The city offers a privileged locale within which these efforts and success stories cohere and can be articulated. However, social work needs an orchestrating focus for these ideas, a conceptual framework within which to locate and map collective and individual action, to capture the diverse nature of the work being undertaken, varying roles, and a framework that will provide recognition and legitimate the social work identity in an age of uncertainties.

Social workers have a key role in city-making processes built on fundamental and enduring concerns with social justice (inequalities and inequities), care (relational dimensions, both individual and collective) and sustainability (viable actions that promote continuity). They have a dual vantage point being deeply immersed as both citizen participants and social actors in city life. Over time, social work has evolved from a focus on its compensatory mandate—what I referred to as the 'street cleaner model'—to challenging the sources of distress, actively reshaping and reframing policy interventions, and crafting new forms of social solidarity: what might be called a 'cooperative city design mode l'. It is timely to consider the city 'as resource rather than a cause', to quote Amin and Thrift (2002: 2). Van Ewijk (2009) has argued that, in the face of trenchant neo-liberal policies, social work has hunkered down and, in retreat, has more forcibly articulated its social justice mandate. However, he fears this is not enough and urges the profession towards what he calls 'citizenship based social work'. Van Ewijk's new designs follow the impact of a threefold devolution within contemporary welfare states characterised by a shift from the state to the market, from the state to civil society and from the state to community. He argues that these shifts signal the diminishing leadership of the central state, with local authorities responsible for localised social objectives and a refreshed role for civil society, municipalities and the market at local level. He suggests social professionals require new competencies and orientations to navigate these positive and negative impacts of this new terrain; that they have a critical role in trying to influence the transformation process underway in the direction of social justice. What could such a model imply for urban social work? I would argue the starting point lies in revisiting, and making an appropriate reconnection with, four key dimensions: *place and space* in urban dynamics; issues of *scale(s)*; the concept of *social sustainability* and engagement with forms of *new civic governance*.

Place and Space

Place has a critical interplay with issues of social justice and wellbeing, both objective and subjective. Many of these relationships are complex. For example, the relationship between health and place suggests both positive and detrimental effects (Curtis 2010). Bai et al. (2012), for example, note that sprawling cities have more overweight people than do compact walkable cities, that the presence of natural environments in cities helps reduce stress and expedite recovery from illness, and those in cities dependent on cars are exposed to increased traffic accidents. But considerations of place move us beyond the quantifiable. Place speaks to relationships of belonging/identity and attachment, to ways of accessing services and to the ways in which individuals, groups and communities collectively mobilise in meeting their needs. It suggests an interest in how people are inscribed in spaces and places, and the meanings they attribute to them through their 'lived' experiences of displacement and disloca- tion, settlement and resettlement, grief and memory; an interest in the variety of ways in which people manage their encounters with strangers and take control over their own destiny.

The city is therefore much more than a backdrop to practice. It is lived and known in places and spaces. Horschelmann and van Blerk (2012), for example, adopting this *relational* perspective of the city, show how constructions of childhood and constructions of the city inter-relate and how childhood identities are formed and shaped via the lived experience of city life. Their approach contests discourses that propose 'the shrink- ing world of childhood' predicated on the dangers and risks of city living by looking at the ways in which children utilise city spaces and places, form place attachments and exercise agency over place. In this vein, Jack (2015) argues that acknowledgement of *place*—and, in particular, place attachments—in children's lives would serve to enhance social work assessments and bring to the fore hitherto absent considerations of child wellbeing (see Chap. 4).

Looking at issues of race and ethnicity, Neely and Samura (2011) make explicit the connections between spatial and racial processes, and suggest that the notion of racialised space provides a language for explain- ing enduring and sustained forms of racial inequality in its varied and, very often, subtle forms today. Space for them becomes a tangible mani- festation of racial inequality in terms of contestation over issues such as residential segregation, global displacement and land theft. In this way, Neely and Samura highlight the role of power relations as embedded in place and space.

Place must be a central consideration. Where we live is intimately connected to wellbeing. Locational disadvantage and the intensification of socio-spatial polarisation at neighbourhood levels are evident in cities across Europe, USA and Australia (Kelaher et al. 2010). So-called neighbourhood or *area effects* have known impacts on health and wellbeing, and call for place-based interventions (Atkinson and Kintrea 2004; Atkinson et. al 2012). Moreover, it has been demonstrated how we, as professionals, frame place and can contribute to stigmatising effects. Research by Atkinson and Kintrea (2004) draws on practitioner accounts to illustrate perceptions of neighbourhood disadvantage in two major UK cities. Their interviews with 50 public service professionals not only confirms a growing body of evidence on the detrimental impacts of stigma on residents' imaginaries, but also indicates the role of neighbourhood disadvantage in compounding lack of opportunity and area level disadvantage. Kelaher et al. (2010) also demonstrate that stigmatised residential identities internalised as a result of living in disadvantaged areas confer fair/poor health status and life satisfaction: first, via stress—which is directly associated with adverse mental and physical outcomes, and, second, via adopted behaviours that undermine health. They provide evidence to suggest that such stigma affects help-seeking behaviour and trust in public services based on residents' perceived lack of respect, prejudice and labelling by professional health service staff. These are important social justice considerations for social work.

Considerations of place and space have also been expanded via geographies of care perspectives (Milligan and Wiles 2010). The concept of care as an ethical imperative of social work and its pragmatic and affective dimensions have been much theorised (Barnes 2012). The gendering of care, the responsibilities and needs of carers—old and young, and issues related the formal and informal workforce of caring are part of these considerations (see Chap. 8). In recent years however, and particularly within human geography, more attention has been given to the spatiality of care, drawing attention to issues of ethics of care across spatial scales stretching from the local and place specific to the global (Milligan et al. 2007; Milligan and Wiles 2010). Whilst much of this work has focused on health care in the *therapeutic landscapes* tradition (Parr and Philo 2003), there are a number of potential avenues for work in relation to social care and support and social work in urban space. Geographers working on this theme have considered the design of care settings, people's relationship to particular welfare hubs or to oases of care in the city. Also considered are the shifts in the location of care following care restructuring such as de-institutionalisation and community care, the relocation of hospitals, clinics and care homes (see, for example, Conradson 2003). In this way, considerations of proximity, distance and temporality are brought to bear on relations of care in the city. Where care takes place is highly significant; how it is performed in localised ideologies of care that are *care-full* and *care-less* spaces and places (Milligan et al. 2007: 137) opens up important emplaced dynamics for social work consideration.

Care technologies are also rapidly changing not only the nature of care in terms of where care takes place, but also how it is supported, overseen and regulated. In all these ways, social geographers are opening up new directions in understanding care as related to place—understandings that are highly relevant to urban practice.

Other perspectives on place throw light on the opportunities the city provides for informalities and sociality in promoting happiness, quality of life, wellbeing, closeness, respect and solidarity within the interpersonal economy (Tonkiss 2013). The built environment can foster such encounters by design or serendipitously in streets, parks and play spaces, and through art and architecture that is people enhancing, promoting care values, reciprocities and opportunities for social cohesion (Fincher and Iveson 2008). Knowledge of these urban dynamics and the analysis of place and space is foundational to urban practice.

Scale

In extending and developing urban practice, social workers will need a better understanding of scale in devising interventions. What is evident in the contemporary city is that multi-tiered levels of influence (local, regional, national, international) and multi-scalar analysis (neighbourhood, suburb, municipality, city and region) are required. Questions of scale include the matrix of *glocal* considerations, and the ways in which assessments and interventions need to consider global connectivity that has local manifestations. Work with migrants (see Chap. 6), unaccompanied minors, human trafficking, migrant care workers and more indicates the ways in which these considerations become critical in social work assessments. Being able to analyse, mobilise and evaluate arenas of influence in order to effect change will be vital to urban practice, as will be transferring knowledges and messages gleaned from local practices from one scale to another.

Operationalising scale at city level often reveals a mismatch between boundaries that are determined by government and those that are apparent in practice. Smith et al. (2009) demonstrate the ways in which different types of intervention are more or less effective on different levels of scale—from the highly local, to supra-local and regional, to the virtual—and in complex combinations. Their work highlights how community empowerment projects need to be attuned to the multiple scales of reference in looking at how 'community' is defined and operates, even *within* area-based initiatives and how such projects need to move beyond simple binaries of place-based or people-based interventions to multi-scaled interventions that can incorporate synergies between neighbourhood-scale and city-scale strategies. Too often, social work effort is framed in 'either/or' ways as a focus on the individualised and localised, or the macro-picture. A more refined understanding of scales of action needs to be demonstrated in relation to the efficacy of social work interventions.

Social Sustainability

Interventions by scale are closely related to issues of social sustainability. Sustainability as a concept is broad and multi-focal; it encompasses overlapping issues of environmental, social and economic sustainability. The concept is particularly relevant to urban practices in social work and there is some literature that considers the concept from a social work perspective (Coates 2003; Mary 2008); however, extensions to urban contexts are, as yet, underworked. McKenzie (2004) has argued that the level of attention paid to the social dimensions of sustainability is rarely given the same weight as that paid to economic and environmental concerns and speaks of (2004: 11) 'a paucity of genuine research within the framework of sustainability into what sustains and promotes an equitable and just society'. McKenzie defines social sustainability as 'a life enhancing condition within communities, and a process within communities that can achieve that condition' and outlines its key features as:

- Equity of access to services;
- Equity between generations;
- A system of cultural relations in which the positive aspects of disparate cultures are valued and protected, and in which cultural integration is supported and promoted;
- Widespread political participation of citizens not only in electoral procedures, but also in other areas of political activity, particularly at local level;
- A system of transmitting awareness of social sustainability from one generation to the next;
- A sense of community responsibility for maintaining that system of transmission;
- Mechanisms for a community collectively to identify its strengths and needs;
- Mechanisms for a community, where possible, to fulfil its own needs through community action;
- Mechanisms for political advocacy to meet needs that cannot be met by community action.

Safe, strengthened and revitalized neighbourhoods and communities lie at the heart of future welfare systems. Social sustainability implies a shift away from macro-level policy and intervention to a focus on innovation at the local level (Oosterlynck et al. 2013). Society is understood by reference to the space (localities) it occupies, bringing into view civic space, location of services, city design, transport, and the potential and capital of the inhabitants themselves and local governance (Dillard et al. 2009). Strategies of social sustainability are being adopted by social services with considerable implications for the social work role (see Evers et al. 2006; WACOSS 2015). For McKenzie, social sustainability is predicated on robust inter-disciplinary partnerships and *communities of practice* that engage a range of professionals working towards specified goals.

Local Governance and Civil Society

The importance of the local welfare state in supporting redistributive policies and initiatives, enhancing cohesion, promoting participation, and in generating and consolidating innovations is an established feature of contemporary welfare restructuring (Evers et al. 2006; Mowbray 2010; Oosterlynck et al. 2013). Greater decentralisation and devolution of function is the norm with the aim of establishing sustainability targets, more democratic inclusion and greater collaboration between a range of professionals in service delivery. Refreshed and proximate forms of governance within the welfare municipality and localised social policy open up critical avenues of influence for social work.

The revival of area-based initiatives is evident everywhere; for example, Social Inclusion Partnerships in England, Community First in Wales, and Social City initiatives in a range of European countries (Evers et al. 2006). It is somewhat surprising that a more comprehensive analysis of the politics of the local state doesn't feature more in social work literature (Manalo 2016). The tendency has been to raise the spectre of the impact of neo-liberal politics and methods and their impact on social work without a critical consideration of the social justice responsibilities of the state and an appraisal of points of leverage. Opportunities for forging change towards social justice objectives are being lost in oppositional stances. Mowbray (2011: 148), arguing specifically in relation to community development intellectuals, suggests that they have ignored the local state in their practice orientation. He suggests a number of reasons why the local state should command the attention of social professionals, notwithstanding its role in land use planning and building design. He argues local government's social reformist activities include:

- Locating and controlling access to urban amenities and services, including transport;
- Influencing the overall supply of housing and other accommodation;
- Shaping the built and natural environment, affecting liveability and climate;
- Collecting taxes and revenues;

- Implementing and extending wider economic policy, including neo-liberal priorities such as the privatisation of public services;
- Providing the institutional means through which people are included or excluded from hierarchies of status, power and influence, affecting overall social relations;
- Regulating behaviour, directly and indirectly, through law enforcement and urban design;
- Advocating or pursuing sectional interests over potentially diverse social, economic and political issues.

Mowbray's nudge is towards practitioners becoming better equipped to engage more broadly with local government and 'move it towards becoming an institution better structured to pursue social justice and environmental sustainability' (2011: 149). The state is the principle institutional actor in the mediation of struggles over welfare—but it is not benign or neutral in its effect. The new welfare framework and the positioning of the state 'as the site of both injustices and their remediation' and 'a terrain of struggle' (Fincher and Iveson 2008: 16) requires activism from outside and within to chip away at policies and negative practices.

Social work is uniquely positioned to play a key role within local area planning as the integration of physical, social, economic, environmental and cultural factors is an established principle of the policy agenda. These devolved and highly localised states are highly differentiated internally in relation to different fields of practice (see Evers et al. 2006; Evers 2010) but their proximity to communities means they are best placed to generate an understanding of needs, to frame the identification of social problems, to reinforce the link between social and spatial considerations, to actively involve citizens in decision-making processes, to provide information and enhance participation in issues that affect wellbeing and quality of life, and to forge new models of service delivery. Evers et.al. (2006) suggests new forms of cooperation and collaboration are rivalling the logic of administrative reforms driven by the philosophy of New Public Management, arguing that a process of learning the new elements of networked cooperative style planning and policy-making is important to all forms of sustainability.

The significance of social work's place in civil society in an era of devolution and direct democracy, when publics are invited to seek greater levels of participation and active citizenship in issues that impact of their wellbeing, cannot be overstated. Social work can maximise robust participation of politically weaker, less organised and disadvantaged social groups, or those that are hard to reach—such as young people, migrants, disabled people and vulnerable others. This can be achieved via advocacy, empowerment, helping them to build their own associations, or creating spaces for public debate and deliberation. Social work has a role in contributing towards ensuring equal opportunities for all and opening up access for all, and in forging new forms of social solidarity. In this respect, it cannot be a lone actor. The ways in which social movements, expressions of citizenry and social action are mobilised in the city are important new knowledges for social work. An understanding of what this implies for the professional, in terms of ways of working is needed and is far greater than responses based simply on the politics of resistance and defensiveness.

The barriers to the pursuit of social justice ambitions are many but Tonkiss (2010) argues for the import of *small acts of urbanism* as critical to moving *from austerity to audacity*. Tonkiss invites us to consider the arenas of space and place beyond the state purview; she invites us to engage with the informal spaces and places that express agency and resilience. This realm is, of course, complex. Tonkiss (2013: 21) has also drawn attention to the notion of the contradicitions of *urban informality* and proposes it as a multi-faceted phenomenon. These arenas—beyond the state of undocumented and informal networks, and autonomous social services—can provide opportunities such as temporary shelter, housing, transient economic opportunities, can mobilise credit and offer forms of mutual support and self-help amongst low-income groups. At the same time, these arenas operate to exploit the vulnerable. Thus, Tonkiss points out: 'the opportunities for self provisioning, mutual aid, petty entrepreneurialism and urban innovation are paralleled by conditions of abandonment, insecurity, racketeering and immiseration' (2013: 21).

Social work will need a sophisticated understanding of the ways in which cities are infra-political environments, as well as subject to the direct interventions of planners, architects and others involved in design. Cities provide a locale for social action and pursuit of social interests as places where both formal and substantive citizenship rights are enacted, but they are also arenas for contestation over rights, including conflicts over settlement and the uses of public spaces.

Conclusion

In revisiting the past, we look to the future. The evolution and development of social work need not create a path of dependency. Particular constructions of the social work task, its mode and methodologies, and particular scripts of the city need not impose the logic of the future. A new departure is implied by an extraordinary confluence of factors that proscribe the contemporary moment. Social work is malleable and adaptable to change, but it also has a core mission and ethical commitment to promote social change in the pursuit of human rights and social justice. The shift from the 'street cleaner model' to the 'cooperative city design model' is afoot. Finding our place in the city mobilises social work values and the ethic of care; it shifts thinking about the role of social work as that of provider to its role as innovator, fixer, creator and entrepreneur in the urban space, creating possibilities and seizing opportunities in a collaborative change effort. It carves out a new relationship with other professionals engaged in city-making, including urban planners, activists and social movements as a *community of practice* (Wenger 2000). It extrapolates social work's capacity enhancing roles, its roles in crafting social solidarities and its social advocacy roles in narrating alternative stories about the city. We have moved *beyond the soup kitchen*. New knowledges suggest the need for the *urbanising* of social work practice; the need to put the city back into social work.

References

Amin, A., & Thrift, N. (2002). *Cities: Reimagining the urban*. Cambridge: Polity Press.

Atkinson, R., & Kintrea, K. (2004). 'Opportunities and despair: It's all in there'. Practitioner experiences and explanations of area effects and life chances. *Sociology, 38*(3), 437–455.

Atkinson, S., Fuller, S., & Painter, J. (Eds.). (2012). *Wellbeing and place.* Farnham: Ashgate.

Bai, X., Nath, I., Capon, A., Hasan, N., & Jaron, D. (2012). Health and wellbeing in the changing urban environment: Complex challenges, scientific responses and the way forward. *Environmental Sustainability, 4,* 485–472.

Barnes, M. (2012). *Care in everyday life: An ethic of care in practice.* Bristol: Policy Press.

Brueggermann, W. (2014). *The practice of macro social work* (3rd ed.). Belmont: Brooks Cole/Cencage Learning.

Bryan, B., Dadzie, S., & Scafe, S. (1985). *The heart of the race: Black women's lives in Britain.* London: Virago Press.

Coates, J. (2003). *Ecology and social work: Toward a new paradigm.* Halifax/Nova Scotia: Fernwood Publishing.

Conradson, D. (2003). Spaces of care in the city: The place of a community drop-in-centre. *Social and Cultural Geography, 4*(4), 507–525.

Corrigan, P., & Leonard, P. (1978). *Social work practice under capitalism: A Marxist approach.* Basingstoke: Palgrave Macmillan.

Coulton, C. (2005). The place of community in social work practice research: Conceptual and methodological developments. *Social Work Research, 29*(2), 73–86.

Curtis, S. (2010). *Space, place and mental health.* Farnham: Ashgate.

Delgado, M. (2000). *Community social work practice in an urban context: The potential of a capacity-enhancement perspective.* New York: Oxford University Press.

Dillard, J., Dujon, V., & King, M. C. (Eds.). (2009). *Understanding the social dimension of sustainability.* New York: Routledge.

Dominelli, L. (2012). *Green social work: From environmental crisis to environmental justice.* Cambridge: Polity Press.

Evers, A. (2010). Mixed welfare systems and hybrid organisations: Changes in the governance and provision of social services. *International Journal of Public Administration, 28*(9–10), 737–748.

Evers, A., Schulz, A. D., & Wiesner, C. (2006). Local policy networks in the programme social city: A case in point for new forms of governance in the field of local social work and urban planning. *European Journal of Social Work, 9*(2), 183–120.

Ferguson, I. (2008). *Reclaiming social work: Challenging neo-liberalism and promoting social justice.* London: Sage.

Ferguson, H. (2008). Liquid social work: Welfare interventions as mobile practices. *British Journal of Social Work, 38*(3), 561–579.

Fincher, R., & Iveson, K. (2008). *Planning and diversity in the city: Redistribution, recognition and encounter*. Basingstoke: Palgrave Macmillan.

Gleeson, B. (2014). *Coming through slaughter* (MSSI issues paper No. 3) Melbourne Sustainable Society Institute, University of Melbourne. http://www.sustainable.unimelb.edu.au/files/mssi/MSSI-IssuesPaper-3_Gleeson_2014_0.pdf. Accessed 5 Sept 2015.

Henderson, P., & Thomas, D. N. (2015). *Skills in neighbourhood work* (4th ed.). London: Routledge.

Horschelmann, K., & van Blerk, L. (2012). *Children, youth and the city*. London: Routledge.

IFSW (International Federation of Social Work). (2012). *A global agenda for social work and social development*. http://ifsw.org/get-involved/agenda-for-social-work/. Accessed 5 Sept 2015.

Jack, G. (2015). 'I may not know who I am, but I know where I am from': The meaning of place in social work with children and families. *Child and Family Social Work, 20*(4), 415–423.

Jani, S. J., & Reisch, M. (2011). The new politics of social work practice: Understanding context to promote change. *British Journal of Social Work, 42*(6), 1132–1150.

Kelaher, M., Warr, D. J., Feldman, P., & Tacticos, T. (2010). Living in 'Birdsville': Exploring the impact of neighbourhood stigma on health. *Health and Place, 16*, 381–388.

Kolko Phillips, N., & Lala Ashenberg Straussner, S. (2002). *Urban social work: An introduction to policy and practice in cities*. Boston: Allyn & Bacon.

Manalo, V. (2016). Engaging local government through neighbourhoods and communities. *Social Work, 61*(2), 163–5.

Mary, N. L. (2008). *Social work in a sustainable world*. Chicago: Lyceum.

McKenzie, S. (2004). *Social sustainability: Toward some definitions* (Hawke Research Institute working paper series No. 27), University of South Australia. http://www.unisa.edu.au/hawkeinstitute/research/ecosocial/eco-links.asp#THREE. Accessed 3 Apr 2015.

Meyer, C. (1976 [1970]). *Social work practice: A response to the urban crisis*, 2nd ed. New York: Free Press.

Milligan, C., Atkinson, S., Skinner, M., & Wiles, J. (2007). Geographies of care: A commentary. *New Zealand Geographer, 63*, 135–140.

Milligan, C., & Wiles, J. (2010). Landscapes of care. *Progress in Human Geography, 34*(6), 736–754.

Mowbray, M. (2011). What became of The Local State? Neo-liberalism, community development and local government. *Community Development Journal, 46*(1), 132–153.

Neal, S., & Agyeman, J. (2006). *The new countryside? Ethnicity, nation and exclusion in contemporary rural Britain.* Bristol: Policy Press.

Neely, B., & Samura, M. (2011). Space geographies of race: Connecting race and space. *Ethnic and Racial Studies, 34*(11), 1933–1952.

Olson, J. (2008). Social work's professional and social justice projects. *Journal of Progressive Human Services, 18*(1), 45–69.

Oosterlynck, S., Kazepov, Y., Novy A., Cools P., Barberis, E., Wukovitsch, F., Sarius, T., & Leubolt, B. (2013, April). *The butterfly and the elephant: Local social innovation, the welfare state and new poverty dynamics* (IMPROVE working papers, discussion paper No.13/03). http://improve-research.eu. Accessed 14 July 2015.

Parr, H., & Philo, C. (2003). Rural mental health and social geographies of care. *Social and Cultural Geography, 4*(4), 471–488.

Pearson, G. (1995). City of darkness, city of light: Crime, drugs and disorder in London and New York. In S. MacGregor & A. Lipow (Eds.), *The other city: People and politics in New York and London.* New Jersey: Humanities Press.

Reisch, M. (2013). What is the future of social work? *Critical and Radical Social Work, 1*(1), 67–85.

Reisch, M., & Andrews, J. (2001). *The road not taken: A history of radical social work in the United States.* Philadelphia: Brunner-Routledge.

Rogowski, S. (2010). *Social work: The rise and fall of a profession.* Bristol: Policy Press.

Smith, S., Bellaby, P., & Lindsay, S. (2009). Social inclusion at different scales in the urban environment: Locating the community to empower. *Urban Studies, 47*(7), 1439–1457.

Stoesz, D., Karger, H. J., & Carrilio, T. (2010). *A dream deferred: How social work lost its way and what can be done.* New Brunswick: Transaction Publishers.

Titmuss, R. (1968). *Commitment to welfare.* London: George Allen Unwin.

Tonkiss, F. (2010). From austerity to audacity: Interview with Fran Tonkiss on the emerging urbanism of small acts. (Authored by Francesca Ferguson) *Ucube 20.* http://www.uncubemagazine.com/sixcms/detail.php?id=12467995&articleid=art-1396020955634-5a47aa6a-80c5-48c9-aba2-f977368bdad9#!/page22. Accessed 4 Jan 2015.

Tonkiss, F. (2013). *Cities by design: The social life of urban form.* Cambridge: Polity Press.

van Ewijk, H. (2009). Citizenship-based social work. *International Social Work,* *52*(2), 167–179.

WACOSS (Western Australia Council of Social Services). (2015). *Model of social sustainability.* http://www.wacoss.org.au/downloads/socialsustainable.pdf. Accessed 14 July 2015.

Webb, S. (2007a). The comfort of strangers: Social work, modernity and late Victorian England, Part I. *European Journal of Social Work, 10*(1), 39–54.

Webb, S. (2007b). The comfort of strangers: Social work, modernity and late Victorian England, Part II. *European Journal of Social Work, 10*(2), 193–207.

Wenger, E. (2000). *Communities of practice* and Social Learning Systems. Organization May 2000 vol. 7 no. 2225-246.

Zapf, M. K. (2010). Social work and the environment: Understanding people and place. *Critical Social Work, 11*(3), 30–46.

3

Reconstructing Urban Social Work

Charlotte Williams

Introduction

Practice constructions of what might be called 'urban social work' require some interrogation. The notion evokes *place*, most specifically cities, as its remit and in doing so marks out some kind of distinction from places elsewhere—namely, suburban, small town, or rural and remote. It conjures certain imaginings of practice engagement with challenging issues such as slums, homelessness, addictions, sex work, racial conflict, mental stress, violence and much more. It may even hint at notions of higher levels of personal risk for the social worker, in terms of safety and security and in terms of job satisfaction. All these assumptions are contestable and require revisiting critically. It is not difficult to imagine that social work perceptions of the city are particularly skewed. Day-to-day contact with the most disadvantaged individuals and communities contributes to depictions of urban life as dark, damaging, precarious and perilous for

C. Williams (✉)
School of Global, Urban and Social Studies, RMIT University,
GPO Box 2476, Melbourne, VIC 3001, Australia

© The Editor(s) (if applicable) and The Author(s) 2016
C. Williams (ed.), *Social Work and the City*,
DOI 10.1057/978-1-137-51623-7_3

those who live and work there. Discourses of 'problem neighbourhoods', rough areas, poor or 'disadvantaged estates' and 'no-go' or high risk suburbs are part and parcel of the social work narrative of the city. Children's social workers in the ethnographic study by D'Cruz (2004: 120), for example, talked of 'working in a war zone' and feelings of being under siege. The city, the inner city and the urban are all subject to multiple constructions and these visualisations of the urban context play a significant role in how practice interventions are perceived. Take, for example, this excerpt from a social work students' blog posted online by Monte Williams and published in the *New York Times* (2000):

> However awash New York City is in Wall Street bonuses and budget surpluses, venture capital and disposable income, it remains for some people one of the world's great social work laboratories—full of poor, troubled people, children at risk and marriages coming apart. And its magnetic pull brings people here from all corners of the country.
>
> Christina Kucera, who recently completed the social work graduate program at Hunter College and is from Columbia, Mo., said, 'Moving to New York, I think I've compromised my safety, but I'm much more concerned for the safety of the people I've worked with. I chose to move to New York because it has one of the largest social service networks in the country,' she said. 'I also chose New York to practise because of the diversity of the people and the complexity of the socio-political climate. Under Giuliani, social services have been cut back. Nevertheless, I think even in these difficult times, New York City is an exciting place to study and practise social work.'

The city in this account is thrilling and, at the same time, full of risk. These competing visions are not solely the domain of social work; yet, social workers have been deeply implicated in scripting the city, particularly in relation to generating understandings of the poor and formulating responses to 'the urban condition'.

So, what is the contemporary narrative of the city? How relevant is the profession in the context of the modern city? What adaptations in thinking and practice methods are necessary? In any consideration of urban themes in twenty-first-century social work, there is a need to balance the prescriptive with the descriptive. What is to be said about social work within the city by social workers themselves? These insights from practice are instructive in reconstructing urban social work. This chapter draws on a small study of social work 'voices' to illustrate the demands of practice in one city context. We hear practitioner views on the nature of urban social work, city change and its impacts, and the possibilities and potentials there are for reworking social work efforts in this arena. Based on these 'soundings', the chapter then proceeds to draw out some principles for a revisioning of social work in the city.

Revisiting Urban Practice: What Practitioners Say

An expert seminar for practitioners was held on the subject of 'Social work and the City' at RMIT University, Melbourne, Australia in August 2015. Melbourne is an interesting case study for consideration in many respects. The rate of growth in a short space of time has been exponential; indeed, Melbourne is considered one of the most rapidly urbanised and densely populated cities in the world. Since the mid-1960s, its population has doubled and continues to rise rapidly. It has also significantly diversified, being a city where almost half of the population (48%) is born in countries other than Australia and languages other than English are spoken at home by 38% of the municipality's residents. By 2050, the number of those over 65 years of age will double and those over 85 will quadruple. The seminar occurred soon after the Victoria government launched its 10-year strategic plan, Plan Melbourne (DTPLT 2014), which refers to the need to build strong communities via social and economic participation, developing local place-based focused programmes and innovative partnerships.

This chapter is based on the findings from this small research study, which included in-depth interviews with a convenience sample of key social work leaders involved in city shaping (n = 6) and a focus group conducted with practitioners (n = 11) working in front-line roles in the city convened as part of the expert seminar. Interviews lasted approximately one hour and the focus group session ran for two hours. The project was subject to RMIT University ethical review. An open invitation to participate was sent to social work Field Educators and other partners of the social work discipline at RMIT. The seminar aimed to open a dialogue about their visioning and values; their skills, strategies and know-how; and the impact on their practice of enabling or restrictive infrastructure and processes. They were asked to share their views of their positioning and response to contemporary challenges of urban living, the types of action and intervention available to them, the nature of their collaborations, innovations in practice, leadership and recognition of the profession at city level. A stimulus presentation was provided to participants on the theme. The participants completed a short questionnaire aimed at gathering basic demographic information and information about their work settings. All attributing details have been anonymised in this account and the names used are purely fictional. The account does not claim to be representative but, rather, to provide a snap-shot into social work discourses of urban practice.

These discussions were considered as qualitative soundings. Transcripts and notes from the focus group were read several times; themes were identified and the quotes that best captured their response to these themes were extracted for analytical purposes. Themes are presented here in composite form with some illustrative quotations for the story they tell of social work and one major city.

Talking About the City: Urban Themes in Contemporary Social Work

Visualising Urban Spaces

It is perhaps unsurprising that the term 'urban social work' has little currency with many of the practitioners in this study. In some respects, the assumption of the city is so complete that, whilst explicating urban themes wasn't too difficult, the identification of an urban social work had less resonance. This oversight was attributed by some to something particularly Australian and associated with the rapid development of Australian cities and the almost quantum leap from the primordial Aboriginal owned landscape or, as Maria put it: '*From a dreaming place to a town straight away....*' '*We not entirely comfortable yet with what it is to live in the city*', Maria proposed, seeing the urban challenge as relatively recent, of perhaps little more than twenty to twenty-five years.

> *We don't tend to think in terms of urban social work. This may be a product of Australian cultural identity and the relatively recent growth of cities in Australia … we are very connected to the rural/remote in our thinking* (Jill).

Other respondents drawing on their experience of working in cities elsewhere, for example London, more readily recognised the term and associated it with the dense high-rise housing estates and the associated multiple layered and complex interlocking social problems. It was the '*them and us worlds*', said Nigel, '*the have's and have nots embedded into the built environment*'. For him, inner city work conjured an '*embattlement ground*' that required a type of '*guerrilla social work*'. He recalled work on these housing estates as full of risk and endangerment.

Cities, of course, vary in their urban forms and development. Melbourne is not characterised by these types of vast poor-housing estates (see Chap. 10). Practitioners suggested its divisions are more subtle and implicitly embedded in mixed neighbourhoods, which becomes apparent in the mismatch between the visualisations of lifestyle in the city and the lived experiences of those pushed out to the margins, or enclosed in discrete patches and '*closed worlds*' (Nigel) within inner city spaces. Nigel spoke of the '*hidden dysfunction*' within the shiny new estates and the billboard image of the perfect Australian family '*doing hidden harm*' all in 'the defence of privacy'.

The theme of the breakdown of the social fabric and loss of community in urban living featured large in the accounts, particularly in what was referred to as the '*vertical communities*' of high-rise social housing. Participants spoke of this loss of connectedness and isolation, in spatial terms as well as in terms of participation and engagement. For example, Maria talked of a '*poverty of participation*', a '*poverty of control over your destiny*' and '*a poverty of intimacy*' that she felt social work should address. Nigel noted: '*What we have lost because of change in the built environment, loss of green space and sites of conviviality and the 360° vision opportunities*'.

These observations locate the urban community geographically but also in terms of forms of association and social networks that afford surveillance and oversight in the collective care effort reminiscent of what

Jane Jacobs in her classic text called the 'eyes upon the street, eyes belonging to those we might call the natural proprietors of the street' (1993 [1961]: 45). The workers made reference to broader concepts of communities of interest and the virtual communities of connectedness that the city generates, confirming, as Delgado (1999) suggests, that any definition of the urban must include multiple dimensions of place and space not simply be in terms of fixed geographies.

The participants' mind maps of the city included not only a proficient sense of geographically referenced disadvantaged areas, but also an intricate mapping of service delivery points, both formal and informal. Catherine referred to '*welfare hubs*' in the city—which she defined as '*known places of safety, help and security*'—where clients feel as though it is their community and feel protected by the proximity of formal and informal services. People are drawn to these places and spaces of welfare in the city, she suggested: '*pulled by anonymity and the proliferation of services and pushed toward them by their marginalisation*'. An acute sense of these 'landscapes of care' (Gleeson and Kearns 2001) as historically embedded places in the city extended to an understanding of other urban oases, including those that were noted as specifically ethnicised or indigenised spaces of Aboriginal life in the city where both formal and informal services had evolved.

Maria commented on the basic human need for intimacy played out in people's search for proximity to others in public spaces, and how social work has a role in fostering connection in everyday lives of the marginalised and vulnerable: '*It's about intimacy, your comfort factor in public space, it's about a sense of say over your destiny where you get to sit every day… about empowerment*'.

In providing these conceptualisations of the relationship between the built environment and human interaction, the participants revealed a considered spatial awareness of urban dynamics. This was not simply the construction of urban social work via the labelling of poor estates, or depictions of social work endangerment out on the streets but, rather, a sophisticated account of cities as human spaces in which mobilities of various kinds can be viewed and an account which speaks to the interconnections between urban and rural. For example, one city council worker spoke of taking an anthropological approach to the assessment of disabled people's pathways through the city towards a service point. He noted the pull of the city for disabled people from regional and remote areas to this central hub for association and the satisfaction of needs, and the ways in which disabled people had to navigate the built environment in their routes from the station. '*We tracked them, watched them, waited and listened to them talk about it and then built our plan to meet their needs*' (James). Miri gave an account of the ways in which an initiative of not-for-profit organisations aimed at supporting children in care within the city had worked with paradoxical intent, acting as a magnet to pull rural youth toward the city, forming new communities of association and, inadvertently, placing them at increased risk via exposure to offenders, drug cultures and other risks. These young people were mobilised in city space as a community of interest coming from a range of locations but sharing an Indigenous Islander heritage.

Angela spoke of the importance of free spaces in the city to the identification of needs. She illustrated how libraries provided spaces of solace and safety for the homeless, those fleeing domestic violence and for vulnerable children, detailing the ways in which they are critical hubs for the identification of needs yet remaining overlooked by formal providers. The focus group discussion illustrated the tensions manifest in such spaces as being open to access for all irrespective of user status, and therefore non-stigmatising, but at the same time imposing conditions. Such places, as Fincher and Iveson (2008: 222) point out 'permit certain forms of socialities and do not permit others'.

City space is about ownership and belonging, and insight into how people mobilise these spaces; the types of support and assistance they need is crucial information to formal providers in building infrastructures of care. For Delgado (1999), 'non-traditional settings' provide for natural collectivities and what Amin and Thrift (2002: 41) have called 'untoward localisations' that the profession has yet to engage with in any systematic way. The importance of free spaces and the informalities of the city have not gone unnoticed by practitioners, although few had any brief to make use of them. Delgado (1999: 70) has argued that these 'urban sanctuaries'—places of retreat, safety and acceptance—are critical to the social work task in urban contexts. The informalities of the interpersonal economy of cities deserve social work attention, as they can be mobilised to plug the gaps in formalised provisioning and extend it; they hold the potential to make real transformations in the social relations of the city.

Practitioners argued they should be exploited, particularly in terms of building new and purposeful types of partnerships for action as part of emergent 'communities of practice' (Wenger 2000).

The spatial and relational mapping undertaken by the participants points to the central value to social work of the task of crafting engagement, conversations, connecting, making ties and knots in the social fabric of the city that lead to sustainable outcomes. Engendering agency and control in an often bewildering environment was suggested as an extremely important lens through which we can look at social work and the city:

> *In a highly dynamic and first world urban environment and habitat how does social work as a practice support or facilitate that sense of destiny at an individual level within the city? And with vulnerable groups?* (Maria).

> *We need to work on building solidarities and promoting dignity and worth as a citizen* (Focus group).

Thus, the visualisations of the city were not static, territorial or stereotyped but, rather, constructed as relational, felt and experienced.

Power, Social Justice and the City

The participants reflected on the ways in which cities, as relational spaces, manifest power within the built environment. In focus groups, they talked at length about city policies aimed at the 'cleansing' and 'sanitising' of urban space of those seen as 'ugly' or undesirable, and the ways in which social work is co-opted to '*keep people off the streets out of the eyes of nice society*' (Catherine). They discussed the exclusivities of the city, drawing on concepts of legitimacy and belonging that might easily have been lifted off the pages of Lefebvre's (1996) 'right to the city'. The talk turned to the social justice considerations in terms of who owns the space of the city, who gets a say in the built environment and who is seen as having a right to be there. This purification of urban spaces, they argued, occurs particularly around high-profile public events such as the Grand Prix or Melbourne Cup horse race, with place-marketing to a worldview, but participants also noted the everyday ways in which this occurs. The focus group discussion here turned on the range of mechanisms deployed to sanitise the streets. They talked about '*surveillance via CCTV but also via public opprobrium*'; about the '*generating of discourses of fear and raising of public anxieties*' of certain groups, such as the mentally ill, and the ways these discourses reduced the spaces available for some. They referred to '*hostile architectural responses*', such as spikes on railings, old tram stops being gated, the removal of drinking fountains and the ways the built environment moves people out as, more and more, '*the public realm has become privatised*' (Focus group).

These issues of access turned on particular groups of people denied their right to the city—in Lefebvre's (1996: 158) terms, 'both the right to inhabit and habituate'—those disabled, those mentally unwell, the homeless, Aboriginal peoples and vulnerable youth and children, amongst others. But they also talked about wider issues of the depersonalising of *the other* and the dehumanising processes of haste and hurry so characteristic of city life. —'*the rush and the rush of the day and how that excludes people*', within the indifference of city-ness (Focus group).

It is not difficult to see from the workers' accounts the ways in which people's lives are framed and lived in the city in multiple taxonomies of place. Fincher and Iveson (2008: 12) point to the range of ways in which people inhabit cities and 'the playing out of their biographies in time and space that is constrained or enabled by relations of power, including those expressed through the built form of the city'. There can be no client group to which this type of analysis cannot be applied. The city magnifies exclusion and marginalisation. Horschelmann and van Blerk (2011) and earlier work by Christensen and O'Brien (2003), for example, have demonstrated the ways in which spaces of childhood and youth are proscribed in city space. Discourses of fear and safety operate to restrict adventure and exploration for children, and to demarcate city space in the 'oughts' and 'shoulds' of public surveillance, with profound effects on children's psychology and identity. Women's safety and older people's freedom or restriction of movement was mentioned in this respect and the ways in which increased surveillance exacerbates discourses of fear and insecurity that powerfully shape their experiences.

These understandings of how individuals and group formations are structured in urban space extended to a consideration of how people contribute to the making of urban spaces and exert agency and control, and the emergence of creative spatial practices.

People are reclaiming (the city) through flash-mobs or pop ups. We need to be aware of how people use space politically (Angela).

It's very intensified and very visible here eg; people come from the rural to mobilise within the city, to have a say over their destiny (Maria)

People bring in their issues from the suburbs and from country towns to march on an issue — even bring rural issues to the city for visibility (John).

Cities are buzzing with initiatives and ideas. Brueggermann (2014) suggests social workers need to be good spotters of spontaneous social movements and community organising in order to enhance how people can and do contribute to the making of urban spaces.

The issues of social worker' power to contribute to, or counter, the framing of issues in city space was taken up by the respondents. Several of the accounts noted the ways in which '*big picture trends becoming highly visible in city space*' (Angela) and '*how these viewings frame and shape policy responses*' (Nigel). These constructions of urban issues can directly shape perceptions and decision-making about priorities and interventions, accordingly highlighting a key role for social work in rescripting the city. The focus group discussion raised concerns about social work's ethical commitments to these social justice issues, putting forward the argument that: '*the public realm has a responsibility to act in more inclusive ways*' (Maria).

Angela raised the issue of social work colluding in the processes of exclusion by reducing people's choices, lifestyles and places where they perform their everyday lives.

We have to ask: Is this practice promoting this person's dignity? Often it's not — its stripping people of the right to choice … and it strips them of their sense of say, of dignity of their citizenship (Angela).

The focus group argued that these sanitising processes lessen the experience for all and that, in banishing difference and diversity from the city, '*all of us are impoverished*'.

The scripts provide evidence that engagement with power and inequalities in cities is multi-dimensional. It requires action at the level of micro-everyday practice in terms of adding value to people's experiences and enhancing their sense of dignity and worth, as well as structural interventions. It requires the narration of inequalities and how they are expressed as needs. It requires the reframing of debates and engagement with a range of professionals including planners, architects, those involved in community safety, health and the army of human service workers working towards individual and community wellbeing.

Constraints, Challenges and Opportunities

Many of the respondents used the phrase 'the urban challenge' or 'challenges of the urban' in identifying a specific focus around which to reconstruct urban social work. The impacts of neo-liberal restructuring formed an underlying theme in all of the conversations. Participants talked about the ways in which their work is constrained by funding streams, being 'hamstrung' by bureaucracy, duplication and siloed thinking, and the shrinking possibilities for creativity and innovation. The short-termism and outcome-focused (rather than process-focused) nature of work was frequently reiterated, as were the ways in which care had been reduced to commercial transactions.

> *The downside is you can't do programs with longevity* (Catherine).

> *Not having the ability to be creative, being bound by legislation....hierarchy, bureaucracy and not being loose enough to go off on a tangent* (Paula).

The impact of neo-liberalism and austerity measures on workplace activity and relations is well-documented (Harris 2014), but the focus of this study prompted some introspection about the impact on ways of working in the city. Miri spoke of the physical retreat of formal services and the loss of connection to the locality—'*We're not amongst them anymore...there is no shopfront feel*'.
Miri suggested that:

> *Increased bureaucracy has withdrawn social work from the street, from the community—to out on the fringe. It's not that same sense of being part of the community...... We have also lost connection with other professionals; there is not that sense of joint functions or joint meetings—we've lost shared work, joint working together forged by co-location of professionals.*

There was acknowledgement of the continued effects of what Webb (2007: 52) called the 'regulation by distance' founded on desk-based management.

I don't know that practice models are so mobile, a lot of service is delivered at the office. It would be interesting to see how outreach operates ...... to do social work like it used to be done (Angela).

Others mentioned the challenge of the turnover of personnel in a very diverse range of agencies. In urban settings, there is almost constant change with '*different people moving in and out of agencies*' (Paula) and '*This is one of the biggest challenges for staff in an urban environment. You have to know every Tom Dick and Harry and keep up with the changes*' (Paula).

Accordingly, trying to change things at area level or city level via collaborations was seen as somewhat difficult.

People move around in their roles quite frequently and because you are dependent on the person it's not structured and quite fragile so the challenge is to make sure it [collaboration] *is cemented in as part of a regular expectation because it's not or only loosely framed...* (Miri).

Issues of collaboration and coordination were identified by almost every participant in the study as a particular challenge in the urban context. Despite the legislative push to mandate more systematic collaboration, the barriers were flagged as a continuing challenge. The duplication of effort with many of agencies doing the same things was frequently identified.

Micro-agencies doing the same work and money is misdirected to these agencies when it could be built via a connection with community to help people in place (Nigel).

This was seen by one respondent as contributing to the sense of disconnect from people and the failure to draw on service users to define the subtleties of service delivery. There were, for Nigel, many lost opportunities through lack of community engagement, and he argued that social work was needed to enable genuine participation.

Others saw the hampering of collaboration as a result of competitive tendering which reconfigured relationships between agencies and, at times, set them against each other, in a particular '*master servant relationship*' between state organisations and the not-for-profit sector fostered by the '*level of scrutiny and increased expectations around funding*' (Miri).

The collaborative effort that exists appears to be ad hoc, lacking systemisation and difficult to sustain beyond personal relationships that too often fall into attrition with staff turnover.

> *Collaboration has to be driven via strong leadership —it's the essence of good practice but it never gets sorted—and therefore it is a constant leadership challenge. You have to work across portfolios—to innovate, garner effort, have a voice* (Jill).

> *The challenge is to do it in a way that is regular and systematic and not as a reaction to an adverse issue or event* (Miri).

> *There are forums but you have to develop them yourself. You have to push it so you've got to find like-minded colleagues in other areas and agencies and you start with that person initially and you've got to grow it—but there is not really an authorising environment* (Miri).

The challenge of greater service user involvement was welcomed by participants. A big shift was noted in attempts to collaborate with clients in the light of more personalised care models reconfiguring the social work task. The imperative to seek client inputs and involvement is now being more securely tied to funding expectations and, at the same time, client expectations are being raised.

Whilst some of the weak sense of collaboration was attributed to lack of leadership, others saw it as related to the pace of work and the pressures day to day.

> *The busy-ness of what people are doing mitigates against a concerted social work approach—we are time poor, too task focussed and need to have things done by yesterday* (Paula).

There was a general agreement of the benefits that could accrue to the profession in a city sphere through better collaboration and organised forums in which to transfer ideas and to reflect and capitalise on achievements and gains, but this was seen as mitigated by reactive crisis driven work:

> *Haste—not having the time to reflect and debrief … always the next crisis walking through the door. The speed of things in an urban area … you don't get time to do this* (Paula).

Place-Based Considerations

The concept of place-making and place-shaping was noted as having infiltrated the political lexicon. These initiatives rely on high levels of community engagement in determining the use of resources and the shape of services within neighbourhoods. Examples were given of place-based initiatives such as Child First in Canada and Sure Start in the UK, and area-based initiatives to tackle income maintenance in neighbourhoods in Melbourne. There was some acknowledgement that place-based consultation is a point of influence in planning for initiatives such as 'inclusionary zoning' and other community development initiatives. Interestingly, respondents in this study, whilst acknowledging the significance of place in policy circuits and its import in individual and community wellbeing, noted it as a very challenging concept and put forward a number of reservations.

They noted issues such as the limitations of identifying community simply in terms of geography, suggesting that communities themselves are transient, unstable and subject to high turnover, given the vulnerable and disadvantaged composition of their populations.

> *We have overlooked an integral factor to the work we might do with clients— their urban environment—this can be used as a resource. Galvanising the community would be very challenging…* (Nigel).

Issues of scale were highlighted:

> *We are challenged by it … Some areas are still really quite large—not a neighbourhood but a large area. Some of the inner urban LGAs* [local government areas] *are dense but not geographically spread and within those there are opportunities to canvas networks* (Miri).

Others addressed the critique of self-help and noted the ways in which self-help and community care have been exploited by political discourse in both weak and strong versions of communitarianism. Care was seen to have been manipulated to shrink government responsibility and workers flagged the need to acknowledge this neo-liberal exploitation underpinning ideas such as place-making and place-shaping.

These considerations of the nature of community, the scale of interventions and the measures of outcomes are all highly significant to a refreshed social work in urban contexts (Delgado 2000). They imply a more adept knowledge and evaluation of how people are connected, and for what purpose and how interventions of different kinds work on different scales of community. Smith et al. (2010) take up this point and offer a useful distinction between locatedness (via various forms of connectivity) and localities (which are geographically determined). They argue that different scales are applicable to different types of intervention strategies, and that practice models need to engage with the various scales implied and their efficacy for different types of activity.

Some caution was also signalled about place-based focus, if little attention was being given to comparing places, transferring messages and learnings, and the evaluation and rolling out of benefits.

It can be a "Trojan horse" in the way it is used politically—often it's partial rather than being rolled out… place by place intervention but things not taken forward in scale and therefore it becomes a political strategy of avoidance (Jill).

Others noted place-making can become an end in itself, eschewing outcomes in an easy rhetoric of making and doing:

It's not outcome focussed, nor ethical—the critical point is—you need to ask: for whom? Why? With whom? Otherwise it's just an empty slogan of the local state (Marie).

The transcripts revealed a healthy scepticism of government policy, terminologies and priority setting. The dialogue illustrated clearly the expanded significance of the local state and social work engagement in localised priorities. Mowbray's (2011) critique of the local state as extending the neo-liberal priorities of central government and of capital becomes even more pertinent in such a climate. Mowbray argues for the need to 'take up questions and engage debate around the overall nature of local government' (2011: 149) as closer analysis reveals that what is often paraded as inclusive, consensual and empowering may, indeed, not be as benign and neutral as suggested.

Practice Issues

The evidence from this study points not only to constraints forged by particular practice assumptions, but also to the potential of new practice opportunities in the city. A tension clearly exists between organisational imperatives pitched towards category and specialism over the notion that geography and genericism may well work better in promoting client interests and wellbeing in a more holistic and integrated way. By and large, the commentary suggested workers are funded for outcomes for specific groups, which can be counterproductive to the work that needs to be done.

> *It's always the client group and focussed on those in direct service. Everyone is funded for very specific outcomes… and open-ended generic work is not funded* (Angela).

Participants argued for the need for work to be more connected and for the need to be freed up for more open-ended holistic approaches with eligibility criteria that allow social work to respond to a range of people and to the complex and overlapping nature of needs. Respondents pointed to the identification of new and complex needs in the city that defy traditional 'stereotypical' social work category and practice models that constrain, rather than promote, preventative and proactive work.

Angela spoke about the identification of new needs and the importance of relaying complexity to policy-makers. Her example referred to the ways in which the casualisation of the labour market had produced particularly precarious roles for women and, thus, dramatically contributed to producing new groups of homeless. She was now seeing women of middle age as homeless for first time. I call them '*the bewildered home-*

less', she said, characterising their sudden encounter with service providers often for the first time in their lives. '*The services are seeing this right now—the messages from practice haven't reached the research agenda as yet as most research is based on the last census*'. These practice messages are highly significant and need to be systematically relayed to policy-makers.

Paula spoke of the use of high-profile incidents to point to issues of safety and security for women and older people in the city, and to lobby for safe spaces in constructing the built environment. High-profile domestic violence cases in public places were given as examples of how these can be used to push policy.

> *Changes of government might lead to a different set of priorities but also things that happen in our back yard can trigger responses* (Paula).

There was apparent scepticism of many political priorities and of catchy new concepts and proposals for interventions and top-down solutions to issues. Participants suggested the need for social work to be proactive in framing big ideas and lobbying to reveal new expressions of need that don't fall into existing categories or ways of thinking about issues.

> *Specific agencies work with specific people but they are now seeing considerable overlap in who is accessing their service—not stereotypical categories but those with complex needs—that could be new categories* (Corrie).

> *I don't think there is that insight yet in the public realm about this. There is still that stereotypical view of who are the vulnerable people limiting the thinking of who is the city … and who we serve* (Angela).

On the horizon, they visualised new practice opportunities unconstrained by path dependencies and social work mobilities that could accommodate factors of space and place in the identification of need. The focus group pursued the example of the library space as an important nexus of community life and the ways in which imaginative co-location or new partnerships with unlikely partners might produce flexible and appropriate responses from social services. This point is argued by Forde and Lynch (2014: 2090), who suggest a critical engagement with community work strategies that incorporate 'social work knowledge and skills of relationship building, collaboration, networking and mobilisation'. Shmulik (2014) similarly argues for the value of flexibility and outreach work as part of contemporary practice.

The arguments put forward by Evers et al. (2006), founded on research-based evidence from 20 major cities, points to the social work role in facilitating new forms of participation and new forms of co-operation beyond path dependencies. They talk about 'changing the routine games' (Evers et al. 2006: 189) towards new learning, 'creating and strengthening socially integrative structures and taking care of them' (p. 193) and integrating weak and vulnerable population groups. They argue social work has a key role in building genuine involvement and participation for socially disadvantaged groups and suggest that 'an enlarged view and contribution from the field of social and community work' (p. 198) can only bolster and enhance the professional standing. In essence, such intervention foregrounds the developmental role of social work in taking advantage of its place in bolstering the social dimensions of activating local economies (Baker and Mehmood (2015). In this way, Evers et al. (2006) suggest the role and identity of social workers is legitimated and upgraded as they find their place in local policy networks.

Care

Themes of care, support, the maintenance of dignity and respect, and engaging with those almost unreachable (Szeintuch 2014) and maintaining sustenance through relationships also shone through in the social workers' narratives of the city.

> *The very vulnerable, just surviving, just coping, they need stability, a bit of joy in their lives, help them to die well and focus on care not throughput. It's about keeping them safe, protecting their wellbeing day by day. We need to remind government about being 'with people', about the importance of relationships* (Catherine).

In this respect, Catherine made reference to the importance of alliances with the vast number of those carrying out care and support work in city life, both formalised and informal (see Baines, Chap. 8). Across the city, acts of social care and support are provided in oases of care from the charity shops and drop-in centres, the parks, community centres and *men's sheds*, religious organisations, and spaces of informality and conviviality that provide therapeutic effects such as cafes, hair and massage parlours. Matrices of care and support can be combined with more formal forms of service delivery, building on natural support systems, nurturing emergent social solidarities, making possible multiple connections. Garnering and capitalising on the effort within civil society is where the resources of hope lie for alternative futures and for cohering tangible discourses of change.

Social Work Leadership and Innovation in the City

The opportunities of the new welfare framework highlighted by the research in Evers et al. (2006) were identified in this study. New civic governance is producing proximities to decision-making and new partnerships are evolving. Participants identified new points of leverage, new and exciting access to decision-making bodies, new coalitions and forums, and new practitioner spaces—both formalised and non-formalised—in which to generate action. Examples were given of the opportunities provided by local area service networks, a relationship with the local council over planning and design of a particular city neighbourhood, and of a coalition of agencies coming together to generate a policy position paper. It was noted that strategic alliances across agencies can have a powerful influencing role and that social work could do more to take advantage of collective effort at city level, both in lobbying and in showcasing achievements.

> Connection to decision makers, to the Ministers, to parliament is very helpful. That centralisation of government when you are in the middle of it... close to decision makers and driving and influencing that is very exciting (Miri).

> Social work can have a leadership role in forging collaboration—we have a skill set that can navigate this landscape, we're an amazing bunch of people (Nigel).

The argument was put forward that partnerships at city level need to be targeted, purposeful, and forged for client priorities and wellbeing.

I think it's about finding the niche of where we need to be rather than the expectation that we need to be everywhere, because I don't think we can be everywhere. It's about where can we make the greatest difference. … And there's no point being in everybody's back pocket if at the end of the day we are duplicating a presence ......or duplicating the actual outcome we are trying to achieve (Paula).

Overall, the sense was of building momentum and capacity, but also that there was little co-ordination or exploitation of the putative leadership role in the city space. The potential to be 'supra-local actors' (Oosterlynck et al. 2013: 31) was being missed in transferring expertise, knowledge, skills and know-how. Yet, it was suggested, social workers do influence at all sorts of levels '*but don't always hold their hand up to being a social worker*' (Jill), infiltrating across the city in ad hoc rather than in systemised ways. Paula argued for using a collaborative forum not only to insert social work perspectives, but also to own them—to use the opportunity for stating the contribution of the profession:

There has to be opportunity for social workers to fall back upon their learnings … we have to take this to the table—if we don't we're just another person at the table.

Others noted that social work is just one of many service delivery actors, urging the profession not to be too fussy about role creep:

So the question becomes how do we engender the collaboration with other professionals that we need in order to drive change? How do we create a groundswell? (Nigel).

Positioning social workers as practice leaders and 'thought leaders' who can push forward the co-ordination of ideas, orchestrating a focus for these developments and taking up roles as moral actors in the visioning of alternative futures, delineates an important role for social work in the city. Fincher and Iveson's (2008) examination of policies of de-institutionalisation of the mentally ill, for example, noted public professionals' inability to assert different alternatives to the mass decampment of people with a mental illness into ghettoised areas of cities. They argue this 'discursive shaping of policy problems and their potential solutions is crucial' (2008: 82), as is the ability to utilise the political context to advantage and point to the responsibility to lobby for 'alternative moral landscapes' (p. 80). Social workers are well-placed to be key narrators, with a particular story to tell about inclusion, social justice and human rights, and the development of community capital.

> *There are some cutting edge co-locations and multi-disciplinary teams. The issue is our ability to transfer messages—as practice leaders—it's now ad hoc and could be more systematic. It's difficult to teach it but the opportunities are vast* (Nigel).

Awareness of lobbying opportunities was flagged, particularly at moments when it is important to assert social work perspectives into local policy networks such as around new development initiatives, arguing for appropriate social service infrastructure.

> *There is a critical need for integrated hubs, new spaces of social work within patch/area—or outreach— we need to ask where is the clinical space, the social service space in any new development* (Marie).

Discussion: Refreshed Urban Practices

These voices from practice clearly articulated a number of significant and pressing issues for the profession in responding to the new urban dynamic. They spoke of countering the '*impacts of the sanitising of the city*', about the emergence of new and complex needs, about contributing to the development of the '*caring and inclusive city*' and about the ways in which social work can be repositioned in the city to maximise effect and impact in terms of sustainability.

The thrust of the collective argument is an appeal to building alliances for change efforts, inserting social work in urban policy circuits, revisiting the focus on the local state, building a variety of new networks and collaborations, and engaging in advocacy work and grassroots mobilisation in broader civil society. Social workers are increasingly positioned as active agents in creating the city and bolstering its redistributive values. Whilst cities vary in size and development, in history and culture, what is clear is that social workers know their city. They have mental maps of service provision, of so-called 'disadvantaged areas', and of their experiences of living within and utilising city space. They are immersed and not detached from the issues impacting on city life as a whole. But their analytical tools are yet to be honed and given theoretical grounding. In concluding the focus group, there was talk of '*Grappling with what our role should be…*' and '*having some theories to strengthen our position*' (Angela).

There were noted gaps in the dialogue which may perhaps be more of a reflection of the free flow of the conversations rather than oversights in practice. Little mention was made of the impact of superdiverse publics on social work practice and the challenges of grappling with very diverse needs (see Chap. 5). Very little was said about the impact of new technologies, disaster management or other environmental hazards of cities. Relationships with the private sector seemed to be evaded, other than to talk about the short-sightedness of private developers and the need for regulation (see Chap. 10).

The social work repertoire is immense and social workers are making a difference, large and small, both through Tonkiss' small urbanisms and through scale to substantive strategic effect. Fran Tonkiss (2010: n.p.) has argued that 'It's easy to dismiss practices of small urbanism as simply niche, transient or low impact' but, as she suggests, they scale up and, accordingly, these interventions matter.

The range and nature of social work competencies applicable and portable to city settings is a given (Kolko Phillips and Lala Ashenberg Straussner 2002; Delgado 1999). A strong value base and a critical consciousness underpin analysis and action. Focus on issues of social justice, care and social sustainability was evident in these discussions. Yet, there appeared a need for a paradigm in which to locate social work activity, to profile its place and reach in city-making and shaping. A key role for development will be models that enhance the agency of disenfranchised and marginalised groups, and expand opportunities to enable their engagement within rapidly changing conditions via what might be called 'participation re-development'. This involves contributing to the enhancement of access to good quality public space, supporting neighbourhood organising and connecting with indigenous efforts in building community capacity. Brueggermann (2014: 146) argues community has never been lost to social work but 'social work must become keen observers of new forms of emergent communal relationships'. For Brueggermann (2014: 146), 'the revolution by other means and ways' will be constructed within the inner cities, the barrios, the slums and the shanty towns of today's cities. These activities at local level will have global impact.

The temptation may be to search out a social work method to delineate an urban social work. The argument put forward here is for a set of principles to guide urban practices, principles that acknowledge that the social work repertoire is broad but that it may need a re-balancing of roles and tasks. There is no attempt to define a simple methodology but, rather, to prompt a re-emphasis of focus, a rebalancing and re-positioning of effort in achieving refreshed urban practices.

What Principles Can We Argue for on the Basis of This?

- Understanding the urban dynamic. A critical consideration of constructions of the urban and its impacts, and of social work's role in framing the city scripts. This would include a reconsideration of the connections between people and place—what place does to people and what people do in place and space in order to identify and mobilise place-based assets.
- An attuned understanding of the local state and the opportunities and constraints of neo-liberal governance that asks: What are the opportunities of new civic governance, what new strategies are implied, who are the new partners and what forms might collaborations take, and where are the points of leverage in pursuing social justice agendas?
- The creation and co-ordination of new forums, platforms and communities of practice to promote productive alliances and the transfer of knowledge, assuming that solutions involve actors across all sectors—public, private and civil society.
- Multi-tiered, multi-scalar action based on an understanding of scale and interventions appropriate to scale; being able to scale up and scale down, cross municipality boundaries, and garner co-operation between tiers of government.

- The development of new practice models, both experimental and consolidated, in forging innovation in service delivery and the creation of new techniques in co-production.
- Creative practices—implying strong and transparent participatory efforts and models, and techniques that enhance social citizenship and social sustainability.
- The significance of 'immersion' in place for the worker—knowing and experiencing—power over place and power in place as citizen participants and social actors.
- Exerting craft in attending to care and intimacies in the city through instilling care values and adding positive value in the crafting of cooperation.
- Engagement with new forms of resistance, new mobilisations as sounding boards for positive change.
- Being consciousness raisers, thought leaders and practice leaders in generating innovation in service delivery, both multi-professional and profession specific.
- Monitoring and evaluating change efforts.

Conclusion: Social Work Futures

Social work is intimately connected to the big issues of our time—social and economic inequalities, fiscal crisis, migration, environmental degradation, and cultural and technological change, as well as changes in the intimate and personal dimensions of life. These global transformations are played out in the city street—in places and spaces across the city: look out of the window of your office; they are part of our everyday walk or ride home. The argument of this text is that there is a need to harness the transformative potential of cities as a privileged locus of change for all and, in doing so, consolidate and assert a confident social work identity. The conceptual apparatus for exploration of social work's role in the city reflects a longstanding engagement with issues of social justice: focused on issues of citizenship, equity and access, redistribution and recognition; issues of care: crafting, creating and bolstering landscapes of care and convivial encounter; and issues of social sustainability: enhancing the capacity of individuals to engage, participate and maintain their contributions over time.

In the new participative society, social service delivery has come closer to home than ever before, bypassing slow bureaucracy and emerging and evolving in new matrices of care and support not via imitation but, rather, via innovation and design. This cannot be left as ad hoc; efforts must be made to garner this energy towards collective good. Social workers have a key role in city-making processes, in supporting redistributive policies, enhancing civic participation, promoting cohesion and working collaboratively with service users and others in consolidating gains and innovations.

References

Amin, A., & Thrift, N. (2002). *Cities: Reimagining the urban.* Cambridge: Polity Press.

Baker, S., & Mehmood, A. (2015). Social innovation and the governance of sustainable places. *Local Environment: The International Journal of Justice and Sustainability, 20*(3), 321–334. doi:10.1080/13549839.2013.842964.

Brueggermann, W. G. (2014). *The practice of macro social work* (4th ed.). Belmont: Brooks Cole/Cengage Learning.

Christensen, P., & O'Brien, M. (Eds.). (2003). *Children in the city: Home, neighbourhood and community.* London: Routledge.

D'Cruz, H. (2004). *Constructing meaning and identities in child protection practice.* Croydon/Victoria: Tertiary.

Delgado, M. (1999). *Social work practice in non-traditional urban settings.* New York: Oxford University Press.

Delgado, M. (2000). *Community social work practice in an urban context: The potential of a capacity-enhancement perspective.* New York: Oxford University Press.

Department of Transport, Planning and Local Infrastructure. (2014). *Plan Melbourne: Metropolitan planning strategy.* Melbourne: Victorian Government.

Evers, A., Schulz, A. D., & Wiesner, C. (2006). Local policy networks in the programme Social City: A case in point for new forms of governance in the field of local social work and urban planning. *European Journal of Social Work, 9*(2), 183–200.

Fincher, R., & Iveson, K. (2008). *Planning and diversity in the city.* Basingstoke: Palgrave Macmillan.

Forde, C., & Lynch, D. (2014). Critical practice for challenging times: Social workers' engagement with community work. *British Journal of Social Work, 44*(8), 2078–2094.

Gleeson, B., & Kearns, R. (2001). Remoralising landscapes of care. *Environment and Planning D: Society and Space, 19*, 61–80.

Harris, J. (2014). (Against) Neoliberal social work. *Critical and Radical Social Work, 2*(1), 7–22.

Horschelmann, K., & van Blerk, L. (2011). *Children, youth and the city.* Abingdon: Routledge.

Jacobs, J. (1993 [1961]). *The death and life of great American cities.* New York: Random House.

Kolko Phillips, N., & Lala Ashenberg Straussner, S. (2002). *Urban social work: An introduction to policy and practice in cities.* Boston: Allyn & Bacon.

Lefebvre, H. (1996). *Writings on cities.* Cambridge: Blackwell.

Mowbray, M. (2011). What became of *The Local State?* Neo-liberalism, community development and local government. *Community Development Journal, 46*(1), 132–153.

Oosterlynck, S., Kazepov, Y., Novy A., Cools P., Barberis, E., Wukovitsch, F., Sarius, T., & Leubolt, B. (2013, April). *The butterfly and the elephant: Local social innovation, the welfare state and new poverty dynamics* (IMPROVE Working Papers, Discussion Paper No.13/03). http://improve-research.eu. Accessed 14 July 2015.

Shmulik, S. (2014). Street work and outreach: A social work method? *British Journal of Social Work.* doi:10.1093/bjsw/bcu103.

Smith, S., Bellaby, P., & Lindsay, S. (2010). Social inclusion at different scales in the urban environment: Locating the community to empower. *Urban Studies, 47*(7), 1439–1457.

Tonkiss, F. (2010). From austerity to audacity: Interview with Fran Tonkiss on the emerging urbanism of small acts. (Authored by Francesca Ferguson) *Ucube 20.* http://www.uncubemagazine.com/sixcms/detail.php?id= 12467995&articleid=art-1396020955634-5a47aa6a-80c5-48c9-aba2-f977368bdad9#!/page22. Accessed 4 Jan 2015.

Webb, S. (2007). The comfort of strangers: Social work, modernity and late Victorian England, Part II. *European Journal of Social Work, 10*(2), 193–207.

Wenger, E. (2000). *Communities of practice.* New York: Cambridge University Press.

Williams, M. (2000, July 30). Social work in the city: Rewards and risks. *New York Times.* http://www.nytimes.com/2000/07/30/nyregion/social-work-in-the-city-rewards-and-risks.html. Accessed 8 July 2015.

4

Social Work Research and the City

Charlotte Williams

Introduction

Generating new knowledge and the evaluation of practice interventions
will be central to a new paradigm of urban practice. A refreshed focus on
the city suggests a plethora of research projects, new research partners
and new methodologies for social work. A research territory awaits. The
applied nature of social work research and its critical mission to address
social justice locates social work research in and of itself as a social work
practice capable of effecting change (D'Cruz and Jones 2013). Social
workers as 'practice ethnographers' (Briskman 2013: 51) are well-placed
to bear witness to the ways in which contemporary issues impact on client groups and the ways in which new needs are being generated, to
assess the impact of major policy initiatives and to contribute knowledge
to the design of new forms of service delivery in seeking to improve urban

C. Williams (✉)
School of Global, Urban and Social Studies, RMIT University,
GPO Box 2476, Melbourne, VIC 3001, Australia

© The Editor(s) (if applicable) and The Author(s) 2016
C. Williams (ed.), *Social Work and the City*,
DOI 10.1057/978-1-137-51623-7_4

97

conditions. Research is a vital component of the professional repertoire and is crucial to the development of urban social work knowledge and identity. Interventions should be informed by research and social justice advocacy should rely on rigorous analysis. The multi-faceted and cross-cutting nature of urban social issues implies increased engagement in inter-disciplinary and inter-professional collaborative research in order to improve service delivery and the experiences of service user groups.

Social work research has a long history of engagement with urban issues. Research may well have been located *in* the city or, indeed, on issues considered particularly urban—such as homelessness, multi-culturalism, prostitution, and so on—but, in many respects, the import of the locale itself was rarely addressed. The relationship between spatial considerations and human behaviour has escaped attention despite a growing body of evidence that implies the need for such interrogation and despite an increased focus on community-level interventions in social policy-making (van Ewijk 2011; Evers et al. 2006). Shaw's round-up of the contemporary scene concluded that social work research is an 'urban desert' (2011: 11). His initial review of major social work databases indicated little contemporary published research on social work and the urban. There is an evident paucity of consideration to place and space in social work research (Jeyasingham 2014; Ferguson 2008). The opportunity to introduce social workers to innovative research methodologies in the context of city life is apparent but to do so requires cross-disciplinary engagement.

This chapter revisits the insights from urban social research practice, outlining key historical traditions such as the social administration approach, the Settlement ethnography and the Chicago School in a consideration of urban social work research orientations. It draws on innovative examples utilised in the context of assessing needs, engaging with communities that are hard to reach and vulnerable, and addressing policy questions in order to demonstrate the nature of an urban social work research.

Urban Research Traditions and Social Work

Part of reconstructing an urban practice has been a consideration of the continuities and discontinuities in social work legacies of the city. In revisiting social work histories, scholars have looked to identify particular research traditions that emerged to underpin the fledgling discipline and to discern the characteristic nature and distinctiveness of these traditions. What are social work's methodological roots? What are the core boundaries, territory of inquiry, theory and methods that have shaped it as a discipline within the broader social sciences? In claiming this territory, certain thinkers, movements and institutional infrastructure become central to understanding the architecture of social work research.

Chapter 1 outlined the development of a rich tradition of urban sociology as the basis for interrogating aspects of city life. What was missing in that account was any sense of the development of the distinctive knowledge base of social work, its research orientations and its influence on urban theory. Indeed, Shaw (2011) argues that this type of analysis has barely been pursued. One of the prerequisites of such an analysis is to identify and make claim to the specificity of social work as a discipline within the wider social sciences. Soydan (2012) proposes that the roots of the social work research tradition lie in two core historical ideas: the emergence of a scientific analysis of society during the second half of the nineteenth century, and the notion that the application of scientific social analysis can be deployed to predict social change (2012: 469). What Soydan (2012: 472) seeks to do in exploring the historical record is look at the interplay between theory and practical action as something distinctive to the development of social work knowledge. He suggests that the emerging discipline relied on a 'theory to practice' orientation and a 'practice to theory' orientation, being influenced both by political movements of the day, such as Fabianism, but also reliant on emerging messages from pragmatic engagement in the field via professional groups within the COS and the Settlement movement.

The emergence of the social administration approach in the latter part of the nineteenth century encapsulates this synergy and provides the most useful starting point for a consideration of the distinctiveness of the social work research tradition, encompassing distinctive themes prevalent in the UK, USA and Europe under conditions of late modernity. The Fabian policy research tradition, with its coupling of scientific-moralism, established the discipline of social administration as the predominant paradigm of social welfare research—in Mishra's terms, as that of 'piecemeal social engineering' (1981: 3). This particular methodology of social investigation was characterised by its empirical and atheoretical orientation, its national focus, its pragmatic and interventionist approach and arguably, its lacked any distinctive disciplinary focus of its own. The pioneering approach of the COS and the Settlement movement, Charles Booth's enumeration and mapping of the city of London and Joseph Rowntree's study of York exemplify this approach. Its methodologies and concerns with the nature of social problems within a discrete national context are also well-represented by later scholars such as Richard Titmuss, Peter Townsend, David Donnison amongst others in the UK, and its ideological certainties held sway in the development of welfare states only to be gradually eroded from the 1970s onwards with the emergence of a more critical social policy (Taylor 1996). The USA followed broadly similar activities conducted under the rubric of social welfare reform. The bedrock of this approach is not so much a concern with building knowledge about social welfare per se, or with analytical theorising but, rather, with a practical understanding of the nature of social problems such as poverty, homelessness, child abuse and deviance, always with a view to finding a solution. It is typified by a preoccupation with facts and the assumed neutrality of facts in shaping interventions and policy solutions.

The pragmatic policy-oriented research orientation that emerged from attempting to quantify the social issues of urban development retains a foundational place in social work research. But other research traditions also hold significance in the development of the discipline. Shaw (2011) suggests that there is a strong case for arguing for the development of a coherent urban social work research tradition based on the Chicago School legacy. Indeed, Shaw's (2011: 16) attempt to disentangle the discipline in his review of the Chicago School finds considerable interdependence between sociological researchers and practitioners, city and university, social work agencies and academics, research and practice in their methodologies and approach to urban welfare issues such that, he argues, the Chicago School studies provide as much of a history for social work research as they do for sociology.

The Chicago School was influenced by Booth's pioneering mapping of the East End of London. These scholars adopted the social survey methodology and utilised the detailed quantitative techniques of the social administration tradition. However, a specific insight of the Chicago School was that social facts are 'located'. Thus, their thinking took a quantum leap forward from Booth's detailed systematic quantification of the city to track patterns between social phenomena. From the Chicago School came techniques focused on the social environment of the city, as social issues were seen to be mediated by place. Their detailed ethnographies revealed the effects of ecological factors on key variables. They noted predictive patterns and associations between variables in specific neighbourhoods or zones, such as the formation of youth gangs and their engagement in deviant activity. What the Chicago academics sought to do, therefore, was to derive macro-level patterns from micro-level interactions and, in doing so, they pioneered attention to spatialities in understanding city life.

The significance of the Chicago School methodology for social work cannot be overstated. These were not detached and dispassionate scholars but, rather, a group who engaged with the city normatively, seeking not only to explain change, but also to predict factors that might underpin interventions. They were closely associated with and informed by social work practitioners and activists in an engaged sociology with ameliorative intent (Shaw 2011). The Settlement movement was similarly based on a methodology that sought out and valued such contacts with knowledge-producing institutions in informing their practice. The Chicago scholars would accordingly influence the Settlement ethnography and suggested an alternative method of social work away from the casework focus to approaches based on community intervention. These avant garde ethnographic techniques have been used for over a century to draw attention to conditions and situations that would otherwise be invisible and form a strong strain of contemporary urban research (see LSE Ordinary Streets ethnography https://lsecities.net).

The COS and the Settlement movement approaches both valorised knowing the district and the importance of sensitive insightful social observation in terms of knowledge of neighbourhoods, residents, and the interiority of social and political life. Whilst these research traditions were predicated on different techniques of enquiry, they were also distinguished by differing theoretical views of the nature of the cause of social problems—from those highly individualised to those focused on societal explanations for human distress. Different ideas about the nature of social problems led to a bifurcation in social work method between the structural and the psychosocial that would be replicated in the focus of social research. Whilst this dichotomy has been largely traversed in contemporary social work research by a more nuanced understanding of the complex interplay of a range of multi-level variables, the mark of these orientations on the development of social work knowledge is profound.

The naming and claiming of disciplinary ground and the research territory of social work is alive and kicking within the discipline (Sharland 2013). Sharland's review of the state of play in the UK thematically outlines the core substantive and methodological strengths and limitations of the field, drawing attention to disciplinary and inter-disciplinary distinctiveness and synergies. An interesting and different perspective was offered by Zimbalist back in the 1970s considering what he called 'waves' or 'cycles of emphasis' in social work/welfare research activity. Zimbalist (1977) reviews the period from the 1870s to the 1960s in the USA (1977: 7) and extrapolates six key research themes of this period: research into the causes of poverty, measuring the distribution of poverty, the social survey movement, quantifying and indexing in social work, evaluation research into the effectiveness of social services, and studies of multi-problem families. What this type of content analysis can only reveal is the ways in which certain social issues become prioritised for attention within a profession, and are funded and supported within research institutions, and how research is subject to 'fashions' and what gets to be counted as social work research at any one time.

The evolution of social work research in the urban context would see a concern 'with the district' recede as modernist concerns to determine broad explanatory frames that could have replicable and transferrable application took precedence. In social work, the focus on specialisms and client category would win out over the particularities of place.

Building Place and Space into Social Work Research

Whilst the principles of both the COS and the University Settlement movement valorised proximity and immersion in place, this is a lost legacy of the social work research tradition. Coulton (2005: 75) has argued that social work practice research:

> has been essentially divorced from where communities are actually located, and the processes within or between them are fostered or impeded by space of distance. Geography has been virtually unaccounted for in most studies of community intervention and researchers have overlooked influences of proximity and distance in community and individual wellbeing.

Zapf (2010) also notes this omission in social work research and practice. He argues that the conventional metaphor of 'person in environment' asserted by Mary Richmond (1861-1928) acknowledged the physical context as a consideration for practice; however, the received professional wisdom interpreted this as social connectedness—the social environment of friends, family and kin—as opposed to the physical and material aspects of place. Zapf suggests that there has been a distortion of the notion 'environment' in ecological theory and that social work literature has foregrounded social functioning, social roles and networks to the neglect of the natural and built world. Whilst Zapf's argument is to reclaim attention to the natural environment, his observations are no less pertinent to consideration of the metropolis. The built environment, urban space and place have been afforded little more than representational value in social work research via oblique reference to place—the housing estate, parts of estates or suburbs, the local authority and disadvantaged neighbourhoods, immigrant areas—in the sense of places where clients live. Alternatively, reference to place has been used as an adjective—for example, *inner city*—to connote disadvantage, rather than demonstrating the ways in which people are placed by disadvantage, or that people are *of* place and the ways in which people use space.

This type of interrogation has been largely confined to the rural (Pugh and Cheers 2010), or indicatively to locate the issues of indigenous peoples (Bennett et al. 2013). Rural settings command attention to locality, identity and belonging, issues of distance and proximity, access to services and the powerful implications of spatiality on social work practice. Rural as *other* commanded this attention whilst the metropolis has been assumed.

Gordon Jack's work (2010, 2015) argues that place matters. His analysis of the literature on childcare social work practice suggests that it gives considerable attention to children's attachment to people but has neglected to consider the role played by their attachment to place. Jack illustrates the significance of place attachment for children's identity formation, their security, their sense of belonging and their sense of independence and adventure. Place exists on different scales: as home, garden, neighbourhood, town or city, region or nation, and place, he argues, is imbued with meaning and association, memory and security in an era of insecurities and uncertainties. Jack (2015) cites examples of the repeated moves and major displacements that children in care experience, even out of authority placements, and notes how social work assessments lack attention to this important dimension of children's wellbeing. Social workers, for Jack, lack place awareness in their assessments and interventions with children, and rely on service-oriented approaches when space-oriented approaches can specifically increase a child's sense of autonomy, control and participation in their environments. Children's ability to shape their own lives can be enhanced by policies aimed at creation of 'child-friendly' cities that consider play strategies, children's participation in designing cityscapes and welfare responses.

In the field of health research, the association of place to health and wellbeing is highly developed. Considerable research exists outside of social work on what has been called 'area effects'—namely, the significance of neighbourhoods, local environments and place-based community in shaping factors such as health and welfare outcomes. There is an established consensus that area effects do exist, and that there are causal connections between poor neighbourhoods and other social problems (Atkinson and Kintrea 2004) —for example, poor health (Cattell 2001), employment opportunities (Kintrea et al. 2010), mental health (Curtis 2010) and child and adolescent outcomes (Leventhal and Brooks-Gunn 2000). There has, however, been some antipathy towards this type of place-based research as a result of political, theoretical and methodological considerations.

Policy trends of the past eschewed the parochial and its specificities in favour of the certainties of universalism. Political and ideological theory looked away from the local towards grand narratives in explaining social inequality and human distress. In addition, the questioning of place-based research and policy as contributing to the stigmatisation of neighbourhoods would see it fall out of favour. Atkinson and Kintrea (2004: 453) note: 'there has been a wariness of cultural explanations of poverty because of their association with discredited individual pathology, under the shorthand term underclass'. The role of stigma in compounding disadvantage cannot be overlooked and has been the subject of considerable research (Atkinson and Jacobs 2010), including the ways in which this stigma is politically framed via research narratives that focus on the social composition and attributes of place at the expense of structural considerations. Critics point to the tensions for academic research of inadvertently feeding into neo-liberal agendas. Studies of area effects, it is argued, have tended to highlight the negative impacts with less regard to the assets and capacities of communities. Lightfoot et al. (2014)) accordingly propose asset mapping as a key social work research tool that focuses on strengths and capacities rather than on deficits, and draws on the skills of community members in the identification, collection and analysis of assets. This type of 'ecometrics' can capture what makes a community a desirable, resilient and sustainable place (Coulton 2005).

Methodological difficulties of operationalising community and the pragmatic difficulties of measuring and transferring impacts and effects of place-based interventions also confound a focus on the geographical locale (Coulton 2005). Neighbourhoods are ecological spaces with both physical and symbolic meaning for residents. They are dynamic and changing internally, and cannot accurately be conceived as closed geospatial entities. Administratively determined locally bounded physical spaces of neighbourhood are not necessarily accurate indicators of neighbourhood affiliation as perceived by residents (Foster and Hipp 2011); neither are they particularly useful spatial referents for new forms of identity, such as transmigrants (Schrooten et al. 2015), gay communities (Wienke and Hill 2013) and others who identify with communities of interest over communities of place. How individuals themselves define neighbourhood can confound any accurate specification of boundaries and therefore prohibit statistical measurement, comparison and replicability of findings.

Research methodologies focused on area effects draw on a variety of measures. Some studies consider the area as a whole via deprivation indexes based on demographic data such as poverty rates, unemployment rates, truancy rates and so on. Others utilise the convenience data of census, postcodes, wards, local government area statistics, estates and other administrative boundaries. General household, citizen and population surveys can also be disaggregated by area to provide interrogative data. The problem of administratively mis-specified boundaries has led academics and community researchers to generate forms of measurement themselves that capture the spatial dimensions of communities, following the Chicago School to delineate patterning of interactions, flows and street networks imbuing simple mapping with spatio-temporal dimensions (see Foster and Hipp 2011; Hillier 2007). These studies use ranking measures constructed by researchers and/or data available from researcher-conducted surveys of residents. Some studies use the perceptions, experiences and accounts of residents and local agents themselves to develop a picture of the experiential impacts of living in a particular neighbourhood. Atkinson and Kintrea's work (2004) is a good example of the latter strategy. They pursued the interplay between area effects and life chances by considering the experiences and explanations of welfare professionals such as social workers, youth and community workers, teachers and others in two major UK cities—one with clear deprivation indicators, and one a more mixed neighbourhood. Taking three core indicators of area effects—isolation, local norms and expectations, and geographically restricted social networks—Atkinson and Kintrea demonstrate the ways in which structural factors are mediated by cultural factors of the norms, values, stories and perceptions of key actors at the level of place. Accordingly, they argue powerfully that there is a strong case for urban sociology of this kind—as 'life chances are in part locally determined' (Atkinson and Kintrea 2004: 452) and qualitative approaches can contribute to the ways in which 'entrenched social problems are reactions to perceptions as well as to objective situations' (p. 452).

The issue of replication also bedevils community-based research. Replicating findings presents pragmatic obstacles and, therefore, resistance to engage with neighbourhood research of this kind. Coulton (2005) identifies a number of the challenges of fidelity and replicability in evaluating small-scale community initiatives, and argues for rigour in moving beyond reliance on single case study approaches. She suggests the internet can facilitate the collection of comparable documentation data from multiple participants and assist in establishing shared templates of definitions and criteria (see, for example, http://betterevaluation.org/).

A number of compelling factors suggest a reorientation to place in social work research. Where people are placed affects their life chances, adds structure to their everyday life, and provides a source of belonging and identification. Geography may affect social interaction and services between communities; and interventions may be more or less effective depending on such spatial properties. Localities also provide opportunities for collective mobilisation, participation, protest and resistance. However, places are not simply geographically located and material; they are also spatial, relative and relational. They become sites where people exercise agency over their lives in seeking to satisfy their needs and wellbeing. Places matter to people. They are also shaped and given meaning as *spaces* in terms of how people use them, attribute meanings, histories and futures to them. The concept of *space* evokes these relational aspects and offers analysis of issues such as power, inequality, difference and diversity.

More recently, inter-disciplinary work between health and geographers encapsulates these considerations. Work on *geographies of care*, for example (see Milligan et al. 2007), opens up these interrogations and permits an understanding of the performative enactments of care in particular settings, spaces and places. Conradson's work (2003a, b) as a student researcher looked at spaces of care in the city and draws on almost incidental ethnography whilst on placement in a drop-in centre on the edge of a council estate in Bristol. Conradson locates care within an 'ethics of encounter', extending the concept of care to consider the daily movements of three service users through various spaces of care in the city—homes, shops, drop-in spaces, as well as statutory welfare and in their co-production of care. Social work, in adopting this type of work, opens itself up to a wealth of research trajectories. Studies of residential and institutional living to date have largely been de-contextualized from wider consideration of place, and warrant theorising and situating in an understanding of care transitions. Research could be extended to non-traditional settings of welfare; for example, the charity shop, the African hairdresser, the Moroccan tea shop—as Delgado's (1999) explorations of the therapeutic potential of such settings suggests, much of the urban informal economy of care is under-researched.

The emergence of the mobilities paradigm in social science opens up the potential to move beyond static and geographically bounded notions of place to consideration of the flows and movements of people, information, speed, distance and rhythms of the city. Attention to place and to the spatial considerations in place (Logan 2012) reveals considerable avenues for social work research. Spatial analysis in terms of proximities, connectedness, exposure and access involves thinking about time and distance, rather than fixed metrics. Such spatial analysis is gaining momentum and its applications are many. It enables considerations such as whether people are living close to transport, child care and play spaces, doctors and health clinics? How do they get to them? It enables the mapping of issues such as youth suicides, capturing the use of enabling technologies by disabled children, work on addictions and their triggers in place, to give a few examples.

Interest in these considerations is emerging in social work. For example, Dharman Jeyasingham (2014: 1879) argues that, with few notable exceptions, social work has not generally engaged with the conceptualisations of space that have been developed in social and cultural geography. Drawing on the work of Lefebvre and reviewing examples of work done largely in children's social work, Jeyasingham argues that three main themes emerge in the ways in which space is constituted in social work research. He suggests the research reveals the construction of a restricted number of *scales* through which practice is understood. These scales relate largely to a small number of sites of action; namely, partial sightings of the local authority; views of, in and around the social work office; or poor estates and clients' homes—such that, he suggests, there is a simplification of relationships between these spaces and social problems. He argues that references such as these privilege social worker knowledge about places at the expense of service user accounts and often reproduce, rather than interrogate, some of the normative ways in which space is constructed. For example:

> social workers in the studies draw a determinate relationship between certain scales of space and social problems such as poverty, parenting problems and child abuse… they develop claims to detailed and privileged understanding of the significance of space for such problems through reference to very specific and precisely delineated locations (Jeyasingham 2014: 1888–1889).

Jeyasingham's analysis is novel. He is particularly critical of the ways in which service user space is signified as distinct from other environments and reproduced as marginal. What he is arguing for is a more expansive and nuanced understanding of the ways in which place and space become significant to understanding practice, rather than the static and stereotypical ways in which these considerations are represented through conventions of practice. He prompts us to look beyond the ways in which normative spatial practices are structured within organisations or professional conventions that shape how social workers do their work to a consideration of how social workers inhabit lived space. Such a trajectory suggests more expansive use of ethnographies in social work and research.

Social Work Urban Research: New Possibilities

Shaw's (2011) assessment of the state of play of urban social work research may not be entirely accurate. He has problems with his database, as he confined it to those studies that explicitly flag the word 'urban' or 'city' and that appear in social work journals. His work is nevertheless indicative. What is evident is that much social work research is located in city settings but fails to engage with urban analysis, begging the question of how to build such an analysis into social work projects.

One of the conventional ways of thinking about urban research is to consider *topics* that are characterised by their frequency, scale or newness in urban contexts. City issues such as prostitution (Van der Meulen 2011), human trafficking (Pearce 2011), homelessness, obesity, racial segregation, migration, asylum, missing persons, youth offending, mass disaster, social cohesion and poverty, amongst others, have all been given this treatment. Several of these issues are demanding new types of analysis based on shifts in policy, changes in urban forms, and/or increased density and heterogeneity, and complex intersections. For example, the nature of homelessness is changing as a result of precariousness in labour markets (see Chap. 8), new forms of poverty are emerging as a result of urban policies (see Chap. 10), and ageing and ethnic diversity are rapidly being redefined in urban contexts. Pathways into prostitution amongst youth, child abuse perpetrator rings, particular forms of addiction amongst older people—all these issues are becoming increasingly apparent in the metropolis. Traditional fields of practice such as child welfare, mental health and disability are being transformed by the issues of city-living characterised by new intersections and complexities. The messy, complex nature and interconnections of wicked issues suggest inter-disciplinary approaches to urban research.

Heterogeneity with proximity and the networks and flows of global communication makes diversity a specificity of city-ness. Schrooten et al. (2015) take up the issue of new migrations, which they argue speaks very directly to an agenda for urban social work research. They point to the dearth of empirical research on the specificity of welfare needs of transmigrants—in particular, the types of risk to which they are exposed. More needs to be known about the strategies new migrants themselves deploy in mobilising to meet their welfare needs and how they engage with self-provisioning not only in place, but also via the maintenance of trans-local and transnational networks. Detailed understanding of the kind of assemblages of care and support they design in meeting their needs that draw on formal, informal and virtual welfare provision could enhance the responsiveness of service delivery. Thus, the city is coming into view via new approaches to ethnicity research; specifically, the nature and resource of superdiverse neighbourhoods and the evaluation of interventions aimed at enhancing social cohesion within them (ICEC 2015). Detailed narrative work with new migrants (Clarke 2009) and ethnographies of diversity in urban space (Berg and Sigona 2013) are building new knowledge about the intersections between variations in migration status and service delivery.

The topics are, of course, endless. The ways in which the urban context has traditionally been constructed in social work focuses on these issues as *inner city troubles* but, by and large, they remain disassociated from the urban characteristics of their manifestation. Social workers frequently don't know how to insert urban analysis into their research; how to ask questions such as: What is the significance of place and space? What difference does city-living or particular urban forms make to the issue under study? What are the place-based considerations in mental health, child protection, domestic violence? How do people use space and scale in mobilising to meet their needs, and how do the factors described in Chap. 1 contribute to our understanding of presenting issues. In sum, what is it that makes this social work research urbanist?

City-ness matters to research design. Density, diversity in proximity and the ways in which intersections of local with global trends are played out in place are part of the characteristic. Networks and flows of communication and their trans-connections are key considerations, including urban/rural. The analysis of the inter-relationship between place, space and human behaviour can be considered in a myriad of ways. Considerations of the impacts of the built environment on movement, access, choice, participation and equality can be illustrated. There may be a focus on the emergence and manifestation of issues that are now seen as typically a result of urban living; for example, obesity. Patterning of service delivery and new forms of service delivery in localised welfare states can be piloted, trialled and evaluated. Environmental concerns, access to green spaces, and concerns with social and environmental sustainability can be demonstrated and developed via research.

In addition, a whole agenda awaits in terms of understanding social work practices in urban contexts and how social workers make use of the opportunities of the city itself in their strategies, techniques and identity building. There is scope for work on the spatial consequences of the use of new technologies such as the mobile phone, laptops and tablet computers, and secure internet connections which are shifting the site of social work practice away from desk-based work to more flexible and mobile forms of working.

Further, a number of conceptual and methodological advances in pursuing urban, place-based research are filtering into the social work circuit.

Rich sociological ethnographies of living in poor neighbourhoods provide deep insights into the spatial dimensions of daily life and the ways in which shared norms and stories are constructed about what people from an area aspire to and achieve. Lisa McKenzie's (2015) *Getting By* narratives bring together the academic and the local community in the production of stories of austerity, injustice and resilience on poor estates in Britain. Studies based on ethnographic observation have used particularly innovative techniques including sounds, signs and other representational text, map-making and other visual methods, go-along and audio-walking techniques, and psychogeography amongst others. Ethnographies open up an understanding of groups that seem somehow out of step with the rhythms of the city—for example, Gypsies and Roma, older people and homeless people—and are useful in engaging with hard to reach and very vulnerable communities. Bryant's (2015) text calls for more critical and creative research methods in social work to understand more closely the complexities of social worlds and people's ways of moving in them.

A range of new technologies is also being deployed for considering how individual wellbeing interacts with the spatial dimensions. The use of applications such as GIS (Geographical Information Systems), QGIS (Qualitative Geographical Information Systems) and hierarchical linear modelling (see Hillier 2007; Logan 2012) to track the spatial dimensions of particular issues are coming into play in social work research. Hillier (2007) argues that the use of GIS can benefit social work by continuing and strengthening the social survey tradition, providing a framework for understanding human needs and assets, improving service delivery, and empowering communities and disenfranchised groups. As social work engages more with these tools, she argues, so they can be refined and developed for use with sensitive and confidential subject matters such as research on child abuse, domestic violence, addictions and access to services at neighbourhood level.

Widening the scope of research under the auspices of social work reveals some more interesting possibilities and trajectories. Theoretical engagement with the conceptual and analytical framework of social geography and critical urban studies opens up new perspectives for social work research on urban issues. There are some ready examples within social work that illustrate this focus.

Sally Holland's work in Wales (Holland 2014; Holland et al. 2011) provides a detailed example of drawing on a spatial approach in social work research. She suggests that too little attention has been paid to the significance of the service user's environment and finds much to recommend in the contemporary 'neighbourhood turn'.

> research that ignores local geographies will miss the opportunity to explore the relational and physical interaction with local environment in people's everyday lives (Holland et al. 2011: 703).

Holland (2014) undertook a qualitative study of two contrasting neighbourhoods, looking at the policy notion that child safeguarding is everyone's business. The research drew on multi-modal methods in capturing community engagement with child safeguarding issues. A range of methods were deployed, including mobile go-along walking interviews, driving interviews with parents, and interview with children and social and community workers. She utilised GPS to track routes and clustered interviews in neighbouring houses in order to build a detailed picture of interactions of perceptions and relationships in place. The research also included careful review of archival and documentary data pertaining to the research locale, including old maps and newspaper reports. The researchers utilised participant observation of meetings in community centres and observed neighbourhood life to provide rich descriptions 'across seasons and at different times of day and evening' (Holland 2014: 696), giving the research a temporal quality.

The analysis by Holland and colleagues (2011) of this type of methodology is illuminating. She makes several claims for this type of spatial approach and argues for the importance of topology as a real and relevant dimension in providing understanding of issues such as child protection. She argues it shifts attention away from deficit models of assessment to a consideration of how communities provide care and support and surveillance. These types of methodological process in themselves can raise community level awareness of issues, generate dialogue and be used to underpin arguments for community level intervention. The findings of Holland's study (2014) are no less instructive. What she is able to demonstrate is the intricate inter-relationship between forms of support—

informal, community and statutory—but most intriguing is what she has to say about the value of social worker immersion: 'that children's social workers be closely located within their local communities, socially and physically' (p. 384). Her findings reiterate ideas about proximity, temporal availability, genericism, and the style and biography of the worker as pertinent to child safeguarding.

Harry Ferguson has perhaps made the greatest contribution to date in terms of the application of the mobilities paradigm to social work practice. In a suite of works (2008, 2009a, b, 2010a, b) Ferguson conceives social work as a flow of 'mobile practices' between the public and the private sphere, thus opening up a research agenda for examining contemporary social work practice in place. He argues that what social workers actually do and where they do it has been largely ignored. Ferguson animates the sphere of activity of the nineteenth-century social worker, demonstrating how the home visit—an activity of walking, cycling or using the horse-drawn carriage—moved social work across the city, exposing and making visible the cruelties of poverty in place. Social work was exposed experientially to places of danger and insecurity in embodied and sensory ways. In Ferguson's work, social workers are animated, they walk, they are 'driven to care' in the therapeutic moments of welfare journeys with clients, they inhabit spaces in client's homes and in office sites in lived experiences of time and space. He argues for a shift from the stasis and structure so familiar to accounts of practice to a consideration of movement, mobility, contingency and affect in what he calls (drawing on Lefebvre) 'the rhythms of practice' (2008: 575).

> it is through movement—professionals getting up from their desks to become co-present with service users and *doing* something, whether in the office or, more often, by leaving it—that the flows that make later-modern social work what it is come into being (Ferguson 2008: 75).

Ferguson's 'liquid social work' (2008) takes for analysis the home visit, the car journey and the social work office/agency to illustrate, 'what happens when social workers leave their desks and go on the move to enter the private lives and spaces, the homes of service users' (2009a: 473). This is all up for grabs in Ferguson's reconceptualising of practice). He posits:

a new relationship appears to be emerging between the informational and the relational, regulation and movement, mobilities and immobilities in welfare practices, all of which require systematic empirical investigation and theoretical development (Ferguson 2008: 568).

This speaks to an agenda for urban social work research.

There are good reasons why a researcher might want to adopt the participative, performative, ethnographic methods that enable them to move along with, see and sense with, and be with research participants. This type of work retains much of the nuance of encounter and animates the context of practice. Go-alongs, ride-alongs, video ethnography and a host of associated methods enable new sensibilities and apprehensions of space. Yet, Merriman (2013) signals some useful cautions about the rush to mobile methods. His critique suggests that, whilst these practices may be informative in terms of innovation and experimentation, he questions whether they add more to the data than conventional methods could elucidate. Further, he suggests that, in their emphasis on movement, they may overlook more passive practices, engagements and experiences— such as 'stillness, waiting, slowness and boredom' (p. 177), and may even be skewed in their focus, paying less attention to infrastructures, technologies, materialities and spaces in which the movement occur. Merriman, as Holland et al. (2011), suggests that mobile methods are often founded on a confidence in new technologies such as GIS, video recordings and mobile apps, and far from providing data analysis in themselves; they are more usefully considered an aid to data analysis.

What this small body of work illustrates, however, is the accommodation of new trajectories of thinking about *people in place* and the significance of place and space for understanding, needs, identities and issues of service provision.

Collaborations and Partnerships

Research progresses through insights and intuition, and is practice driven. The city offers new collaborative partners in the research endeavour. Relationships can be established between the academy and the community, between agencies and their service users, for the co-production of knowledge and for the validation of different forms of knowledge useful to social work. This type of affiliation is heavily supported by university mission statements. Most institutions today fully sponsor connectedness to the city, and seek to foster deep partnerships with agency and industry in forging relationships between 'town and gown'. The wind is behind us in this respect. Funding streams support collaborative inter-professional and cross-disciplinary work, looking for methodological innovation and creative ideas about research practice.

Begun et al. (2010) explore the nature of such partnerships and the conditions that support their effectiveness. They propose four key considerations in establishing rewarding partnerships; these include the multi-directional exchange of expertise and know-how; the fact that these relationships have to be established as longitudinal and developmental, in order to build trust and understanding; that they should be based on clear understanding of respective motivations and expectations; and that there should be clarity about funding arrangements and budgets. Loughran and McCann's (2015) study of drug problems in three communities in the city of Dublin rehearses several of these principles in their community-based participatory research strategy. Longstanding relationships with drug agencies in the city opened up the possibility for high user and agency involvement in the design and conduct of the research. They reflect on the nature of researcher partnerships as 'affiliated'— where the researcher works but does not live on the research patch, and 'immersed'—where the researcher both lives and works within the community (Loughran and McCann 2015: 713). What is interesting about Loughran and McCann's (2015) account is that they demonstrate very powerfully a research strategy built on localised knowledge, insights from local informants and community sources to which the university academic would not normally have had access. Local relationships enabled access to hard to reach participants in their study and provided the medium for knowledge transfer. These research techniques are known and used in social work (van Ewijk 2011), and can only be enhanced by a deeper and more explicit examination of some of the place-based considerations raised in this chapter.

Conclusion

For all the borrowings across critical geography and urbanology, when the dust settles we will need to find our place and to define a focus and parameter for social work research in the city aimed at extending the profession's social justice ambitions. From endless possibilities, we need to configure our attention to key themes that build on the research traditions of the discipline; to polish our disciplinary lens. The challenge and the opportunity are to devise methodologies that pay attention to the micro-issues of everyday interactions in localities and yet are also attuned to the trans-local, transnational connections of contemporary moment. The field is wide open. Part and parcel of carving out and legitimating the role and identity of social work in the city will be establishing the research niche focused on key social work concerns with social justice, care and sustainability.

References

Atkinson, R., & Jacobs, K. (2010). Damned by place, then by politics: Spatial disadvantage and the housing policy-research interface. *International Journal of Housing Policy, 10*(2), 155–171.

Atkinson, R., & Kintrea, K. (2004). 'Opportunities and despair: It's all in there'. Practitioner experiences and explanations of area effects and life chances. *Sociology, 38*(3), 437–455.

Begun, A. L., Berger, L. K., Otto-Salaj, L. L., & Rose, S. J. (2010). Developing effective social work university-community research collaborations. *Social Work, 55*(1), 54–62.

Bennett, B., Green, S., Gilbert, S., & Bessarab, D. (2013). *Our voices: Aboriginal and Torres Strait Islander social work*. Melbourne: Palgrave Macmillan.

Berg, M. L., & Sigona, N. (2013). Ethnography, diversity and urban space. *Identities: Global Studies in Culture and Power, 20*(4), 347–360.

Briskman, L. (2013). Courageous ethnographers or agents of the state: Challenges for social work. *Critical and Radical Social Work, 1*(1), 51–66.

Bryant, L. (Ed.). (2015). *Critical and creative research methodologies in social work*. Farnham: Ashgate.

Cattell, V. (2001). Poor people, poor places, and poor health: The mediating role of social networks and social capital. *Social Science and Medicine, 52*, 1501–1516.

Clarke, K. (2009). Negotiating migrant community needs through social work research. *Qualitative Social Work, 10*(1), 8–27.

Conradson, D. (2003a). Spaces of care in the city: The place of a community drop-in-centre. *Social and Cultural Geography, 4*(4), 507–525.

Conradson, D. (2003b). Doing organisational space: Practices of voluntary welfare in the city. *Environment and Planning, 35*(11), 1975–1992.

Coulton, C. (2005). The place of community in social work practice research: Conceptual and methodological developments. *Social Work Research, 29*(2), 73–86.

Curtis, S. (2010). *Space, place and mental health*. Farnham: Ashgate.

D'Cruz, H., & Jones, M. (2013). *Social work research in practice: Ethical and political contexts*. London: Sage.

Delgado, M. (1999). *Social work practice in non-traditional urban settings*. New York: Oxford University Press.

Evers, A., Schulz, A. D., & Wiesner, C. (2006). Local policy networks in the programme Social City: A case in point for new forms of governance in the field of local social work and urban planning. *European Journal of Social Work, 9*(2), 183–200.

Ferguson, H. (2008). Liquid social work: Welfare interventions as mobile practices. *British Journal of Social Work, 38*(3), 561–579.

Ferguson, H. (2009a). Driven to care: The car, automobility and social work. *Mobilities, 4*(2), 275–293.

Ferguson, H. (2009b). Performing child protection: Home visiting, movement and the struggle to reach the abused child. *Child and Family Social Work, 14*, 471–480.

Ferguson, H. (2010a). Walks, home visits and atmospheres: Risk and the everyday practices and mobilities of social work and child protection. *British Journal of Social Work, 40*, 1100–1117.

Ferguson, H. (2010b). Therapeutic journeys: The car as a vehicle for working with children and families and theorising practice. *Journal of Social Work, 24*(2), 121–138.

Foster, K. A., & Hipp, J. A. (2011). Defining neighbourhood boundaries for social measurement: Advancing social work research. *Social Work Research, 35*(1), 25–35.

Hillier, A. E. (2007). Why social work needs mapping. *Journal of Social Work Education, 43*(2), 205–221.

Holland, S. (2014). Trust in the community: Understanding the relationship between formal, semi-formal and informal child safeguarding in a local neighbourhood. *British Journal of Social Work, 44*(2), 384–400.

Holland, S., Burgess, S., Grogan-Kaylor, A., & Delva, J. (2011). Understanding neighbourhoods, communities and environments: New approaches to social work research. *British Journal of Social Work, 41*, 689707.

ICEC (Interethnic Coexistence in European Cities). (2015). www.iceproject.com.

Jack, G. (2010). Place matters: The significance of place attachments for children's well-being. *British Journal of Social Work, 40*(3), 755–771.

Jack, G. (2015). 'I may not know who I am, but I know where I am from': The meaning of place in social work with children and families. *Child and Family Social Work, 20*(4), 415–423.

Jeyasingham, D. (2014). The production of space in children's social work: Insights from Henri Lefebvre's spatial dialectics. *British Journal of Social Work, 44*(7), 1879–1894.

Kintrea, K., Bannister, J., & Pickering, J. (2010). Territoriality and disadvantage among young people: An exploratory study of six British neighbourhoods. *Journal of Housing and the Built Environment, 25*, 447–465.

Leventhal, T., & Brooks-Gunn, J. (2000). The neighbourhoods they live in: The effects of neighbourhood residence on child and adolescent outcomes. *Psychological Bulletin, 126*(2), 309–337.

Lightfoot, E., Simmelink McCleary, J., & Lum, T. (2014). Asset mapping as a research tool for community-based participatory research in social work. *Social Work Research, 38*(1), 59–64.

Logan, J. R. (2012). Making a place for space: Spatial thinking in social science. *The Annual Review of Sociology, 38*, 507–524.

Loughran, H., & McCann, M. E. (2015). Employing community participative research methods to advance service user collaboration in social work research. *British Journal of Social Work, 45*(2), 705–723.

McKenzie, L. (2015). *Getting by: Estates, class and culture in austerity Britain.* Bristol: Policy Press.

Merriman, P. (2013). Rethinking mobile methods. *Mobilities, 9*(2), 167–187.

Milligan, C., Atkinson, S., Skinner, M., & Wiles, J. (2007). Geographies of care: A commentary. *New Zealand Geographer, 63*, 135–140. http://www.researchgate.net/publication/249470500_Geographies_of_care_A_commentary. Date accessed 17 Sept 2015.

Mishra, R. (1981). *Society and social policy: Theories and practice of welfare.* London: Macmillan.

Pearce, J. (2011). Working with trafficked children and young people: Complexities in practice. *British Journal of Social Work, 41*(8), 1424–1441.

Pugh, R., & Cheers, B. (2010). *Rural social work: An international perspective.* Bristol: Policy Press.

Schrooten, M., Geldof, D., & Withaeckx, S. (2015). Transmigration and urban social work: Towards a research agenda. *European Journal of Social Work.* doi:10.1080/13691457.2014.1001725.

Sharland, E. (2013). Where are we now? Strengths and limitations of UK social work and social care research. *Social Work and Social Sciences Review, 16*(2), 7–19.

Shaw, I. (2011). Social work research: An urban desert? *European Journal of Social Work, 14*(1), 11–26.

Soydan, H. (2012). Understanding social work in the history of ideas. *Research on Social Work Practice, 22*(5), 468–480.

Taylor, D. (1996). *Critical social policy: A reader: Social policy and social relations.* London: Sage.

Van der Meulen, E. (2011). Action research with sex workers: Dismantling barriers and building bridges. *Action Research, 9*(4), 370–384.

van Ewijk, H. (2011). Collaboration in community research. *European Journal of Social Work, 14*(1), 41–52.

Wienke, C., & Hill, G. J. (2013). Does place of residence matter? Rural-urban differences and the wellbeing of gay men and lesbians. *Journal of Homosexuality, 60*(9), 1256–1279.

Zapf, M. K. (2010). Social work and the environment: Understanding people and place. *Critical Social Work, 11*(3), 30–46.

Zimbalist, S. E. (1977). *Historic themes and landmarks in social welfare research.* New York: Harper & Row.

Part II

Social Issues and the City: New Directions in Practice

Charlotte Williams

Introduction

By all accounts, cities are where the action is. In Australia, a Minister for Cities has been appointed by the incoming Liberal government (2015) and, in the UK, the government has acknowledged the significance of cities in comissioning a series of cross-disciplinary position papers under the Foresight Future of Cities Program.[1] In the Foresight essays, a number of academic commentators propose future scenarios for cities based on their expert reading of the present. If I were to be invited to provide a 'Foresight' on social work futures and the city, I would perhaps be wary of designing a utopia in which social work services would be largely redundant, and individuals and communities self-determining and self-sustaining,

---

[1] https://www.gov.uk/government/collections/future-of-cities.

C. Williams (✉)
School of Global, Urban and Social Studies,
RMIT University,
GPO Box 2476,
Melbourne, VIC 3001, Australia

© The Editor(s) (if applicable) and The Author(s) 2016
C. Williams (ed.), *Social Work and the City*,
DOI 10.1057/978-1-137-51623-7

121

or of formulating the dystopia of neglected or misplaced interventions, runaway technological determinism, bitter and entrenched inequalities, rising levels of mental stress, disenfranchisement, individualisation and exclusion. Such reading of the runes would be folly, given the complexities of human behaviour, human agency and resilience, and the serendipities of the city. But, as this text has argued, social work does have a stake in city-making and therefore we must be empowered to propose visions of 'the possible city' (Tonkiss 2013).

So, taking the next best option in hand, I invited experts in their field to suggest new perspectives and issues for practice that are emerging in the light of the new urbanisms. The chapters that follow explore a contemporary social issue/policy field of significance in modern city life outlining the ways in which this issue is manifest and the debates it raises for consideration in the future. The selected areas are by no means exhaustive,[2] but they are illustrative of a number of dominant debates characterising the concerns of the urban age: diversity, ageing, poverty and inequality, disability and care. Collectively, they highlight some of the key issues shaping practice: welfare austerity, rights, power over place, dignity and caring, social sustainability, new ways of working, change and innovation in service delivery. These cross-cutting issues demand sophisticated responses and point to new forms of practice and new forms of service delivery. The onus is on social work to generate 'alternative moral landscapes' (Gleeson and Kearns 2001) to advocate and insert alternative perspectives on social issues and, as Zufferey suggests in Chap. 9, to generate 'counter discursive strategies' that circumvent 'disrespectful urban policies'.

Cities today are *divercities*.[3] Immigration, socio-economic inequalities, spatial segregation and a diversity of identities and lifestyles are all contributing factors. There can be no social work caseload in urban contexts that is not superdiverse. The challenges faced by urban policy-makers and service provider institutions to meet the needs of an increasingly diverse

---

[2] For example, there exists very useful text on Children, Youth and the City (Horschelmann and van Blerk 2012) and mental health and the city (Curtis 2010), see also LSE cities: https://lsecities.net/media/objects/articles/urban-stress-and-mental-health/en-gb/.

[3] See DIVERCITIES, financed by the European Commission under the 7th Framework Programme (Project No. 319970).

population are numerous and complex, but traditional approaches to ethnic diversity are rapidly being undermined by this new phenomenon. In Chap. 5, which opens Part II, Geldof tackles the implications of 'superdiversity': characterised by the diversification of diversity itself, the newness and the churn of migrations. Within the microcosm of superdiverse neighbourhoods in the city, global transnational processes are being played out. Geldof uses the term 'transmigrants' to capture the multiple spaces inhabited by individuals who stand betwixt and between legal, cultural, social and political contexts, managing and negotiating multiple affiliations—local, national, transnational. He sets out the challenge for more research in this area to map and understand these complex assemblages and mobilisations made by individuals and groups. Geldof illustrates this contemporary transition as both a quantitative and qualitative transition which has clear consequences for the delivery of social services, including social work, moving well beyond ethnic essentialism and traditional universalism. He concludes with two scenarios, one envisioning urban diversity positively and the other from a negative perspective. Clearly, a re-think of public policies and governance models is needed to make more intelligent use of diversity's potential.

What Geldof's chapter shows, and what the chapters by Phillipson and Ray on ageing and Prince on disability confront, are the limitations of the notion urban citizenship and, thus, the challenges to any idea of 'citizenship focused social work' (van Ewijk 2009). In the Introduction to the book, I tentatively adopted van Ewijk's concept for its utility in proposing a revisionist social work. The caution, of course, is to recognize those groups excluded or denied substantive citizenship and those placed beyond the state's purview as citizens-in-waiting. Phillipson and Ray (Chap. 6) set out some of the evidence on the challenges posed to those growing older in urban environments and argue for enabling, age-friendly practice that promotes the visibility and participation of older people, and actively forges alliances and partnerships with older people in challenging and campaigning for policies that directly benefit them. This may seem axiomatic but the point these authors make is that there is, as yet, little evidence that social work is actively supporting age-friendly developments, or any coherent engagement with the age-friendly movement.

Prince (Chap. 7) confronts the issue of urban power as manifest in the disabling environment of cities. For him, all cities are disabling. Prince also takes a citizenship-based approach, challenging the urban practices of ableism as they exclude and marginalize people with disabilities. Disabled people, he suggests, have not always enjoyed a positive relationship with social work. He outlines an urban practice which insists on respectful empowering practices in the carving out of inclusive and democratic spaces. What Prince insightfully shows is the contestation mounted by, and the potent force of disability activism in, establishing sites of resistance towards the reshaping of cities and city living. This is an embodied politics of resistance which resonates with Baines' (Chap. 8) examination of care and the city as a site of innovation and struggle, as well as a site in which to foster solidarity and change. Baines demonstrates the reconfiguration of care under neo-liberal politics and the scarring of care practices by the downward pressures of austerity measures towards 'thin, technical, tightly quantified care to those in need'. She argues that these pressures have, in many instances, produced a compromising of ethical standards amongst the formal care workforce. However, she also points to the potential of informal care economies in forging change and urges social workers, as practice leaders, to work on building solidarities and coalitions for collective action, capitalising on the potent politicization of care towards productive change. In my reading of Baines, I glimpsed the bedtime city and the army of care workers moving through the time and space of the city: a workforce that is highly gendered and racialised, highly fragmented and disparate, operating within and between different dimensions of the 'an imaginary care space'.

Urban policies require critical examination, in as much as they are damaging to and undermining of vulnerable groups, and/or serve to reproduce or generate inequalities. The push of deregulation, privatisation and economic development at the expense of human wellbeing is a theme in the chapters by Zufferey on homelessness (Chap. 9) and Martin and Goodman on poverty (Chap. 10). Redevelopment projects can be hostile to human wellbeing, exclusive and exacerbating of the polarisation between haves and have-nots, and act to increase marginalisation. Zufferey poses these as issues of human rights, dignity, respect and power. Her argument is that multi-level action on the part of social workers is required in responding to homelessness. She proposes two scenarios: one in which social work is submissive to urban policies and state regulations that deploy surveillance, policing and hostile architecture in response to the issue of homelessness; the other in which human rights are foregrounded and social work must find ways to circumvent oppressive urban policy and practices. Her examination of Housing First initiatives as an innovation in interventions demands a mind shift for social work in the ways in which priorities emerge in assessment and in reconfiguring their relationship with service users. This mind shift is also required in relation to thinking about the nature and response to new forms of poverty. Poverty and its spatial referents have been a neglected theme in social work discourse. Martin and Goodman's chapter takes us beyond the stereotypical view of the inner city high rise poverty to consideration of new forms of spatial disadvantage and newly impoverished groups. Their citizen focused perspective points to a poverty of place in terms of access to jobs, community and cultural provisioning for many young families, migrant families and others who are forced out to cheaper housing options in city suburbs. These new patterns of social inequality are notably less visible forms and more complex in the relationship they reflect between spatial and social determinants. In examining this issue in the development of the city of Melbourne, Martin and Goodman argue for greater collaboration between social work and urban planning in responding to the deficiencies of the built environment, more nuanced community consultation and engagement, and concerted advocacy on the part of both professions.

The call to collaboration, inter-disciplinary practice and education aptly concludes the book with Costello and Raxworthy's chapter on learning together (Chap. 11). These authors appeal to the common tradition and value base of the professions as a starting point for working together, and suggest the role of educational institutions in preparing the ground for inter-disciplinary practice. Their argument is that the complexity of social issues in the contemporary city demands inter-disciplinary working, but that it cannot be assumed that we know how to collaborate and how to form genuine partnerships. Moving beyond the siloed thinking of our disciplines requires an imaginative leap, skill, creativity and confidence; it involves deep engagement with concepts such as partnership, innovation and transformation in imagining futures. This is the very ambition that underpins this book.

References

Curtis, S. (2010). *Space, place and mental health*. Farnham: Ashgate.

Gleeson, B., & Kearns, R. (2001). Remoralising landscapes of care. *Environment and Planning D: Society and Space, 19*, 61–80.

Horschelmann, K., & van Blerk, L. (2012). *Children, youth and the city*. London: Routledge.

Tonkiss, F. (2013). *Cities by design: The social life of urban form*. Cambridge: Polity Press.

van Ewijk, H. (2009). Citizenship-based social work. *International Social Work, 52*(2), 167–179.

5

Superdiversity and the City

Dirk Geldof

Introduction: The Nature of the Contemporary City

The impact and scale of migrations and mobilities are possibly the most predominant issue in the contemporary transformation of cities. Cities are the sites of negotiations of differences. They are plural spaces, characterised by a superdiversity (Vertovec 2007, 2011; Geldof, 2016) that demands the particular attention of social work in terms of solidarities, cohesion and appropriate cross-cultural responses.

Many cities are more ethnically diverse than ever before, with several cities having majority ethnically diverse populations—such as Luton, Birmingham and Slough in Great-Britain; Brussels in Belgium; Amsterdam or Rotterdam in the Netherlands.

Minority ethnic groups are over-represented in the most deprived neighbourhoods in cities; they are significantly disenfranchised and

D. Geldof (✉)
University of Antwerp, Odisee University College and Karel de Grote
University College, Antwerp & Brussels, Belgium

© The Editor(s) (if applicable) and The Author(s) 2016
C. Williams (ed.), *Social Work and the City*,
DOI 10.1057/978-1-137-51623-7_5

highly internally differentiated. Often, these neighbourhoods are associated with problems of social cohesion, belonging and investment. They are framed as deprived neighbourhoods and ghettos, with a strong focus on segregation and (a lack of) integration (Vaughan and Arbaci 2011). Sporadic riots in the *banlieues* (suburbs) in France, or in the northern cities of the UK, attest to the ways in which public space has been claimed for protest and resistance and for struggles over welfare provision and equality. At the same time, these cities are succesful as a result of such diversity and become increasingly so. People with a migrant background are not only part of the city, to a large extent they constitute what these cities *are*. They are also entrepreneurial in mobilising to meet community needs. Arrival cities and arrival neighbourhoods are not only densely populated, but also very dynamic neighbourhoods, in the formal and the informal economy.

Urban social work has a strong body of knowledge in cross-cultural and inter-cultural practice, but what innovations are there in the field that rethink ideas about people, place and community? In this chapter, I analyse the context of superdiversity as the urban condition of the twenty-first century and the challenges for and responses from social work.

Superdiversity as the Urban Context

The city has always been a focal point in sociology as well as in social work, going back to the Settlement movement and Toynbee Hall in London to Hull House and Jane Adams in the USA. In sociology, the focal point has ranged from Robert Park and his colleagues in the Chicago School and their focus on transition zones and vulnerable (or deviant) groups to Saskia Sassen's analysis of global cities (Sassen 2001 [1991]). Gradually, diversity is also becoming an issue in urban planning (Eckhart and Eade 2012).

Very often, urban segregation patterns and inequality were analysed, largely in terms of division, exclusion, gentrification or even ghettoisation. Attention in sociology as well as in social work was often focused on the position of vulnerable minorities vis-à-vis the dominant majority. Increasingly, attention was paid to the position of ethnic minorities in the city and their integration into the dominant society. Although socio-economic inequalities still lead to divided cities, these inequality patterns can no longer be understood through an exclusive focus on ethnic segregation patterns since, in the twenty-first century, most western European countries and the USA are making a transition towards superdiversity, especially in the larger cities.

Steven Vertovec introduced the concept of superdiversity in 2005/2007 (Vertovec 2005, 2007, 2012; Crul et al. 2013; Blommaert, 2013; Geldof 2013). In my book *Superdiversity in the Heart of Europe* (Geldof 2016), I define superdiversity in terms of a quantitative and a qualitative transition.

The increasing diversity in our societies is part of the quantitative transition, certainly in the larger cities. Many western European urban areas have become arrival cities, just as have many cities in the south (Saunders 2011). They are the main destination of international migrants. The strong acceleration of migration since World War II—especially since the 1990s—due to globalisation and the enlargement of the EU towards the east, has confronted most western European cities with an increasing diversity, 'layering' new migrations on top of established diversity (Vertovec 2011).

Increasingly, cities are becoming 'majority-minority cities': cities in which the majority of its inhabitants have their roots in migration, cities in which there is no longer a majority of one ethnic group (the native population) but only a wide variety of ethnic minorities. This is already the case in the heart of Europe in cities such as Brussels, Rotterdam or Amsterdam, and, by 2020, Antwerp (Geldof, 2016).

This shift is not only the result of increasing migration since the 1990s, but also a consequence of the demographic reality that people with a migrant background are more represented amongst the younger population (Crul et al. 2013; Kochan 2014; Geldof 2016;). Even without new migration, diversity will increase further, as a result of the demographic structure of urban populations. Among the elderly, there are fewer citizens with a migrant background. However, in progressively more cities and in metropolitan regions, the majority of the children and young people have a family history of migration. They are today's parents, or will become those of tomorrow. They are *Inheriting the City* (Kasinitz et al. 2010).

Even more important in defining superdiversity is the qualitative transition. Vertovec coined superdiversity as being *the diversification of diversity*, that is:

> not just in terms of bringing more ethnicities and countries of origin, but also with respect to a multiplication of significant variables that affect where, how and with whom people live (Vertovec 2007: 1025).

Superdiversity is about the dynamic interplay of these factors. It is about new, small and scattered, multiple-origin, transnationally connected, socio-economically differentiated and legally stratified immigrants.

Since the early 1990s, European societies have gone through a crucial change in their migration patterns. In the mid-1960s, migration towards western European countries such as Belgium, the Netherlands, France or Germany was initiated by the national authorities. So-called 'temporary foreign workers' were recruited in a rather limited number of countries of origin. In today's era of superdiversity, migration is worldwide. Migration changed from 'large numbers moving from particular places to particular places' to 'small numbers moving from many places to many places' (Vertovec 2011: 8).

As a consequence, Western societies and cities are characterised by an increasing diversity in the nationalities and countries of origin of their inhabitants, and an increase in the different languages spoken, religions practised and in lifestyles. We also see an increasing diversity in migration motives, statuses of migrants and their socio-economic positions (Vertovec 2007; Williams and Graham 2014).

Growing interest in Vertovec's concept of superdiversity prompts us to develop the concept, theoretically and empirically. We should avoid the tendency to see superdiversity simply as a synonym for 'multicultural' or 'diversity'. Superdiversity is about an ongoing process of differentiation (Meissner and Vertovec 2014). Superdiversity is a lens through which and with which to understand the transition of urban societies towards majority-minority cities and the further diversification of diversity. It is about the complex but fascinating dynamic interplay of different kinds of diversity.

This has consequences for social work. People with migrant backgrounds often live in precarious social situations, together with the 'original' inhabitants of deprived neighbourhoods. Both are threatened by processes of social exclusion. Both are fighting for recognition and for a social status, vital to their social integration and identity. However, in many cities they are placed in competition and must interact in direct encounters within their neighbourhoods. Urban social problems in the twenty-first century are social problems, but additionally have an ethnic dimension on top of the structural problems of exclusion in the labour market, in the housing market or in the educational system.

This ethnic dimension makes social work in an urban context increasingly different from social work elsewhere. The context of the city is specific. Both the scale of the city and the concentration of social problems in cities and in deprived neighbourhoods within these cities are relevant. At the beginning of the twenty-first century, the migration processes that have occurred since the mid-1990s have changed our cities and their social landscape profoundly (Geldof 2011; Beck and Beck-Gernsheim 2011).

This leads to new patterns of inequality, segregation and prejudice, as well as to 'new experiences of space and contact and new practices of cosmopolitanism, creolisation and conviviality' (Vertovec 2011: 8). Commonplace diversity emerges in superdiverse neighbourhoods (Wessendorf 2013, 2014). Public and semi-public spaces such as shops, libraries or (internet) cafes become the places for commonplace intercultural contact, with a normalisation of diversity and the development of forms of civility in dealing with other citizens (Wessendorf 2013, 2014; Lofland 1973). This new dynamic also has an influence on public services and social work (Geldof 2011, 2016).

Beyond Methodological Nationalism

Superdiversity is not only a way of understanding the dynamics of urban contexts; it also confronts us with the need for a paradigmatic shift. In order to understand the real social situation in European cities, we have to leave the old methodological nationalism behind (Beck 2004, 2007, 2008; Geldof 2016). Nationality is no longer a useful category if we wish to understand demographic, social or ethnic evolutions in European cities. Increasingly, citizens have multiple identities, partly rooted in migration processes. They belong to local and global networks, with transnational lifestyles. They mix and combine places, cultures and lifestyles.

Ambivalence becomes a crucial concept. We can no longer understand the dynamics in urban societies using the old national 'either/or' framework. People live in an 'and/and' world. They are, simultaneously, inhabitants of their neighbourhood and of their city, and nationals with a passport from their new country, while still holding one from their country of origin. Their family is both here and in their country of origin, and often in other European cities as well. These new transnational networks must be taken into account in order to understand daily life.

Social workers also need to be aware of the growing difference between the official city and the daily city. In superdiverse or cosmopolitan cities—I consider both concepts as synonymous—urban life includes inhabitants that are not officially registered in the city. They live in our cities as undocumented migrants, or as asylum seekers, as transmigrants or intra EU-workers, as tourists, as Case 5.1 from Antwerp illustrates.

Case 5.1: Undocumented Migrants are Part of the Urban Context

Every superdiverse city hosts a number of undocumented migrants. Estimations about their numbers can differ substantially, depending on the methodological choices, but often also depending on political interpretations. For social work, this is a group that matters, as the case of Antwerp (Belgium) illustrates.

Antwerp is a city with 515,000 official inhabitants. In 2009, Belgium organised an exceptional collective regularisation for undocumented migrants that had already been staying in the country for several years and who had already undertaken steps towards integration. As a result, more than 7,000 applications were made in Antwerp by undocumented migrants. For every 1,000 official inhabitants in Antwerp, 15 undocumented migrants applied for regularisation. In the superdiverse neighbourhoods of the north of Antwerp, more than 50 applications were made for every 1,000 officially registered inhabitants of those neighbourhoods, or 1 undocumented migrant for each 20 officially registered citizens (Geldof 2012, 2016). The case of Antwerp pins our attention on the real population, which differs from official data, because hidden groups become visible. If social workers want to understand social and economic reality in superdiverse neighbourhoods and cities, they have to go beyond samples and beyond official population data; they have to pay attention to hidden, often vulnerable groups.

> Working with undocumented migrants is part of social work in every city. Social workers often have to walk a tightrope between the ethical principles of their profession and the legal framework of their organisation or city (Jönsson 2014).

Understanding superdiversity requires an inter-disciplinary approach. Attention to the use of space and place as a geographical dimension is a crucial element in fully understanding the impact of superdiversity. Superdiversity is part of globalisation processes, but it crystalises geographically in specific neighbourhoods, cities and specific regions. Some time ago, Saskia Sassen illustrated the 'rootedness' of globalisation processes in global cities (Sassen 2001 [1991]). These global cities are often today's superdiverse cities. In her recent book *Expulsions* (2014), Sassen looks at processes and places of expulsion in our capitalist societies. Refugee camps, undocumented migrants in Calais or Le Havre or in the South of Italy after reaching Lampedusa, or thousands of refugees dying in the Mediterranean, may be considered examples of superdiverse expulsion, but we can also find the hidden results of expulsion in our cities (Geldof and Oosterlynck 2015).

Policy Responses to Migration and Diversity

Migration has been, and still is, on the policy agenda in many different ways. Most Western countries wanted labour migration after World War II, and certainly in the golden 1950s and 1960s. In the same period, decolonisation took place. Migrants in those days were mostly labour migrants. Most governments and migrants themselves considered their presence in European countries as temporary.

The oil-crisis in 1973 and the economic crisis thereafter created an important policy change. Gradually, most migrants had become permanent residents in their new countries. Attracting new migrants was no longer an objective, due to the crisis. Integration of people who had migrated in previous decades and integration of new migrants became the dominant challenge. Integration in those days was seen as a two-way process. Newcomers had to adapt to the dominant society but, at the same time, Western societies were willing to change their policies and institutions to make this possible. Language courses and settlement services were organised, pathways towards full citizenship offered access to nationality and equal rights, and religious diversity was evident and accepted in most Western liberal democracies. Multi-culturalism became the dominant discourse and policy frame in the 1990s. Bauböck (2002, 2008) distinguished a celebrative multi-culturalism, which welcomes diversity as an enrichment, a multiculturalism of mutual tolerance and a more profound, structural multiculturalism based on recognition.

However, at the beginning of the twenty-first century, and certainly after the terrorist attacks of 9/11, political discourses changed. Scholars, public opinion-makers and politicians from the political centre, and even from the left, declared the 'failure of integration' and the 'end of multi-culturalism'. A discourse of 'new realism' occurred, beyond the supposed 'political correctness' of multi-cultural approaches (Kymlicka 2010, 2012; Vertovec and Wessendorf 2010). It was critical of tolerance and of social work approaches to diversity, their being considered as too 'soft' and too tolerant towards migrants and as hindering 'real' integration.

As a result, the focus shifted towards a neo-assimilation. Since the mid-2000s, there has been a strong neo-liberal tendency towards individualisation of the debates about integration and inter-culturalisation. According to Williams and Graham (2014: i4):

a plethora of government agents, including social work, have been engaged in assisting the migrant to settle and assimilate. Policies of multiculturalism that once venerated and celebrated heterogeneity have gradually given way in the present neo-liberal area to a neo-assimilationism, a conditional integration proscribed by the ability of the migrant to adapt to dominant values and ways of life.

Integration became the individual responsibility of migrants, and inter-culturalisation became an individual competence which side stepped the (white middleclass) culture of organisations, institutions or politics. Social work came under pressure and was reoriented towards or replaced by more disciplinary approaches initiated by local and national authorities. Security issues gained weight on the political agenda, first with a focus on criminality, more recently on the potential threat of radicalisation in Islam and the risk for terror.

Case 5.2: The Institutionalisation of Integration Work in Flanders (Belgium)

As many other European countries, Belgium organised labour migration in the golden 1950s and 1960s and attracted temporary foreign workers in southern Europe, Morocco and Turkey. Because the Belgian government considered this labour migration as temporary, no integration policies or language courses were set up in those days. NGOs, community workers and social workers engaged themselves in supporting these labour migrants and their families in Belgium.

From the 1970s on, these organisations were gradually recognised as local integration initiatives and supported by the Belgian, Flemish and local authorities. In the beginning of the twenty-first century, the Flemish Parliament introduced obligatory integration trajectories for new migrants. They were organised by the local authorities, in collaboration with the local integration initiatives. Integration was strongly monitored (Vanduynslager et al. 2013).

In 2013, the Flemish Parliament decided to further reorganise the integration sector. The subsidised NGOs had to become a part of an external Government Agency for Integration (Extern Verzelfstandigd Agentschap Integratie en Inburgering) from 2015 on. This agency supports the Flemish integration policy.

For some, this is an example of positive institutionalisation: since the 1970s, authorities have gradually recognised the work of NGOs in supporting migrants and their integration, which they have subsidised and regulated. Nowadays, the Flemish authorities see it as their responsibility to organise such integration.

Many social workers, however, consider this as an instrumentalisation of the dynamic of these organisations in a less empowering and much more assimilating framework. They fear that giving voice to migrants and the critical function of social work will not find a place in the new agency (Groffy and Debruyne 2014). Interesting, however, is that in the superdiverse cities migrants themselves are simultaneously raising their voices and setting up new organisations to take up this role.

The reality of superdiversity in urban contexts confronts us today with a strong paradox. The dominant policy framework builds on and strengthens an us-versus-them-discourse. A (white) majority tries to enforce and impose integration—often limiting it to assimilation—on minorities and newcomers. At the same time, the transition towards superdiversity and majority-minority cities, including the rise of an ethnic middle class in these cities, confronts us with a new reality and the need for new policy frames.

Social Work and Superdiversity

From 'the age of migration' (Castles and Miller 2009) we have entered 'the age of superdiversity'. In this context, migration is not just a specialism of social work but, rather, a central concern for the profession, as all societies are fundamentally and ever more deeply migrant societies (Williams and Graham 2014: i15). With the demographic changes in European cities, the context for urban social work also changes. Urban social work operates within crucial tensions: structural versus cultural changes, changes at the macro level versus those at the micro level, targeting the geographical dimension versus the categorical dimension and, not least, combining an ever stronger assimilationist mandate with a rights-based and empowering focus towards recognition and citizenship.

This increasing superdiversity is becoming the specificity of, and one of the main challenges for, urban social work. It requires organisational challenges and (further) inter-culturalisation of social work organisations. Sometimes, specific methodologies are required to reach the same empowerment objectives, given the diversity of citizens in such diverse urban contexts. The main need for social work in an urban context in Europe is the need to operate in a more inter-cultural way—which requires a profound empathy for the living conditions of all citizens—with respect to the broadening variety of ethnic backgrounds. Finally, we also need new policy frameworks to deal with the reality of superdiversity.

What role can social work play in this transition? And to what extent can the emerging paradigm of superdiversity help social workers or other professionals in urban contexts to develop their skills and to find answers to challenges of novelty, complexity and newness among their clients? Empirical work in progress is illustrative (Phillimore 2015).

Paolo Boccagni (2015) is one of the first to analyse the potential of superdiversity as a new lens for social work practice. He describes super-diversity as the 'accelerated interdependence between ethnicity and other diversity traits', which results in more complex underlying social identifications' (Boccagni 2015: 608). What, then, is the added value of super-diversity, compared with pre-existing elaborations of anti-oppressive and culturally sensitive social work practice? Against tendencies to over-culturalise migrants' patterns of disadvantage—often latent even in the routine of social work agencies and practitioners—the notion of superdi-versity may be a good reminder of the more complex and varied sources of inequality to which migrants are exposed as welfare recipients. While much literature still seems to be stuck in the age-old stalemate of cul-turalised versus culturally blind accounts, a superdiversity-oriented per-spective may well provide a reasonable way ahead (Boccagni 2015: 615; Geldof 2013, 2016).

According to Boccagni, the actual diversity lens is marked by an ambiguous coexistence of two stances: the overcoming of any essentialising and reifying understanding of ethnicity or of culture, and the risk of downplaying 'the specific roots and processes' of social inequality, discrimination and racism, due to the lack of a consistently structural focus. An appropriate use of diversity additionally requires awareness of the structural roots of minorities' disadvantage, including institutional racism.

Superdiversity is familiar, but slightly distinct from the notion of inter-sectionality, argues Boccagni. Inter-sectionality, primarily theorised by feminist scholars (Crenshaw 1989), does not (always) cover an equally wide spectrum of axes of differentiation—including factors such as legal status, age, religion, language, length of stay and so on. The focus of inter-sectionality is on patterns of oppression; superdiversity focuses on processes of differentiation. For Boccagni, superdiversity points to the relevance of how social actors perceive, make sense of and react to the situated inter-section between multiple attributes over the life course. It stimulates moving beyond the identity politics waged in the name of diversity, while recognising the importance of individual trajectories (rather than cross-sectional categorisations) of migration, labour market participation and legal statuses. Superdiversity thus can serve as a lens to further de-essentialise ethnic and cultural differences, and also to focus on the underlying concurrent processes of societal differentiation, individual identification and group (dis)alignment. In this way, superdiversity can help social workers to understand the implications of accelerated societal diversification processes—particularly in large urban areas—for social work theory and practice (Boccagni 2015: 611).

Boccagni also positions superdiversity in dialogue with the anti-oppressive (Dominelli 2002), anti-discriminatory (Thompson 2006) and anti-racist (Dominelli 2008) tradition in social work. These different but related approaches have their emphasis on the structural inequalities and power imbalances underlying social work practice in common, including those between clients and practitioners. A stronger awareness of this inescapable power dimension should be integrated into the debate on superdiversity. This could provide a more nuanced account of the practical influence of a social worker's background (Boccagni 2015: 613).

Paying more attention to power imbalances can help to avoid a risk in using the frame of superdiversity. Boccagni warns that:

> while clients' shared identities and backgrounds may be less rigid or unidimensional than they were perceived to be in the past, such fluidity risks being a poor substitute of traditional frames for collective action such as gender, disability, sexuality or even ethnicity (Boccagni 2015: 615).

Social work in superdiverse cities also needs to acknowledge the ways in which migrants organise themselves to meet their welfare needs. We see the emergence and growth of organisations within civil society, set up within groups and communities. Sometimes, they build on religious institutions such as mosques or African or Latin American evangelic churches (sometimes hosted in old shops or theatres) which start to provide social services.

They can cover a wide range of support services, from distribution of food and clothes to housing support, legal advice, psychological support and advocacy (Schrooten et al. 2015, 2016). The agency of these groups and how they mobilise to meet their own needs challenges the existing framework of social work in superdiverse cities.

Challenges for Social Workers

How, therefore, to respond to superdiversity? The diversification of diversity confronts us with the necessity to evaluate and partly rethink our actual way of dealing with diversity: as professionals, at organisational and institutional levels, and at policy levels.

Professionals Responding to Superdiversity: Inter-Cultural Competences, Cultural Sensitivity and Inter-Sectionality

Professionals in urban environments are daily confronted with superdiversity. Superdiversity is the reality in the work of teachers, nurses and doctors, social workers, policeman, civil servants and others in the social professions. The growing diversity and the diversification of diversity are mostly seen as a challenge for these professionals. Are they and are we prepared to work as professionals in a superdiverse context, in our schools, in social work, in health care, in policing?

The transition towards superdiversity is mostly framed in terms of developing individual inter-cultural competences, culturally or diverssensitive competent practices or cultural awareness (e.g. Davis 2009). This includes a discourse of mutual respect, openness, tackling prejudices, avoiding stereotyping, and recognising the other as an individual rather than as a member of an ethnic group. In the context of superdiversity, inter-cultural competences will become even more important. The frame of inter-sectionality underpins inter-cultural responses but needs to be broadened to address superdiversity. Although the different sensitivity approaches incorporate some structural perspectives, they are often and usually applied in a reflexive-therapeutic way, rather than seeking broad social change. The latter is more to be found in anti-discrimination approaches or anti-oppressive social work (Dominelli 2002, 2008; Payne 2014). Raising inter-cultural competences is necessary and important for professionals to understand and to work with the diversities they have to deal with in practice, but it is not sufficient. Acting in a world of super-diversity not only requires individual skills and competences, but also involves organisational and societal changes as well.

Superdiversity as an Organisational Challenge

Greater attention should also be given, in the debate on diversity-oriented social work practice, to the organisational cultures and settings of social work agencies. In a sort of tacit over-individualisation of cultural competence, organisational influences are often downplayed, contrary to individual workers' inter-cultural attitudes and skills (Boccagni 2015: 616).

How well are our organisations and institutions adapted to the increasing superdiversity? Is superdiversity yet a reality in social work or non-profit organisations, or in companies? And if so, is this at all levels in these organisations, in leading positions as well as in unskilled jobs? This requires policies inside these organisations to measure and manage diversity, to tackle or avoid discrimination, to train people's inter-cultural skills and competences, to increase inter-culturalisation, and to train and support professionals. Research evidence suggests that successful inter-cultural practices are not only a question of individual competences, but also must be embedded in an organisational structure actively involved in an inter-cultural trajectory (Boccagni 2015; Phillimore 2014; Van Robaeys 2014). Today we are only witnessing the start of these processes in most of our organisations and institutions.

Superdiversity and Urban Policies

Superdiversity is a policy challenge. National and urban authorities have to set up frameworks and legislation to stop racism; to avoid discrimination; to offer equal opportunities in educational systems, in the labour market, in the housing market and in criminal justice systems. Since the mid-1990s, a very polarised debate has taken place in favour or against multicultural society (Vertovec and Wessendorf 2010). While that debate dominated the political agenda, the transition towards superdiversity took place. Today, the question is no longer whether we want superdiversity: superdiversity has become the reality of the twenty-first century. Today's debate is about the different ways to respond to superdiversity. It is no longer about policies for minorities or individuals; the future is about the co-creation of superdiverse policies.

However, this does not imply that categorical measures or policies have no relevance. We should be careful to ensure that studies on superdiversity will not be misused to further individualise the debates on integration. Even in today's superdiverse cities, we will need a balanced combination of generic and structural measures, combined with tailor-made approaches that respect the diversification of diversity. Without essentialising people or groups, structural adaptations of major institutions—such as our educational system, or the functioning of the labour and housing markets—remain necessary to adapt them to a world of growing superdiversity.

Transmigrants as a New Challenge

The shift towards superdiversity in large cities raises numerous challenges for social work practice. One of them is finding ways to work with transmigrants. In our superdiverse cities, the increase of flexible migration strategies is gaining a foothold. Many contemporary migrants come and go—not always being sure how long they will stay in sending or receiving countries, when they will stop migrating, or where they will settle (Glick Schiller et al. 1995). Temporality and 'liquid migration' become features of the urban context. However, the amount of research on transmigration, on its impact on urban life, or in specific sectors as social work is still limited (Schrooten et al. 2015, 2016).

The social life of these 'mobile migrants' or 'transmigrants' is not only oriented towards their new countries, but consists of complex networks and contacts beyond boundaries. They shift between different modus operandi and between different visible and invisible networks—local and global. Transmigrants balance themselves on a tightrope, vacillating between maintaining 'some functional sense of local "rootedness" while at the same time gaining access to opportunities that are more transnational, even global, in scope' (Simone 2001: 84).

Transmigrants are defined neither by the cause of leaving their country of origin nor by the endpoint of their journey but, rather, by 'the lived condition of straddling borders, whether by choice or by necessity' (Hunter et al. 2010: 223). In contrast to the traditional image of migrants as people who stop shifting country boundaries after a while and reinforce their rootedness in the region of arrival, the concept of transmigrants focuses on how an increasing number of present-day migrants adopt a strategy of shifting between and engaging in lives in different places, countries and cultures.

The reality of transmigration requires an enhanced understanding of the multiple spaces inhabited by transmigrants, and of the complex legal, cultural, social and political contexts that push and pull families across national and local borders (Webster et al. 2010: 208). This is a very challenging shift for urban social policy and for social work in an urban context.

Almost all transmigrants maintain transnational social ties with people located in more than one national territory. Even so, rather than the national level, the local level is often more important for transmigrants, as their social relations are situated in specific localities, involving a network surrounding their local community of origin. To grasp this perspective 'from below', it is therefore important for social workers to look at the articulation of global and local dynamics in local contexts such as neighbourhoods, homes and families (Greiner and Sakdapolrak 2013).

Research with Moroccan, Brazilian and Ghanaian transmigrants in the superdiverse Belgian cities Brussels and Antwerp indicates that newly arrived migrants are increasingly mobile and engage in transnational networks spanning multiple locations. The condition of transmigration impacts on welfare needs, on decisions to migrate and on the ability to build up social capital in new locations. Policy and social services should become aware of this new reality. Transmigration influences our understanding of rootedness/identity, integration, social policy and social work, certainly in arrival cities (Schrooten et al. 2015, 2016; Withaeckx et al. 2015). It is one of the many aspects of superdiversity and urban social work that needs further research.

Discussion: Themes in an Urban Context

The diversity in the cities has also an important spatial dimension. This was already analysed in the early work of the Chicago School almost a century ago, with a focus on transition zones where arriving migrants found a place to stay. It resonates in the actual work of Doug Saunders (2011) on the role of arrival cities and neighbourhoods.

Spatial segregation has, to some extent, always been a reality in cities: socio-economic inequalities translate themselves in different housing preferences and possibilities. European cities were transformed in the nineteenth century—inspired by Haussmann—to improve the living conditions of poor workers in the poor and over-populated neighbourhoods, and/or to avoid revolutionary protest against the severe exploitation of the workers in a period of early capitalism.

Debates about spatial segregation have regained attention during the last decades. Starting with the organised labour migration of the 1950s and 1960s in Europe, but ongoing until now, most migrants could only afford a house in the poorer neighbourhoods. Long before we could talk about superdiverse cities, these neighbourhoods became superdiverse. The concentration of migrants in deprived neighbourhoods has been a concern for many researchers, politicians and professionals. For social work, especially for community work, these neighbourhoods were the places where categorical and territorial neighbourhood approaches were combined to improve the living conditions, to empower the inhabitants and to bridge the gap between deprived people with and without a background of migration. In the closing decades of the nineteenth century, tensions between migrants and the original inhabitants in neighbourhoods and suburbs of major cities often formed the basis for the development of extreme right and racist parties all over Europe. Such neighbourhoods were framed as poor, deprived neighbourhoods with highly concentrated populations, dangerous and criminal localities, even described as ghettos; this, despite the work of Loïc Wacquant (2008), who argues that ghettos exist in American cities but not in European cities. Even in the French *banlieues*, local and national authorities remain strongly involved and keep up investment, although not enough to improve the living conditions sufficiently. Such framing opened in the last two decades the door for gentrification policies in most European cities, with governments trying to obtain a social mix in neighbourhoods by attracting middle-class inhabitants. As a result, poorer inhabitants were often forced to move to other deprived neighbourhoods where they still could afford the rent.

Todays' superdiversity does not stop processes of spatial segregation; neither does it stop policies of gentrification. However, the transition towards majority-minority cities and the rise of an ethnic middle class in the cities leads to an increase of diversity throughout the city. Spatial segregation will remain, but the focus on socio-economic differences will become more important, as the diversification of diversity will contribute to social mobility and forms of social-mix-from-below.

Furthermore, the superdiverse neighbourhoods are becoming the places where we see the normalisation of diversity. Susanne Wessendorf (2014) defines it as commonplace diversity in her study of Hackney in London. Such neighbourhoods are not only an integral part of the city, superdiversity becomes the city.

Scenarios for the Future

Superdiversity is not something that is good or bad. It is not an ideological, political or normative concept. Superdiversity offers a theoretical tool with which to understand and to study the transitions in our societies and cities. Superdiversity can strengthen or weaken our cities and societies. This depends on the way we deal with the increasing reality of superdiversity in the future. The Dutch sociologist Maurice Crul and his colleagues (2013) have drawn attention to two scenarios for the future as a frame for reflection.

On the one hand, we see in our cities elements leaning towards scenarios of polarisation, fear and humiliation: polarisation around Islam, radicalisation, daily racism, ethnic poverty, high unemployment among young people from migrant backgrounds and lack of inter-ethnic friendships, all of which can create a breeding ground for fear and humiliation. If we let this scenario come true, superdiversity can become socially explosive, including riots—as we have witnessed in different cities. Rising social inequality here goes hand-in-hand with ethnic divides.

But, at the same time, and in the same cities, we witness the rise of a scenario of hope and empowerment: the number of students with an ethnic background increases, a new ethnic middle class stands up, ethnic business booms, inter-ethnic friendships are the new normality for youngsters in our cities. Maurice Crul and his colleagues conclude that majority-minority cities provide opportunities for establishing social mobility and a more equal society.

This scenario of hope and empowerment, however, will not become a reality for everyone without adequate policies and empowering social work practices. It is up to all professionals in schools, companies, sports clubs and other social settings to create the conditions for this new future. This is a change which will certainly be accompanied by conflicts and disillusionment, but there is no way back (Crul et al. 2013: 83). Demographic developments point in only one direction: the twenty-first century will be a century of superdiversity.

More than a decade ago, Lena Dominelli (2002: 290) concluded that:

> dynamics of people to exercise agency and constant changes in social categories of ethnicity push social work practice to look for problem-solving mechanisms far beyond the traditional positions of essentialism and universalism. [...] Furthermore the challenge of developing theoretical frameworks for social work practice and exploring empirical bases of such frameworks will take place in cross-roads between the demand for context specific practices and the need for more generalizable knowledge. This in its turn presupposes international and global collaboration between the actors in social work, whether they are practitioners or researchers.

In today's superdiverse cities, this is still the challenge, because urban social work in the twenty-first century is superdiverse social work.

References

Bauböck, R. (2002). Farewell to multiculturalism? Sharing values and identities in societies of immigration. *Journal of International Migration and Integration, 3*(1), 1–16.

Bauböck, R. (2008). *Beyond culturalism and statism. Liberal responses to diversity.* Eurosphere working paper no. 6, 2–34, Florence.

Beck, U. (2004). *Der kosmopolitische Blick, oder: Krieg ist Frieden.* Suhrkamp: Frankfurt am Main.

Beck, U. (2007). *Weltrisikogesellschaft: auf der Suche nach verlorenen Sicherheit.* Suhrkamp: Frankfurt am Main.

Beck, U. (2008). *Die Neuvermessung der Ungleichheit unter den Menschen: Soziologische Aufklärung im 21 Jahrhundert.* Suhrkamp: Frankfurt am Main.

Beck, U., & Beck-Gernsheim, E. (2011). *Fernliebe. Lebensformen im globalen Zeitalter.* Berlin: Suhrkamp.

Blommaert, J. (2013). *Ethnography, superdiversity and linguistic landscapes. Chronicles of complexity.* Bristol: Multilingual Matters.

Boccagni, P. (2015). (Super)diversity and the migration-social work nexus: A new lens on the field of access and inclusion? *Ethnic and Racial Studies, 38*(4), 608–620.

Castles, S., & Miller, M. J. (2009). *The age of migration: International population movements in the modern world* (Vol. 4). Basingstoke: Palgrave Macmillan.

Crenshaw, K. (1989). Demarginalizing the intersection of race and sex: A black feminist critique of antidiscrimination doctrine, feminist theory and antiracist politics. *The University of Chicago Legal Forum, 140*, 139–167.

Crul, M., Schneider, J., & Lelie, F. (2013). *Superdiversity: A new perspective on integration.* Amsterdam: VU University Press.

Davis, T. (2009). Diversity practice in social work: Examining theory in practice. *Journal of Ethnic and Cultural Diversity in Social Work, 18*(1–2), 40–69.

Dominelli, L. (2002). *Anti-oppressive social work theory and practice.* Basingstoke: Palgrave.

Dominelli, L. (2008). *Anti-racist social work.* Basingstoke: Palgrave.

Eckhart, F., & Eade, J. (2012). *The ethnically diverse city* (Future Urban Research in Europa, Band 4). Berlin: Berliner Wissenschaftsverlag.

Geldof, D. (2011). New challenges for urban social work and urban social work research. *European Journal of Social Work, 14*(1), 27–39.

Geldof, D. (2012). Stadsbewoners zonder papieren. Een verkennende analyse van de regularisatieaanvragen in Antwerpen in 2000 en 2009. *Ruimte en Maatschappij. Jrg., 3*(3), 1–24.

Geldof, D. (2013, 5th revised edition 2015). *Superdiversiteit. Hoe migratie onze samenleving verandert.* Leuven/Den Haag: ACCO.

Geldof, D. (2015). Nood aan een nieuwe democratiseringsgolf. De transitie naar superdiversiteit als uitdaging voor hoger onderwijs. *Tijdschrift voor Onderwijsrecht en Onderwijsbeleid (T.O.R.B.), 2014–2015*(4), 67–77.

Geldof, D. (2016). *Superdiversity in the heart of Europe: How migration changes our society.* Leuven/Den Haag: ACCO.

Geldof, D., & Oosterlynck, S. (2015). Van globalisering tot uitstoting. Het uitdagende oeuvre van Saskia Sassen. In S. Sassen (Ed.), *Uitstoting: Brutaliteit en complexiteit in de wereldeconomie* (pp. 7–18). Leuven/Den Haag: ACCO.

Glick Schiller, N., Basch, L., & Blanc-Szanton, C. (1995). From immigrant to transmigrant: Theorizing transnational migration. *Anthropological Quarterly, 68*(1), 46–63.

Greiner, C., & Sakdapolrak, P. (2013). Translocality: Concepts, applications and emerging research perspectives. *Geography Compass, 7*(5), 373–384.

Groffy, L., & Debruyne, P. (2014). Integratie is dood. Lang leve de integratie! Van integratiepioniers naar migratiebeheer in tijden van superdiversiteit. *OIKOS, 69*(2), 44–64.

Hunter, C. A., Lepley, S., & Nickels, S. (2010). New practice frontiers: Current and future social work with transmigrants. In N. J. Negi & R. Furnham (Eds.), *Transnational social work practice.* New York: Columbia University Press.

Jönsson, J. (2014). Local reactions to global problems: Undocumented immigrants and social work. *British Journal of Social Work, 44*(1), i35–i52.

Kasinitz, P., Mollenkopf, J. H., Waters, M. C., & Holdaway, J. (2010). *Inheriting the city: The children of immigrants come of age.* New York: Russell Safe Foundation.

Kochan, B. (Ed.). (2014). *Migration and London's growth.* London: LSE.

Kymlicka, W. (2010). The rise and fall of multiculturalism? New debates on inclusion and accommodation in diverse societies. In S. Vertovec & S. Wessendorf (Eds.), *The multiculturalism backlash. European discourses, policies and practices* (pp. 32–49). London/New York: Routledge.

Kymlicka, W. (2012). *Multiculturalism: Success, failure, and the future.* Washington, DC: Migration Policy Institute.

Lofland, L. (1973). *A world of strangers: Order and action in urban public space.* New York: Basic Books.

Meissner, F., & Vertovec, S. (2014). Comparing superdiversity. *Ethnic and Racial Studies, 38*(4), 541–555.

Payne, M. (2014). *Modern social work theory* (4th ed.). Basingstoke: Palgrave Macmillan.

Phillimore, J. (2015). Delivering maternity services in an era of superdiversity: the challenges of novelty and newness. Journal of Ethnic and Racial Studies, 38(4): 568-582.

Sassen, S. (2001 [1991]). *The global city*, 2nd ed. New York/London/Tokyo/Princeton/Oxford: Princeton University Press.

Sassen, S. (2014). *Expulsions: Brutality and complexity in the global economy.* Cambridge, MA: Harvard University Press.

Saunders, D. (2011). *Arrival city: How the largest migration in history is reshaping our world.* London: William Heinemann.

Schrooten, M., Geldof, D., & Withaeckx, S. (2015). Transmigration and urban social work: Towards a research agenda. *European Journal of Social Work.* doi: 10.1080/13691457.2014.1001725.

Schrooten, M. , Withaeckx, S., Geldof, D. & Lavent, M. (2016). Transmigration. Social work in a world of superdiversity. Leuven/Den Haag: AccoSimone, A. (2001). On the worlding of African cities. *African Studies Review, 44*(2), 15–41.

Van Robaeys, B. (2014). *Verbinden vanuit diversiteit. Krachtgericht werken in een context van armoede en culturele diversiteit.* Leuven: Lannoocampus.

Vanduynslager, L., Wets, J., Noppe, J., & Doyen, G. (2013). Vlaamse migratie en Integratiemonitor 2013. Steunpunt Inburgering en Integratie/Studiedienst van de Vlaamse Regering (Brussels).

Vaughan, L., & Arbaci, S. (2011). The challenges of understanding urban segregation. *Built Environment, 37*(2), 128–138.

Vertovec, S. (2005). Opinion: Super-diversity revealed. BBC News, September 20. http://news.bbc.co.uk/2/hi/uk_news/4266102.stm

Vertovec, S. (2007). Superdiversity and its implications. *Ethnic and Racial Studies, 29*(6), 1024–1054.

Vertovec, S. (2011). *Migration and new diversities in global cities: Comparatively conceiving, observing and visualizing diversification in urban public spaces.* MMG working paper 11–08. Göttingen: Max Planck Institute for the Study of Religious and Ethnic Diversity.

Vertovec, S. (2012). 'Diversity' and the social imaginary. *European Journal of Sociology, 53*(3), 287–312.

Vertovec, S., & Wessendorf, S. (Eds.). (2010). *The multiculturalism backlash. European discourses, policies and practices.* London/New York: Routledge.

Wacquant, L. (2008). *Urban outcasts: A comparative sociology of advanced marginality.* Cambridge: Polity Press.

Webster, S. K., Arenas, A.-T., & Magaña, S. (2010). Incorporating transnational social work into the curriculum. In N. J. Negi & R. Furman (Eds.), *Transnational social work practice* (pp. 205–221). New York: Columbia University Press.

Wessendorf, S. (2013). Commonplace diversity and the "ethos of mixing": Perceptions of difference in a London neighbourhood. *Identities, 20*(4), 407–422.

Wessendorf, S. (2014). *Commonplace diversity. Social relations in a super-diverse context.* Basingstoke: Palgrave Macmillan.

Williams, C., & Graham, M. (2014). A world on the move: Migration, mobilities and social work. *British Journal of Social Work, 44*(Supplement 1), i1–i17.

Withaeckx, S., Schrooten, M., & Geldof, D. (2015). Living across borders: The everyday experiences of Moroccan and Brazilian transmigrants in Belgium. *Crossings: Journal of Migration & Culture, 6*(1), 23–40.

6

Ageing in Urban Environments: Challenges and Opportunities for a Critical Social Work Practice

Chris Phillipson and Mo Ray

Introduction

Two major forces are set to shape the quality of daily life in the twenty-first century: population ageing, on the one hand, and urban change, on the other. By 2030, two-thirds of the world's population will be residing in cities. At that point, many of the major urban areas in the developed world will have 25% or more of their populations aged 60 and over (OECD 2015). Cities are now regarded as central to economic development, attracting waves of migrants and supporting new knowledge-based industries. However, it remains uncertain as to whether what Katz et al. (2008: 474) describe as the new 'urban age' will create oppor-

C. Phillipson (✉)
Manchester Interdisciplinary Collaboration for Research on Ageing (MICRA),
University of Manchester, Manchester, UK

M. Ray
School of Social Science and Public Policy, University of Keele,
Staffordshire, UK

© The Editor(s) (if applicable) and The Author(s) 2016
C. Williams (ed.), *Social Work and the City*,
DOI 10.1057/978-1-137-51623-7_6

tunities or promote conflicts within urban space, the latter reflecting inequalities in access and influence amongst different social and generational groups.

This chapter examines the implications of urban change for a critical social work practice with older people. The introduction to this volume notes the extent to which social work was itself a creation of city life—notably with the expansion of urban growth consequent on industrialisation from the eighteenth and nineteenth centuries onwards. And older people are themselves an important part of this story, with declining mortality reflecting improvements in urban public health, and reforms associated with the introduction of state pensions integral to the economic growth associated with the development of urban societies. Studies demonstrating both the strengths and challenges of living in urban areas have been an important theme in social research, at least since the 1940s. In the UK, work by Sheldon (1948) in Wolverhampton, and Townsend (1957) in Bethnal Green (London), demonstrated the persistence of strong (predominantly) family-based ties within densely populated urban communities (see also, Phillipson et al. 2001). Isaacs et al. (1972) also highlighted the importance of family support, but noted the pressures on carers in providing support within hard-pressed working-class neighbourhoods. More recent research (notably that in the United States) has focused on problems facing isolated groups of urban men and women who having outlived their social networks, and face pressures arising from chronic ill-health, deprivation and social exclusion (Klinenberg 2002; Portacolone 2013).

A key issue arising from the above review is the importance of linking urban change, on the one hand, and pressures facing people in later life, on the other. Both dimensions have important implications for a critical social work practice and will be discussed, first, through outlining the background to ageing within cities and the development of the idea of what the World Health Organization (WHO) (2007) terms 'age-friendly cities'. Second, the chapter reviews evidence about the importance of urban neighbourhoods for older people and their contribution to experiences of social inclusion and exclusion. Third, the chapter explores ideas for a critical social work practice focused on different aspects of the lives of older people living in urban areas.

Urbanisation and Ageing

Although ageing and urbanisation can rightly be viewed as major trends for the present century, they have been kept largely separate for the purpose of research. This has happened despite urging from pioneer researchers of urban society such as Lewis Mumford (1956) that we should be seeking 'age integration', rather than 'age segregation', in our cities. Against this, the direction of urban policy over the post-war period appears to have been in the opposite direction, with age-segregated provision such as sheltered housing (developed in the UK in the 1950s and 1960s) through to retirement communities and the more recent evolution of urban retirement villages. However, policy developments aside, cities are where the majority of people now live their lives and where they will spend their old age. At the same time, cities are also where—despite potential barriers—older people can make a substantial contribution to the quality of life within their communities. Realising the benefits to cities of an ageing population will, however, require attention to the link between urban change and community development. Here, a report from the Organisation for Economic Cooperation and Development (OECD) (2015: 18) argues that:

> Designing policies that address ageing issues requires a deep understanding of local circumstances, including communities' economic assets, history and culture. The spatially heterogeneous nature of ageing trends makes it important to approach ageing from an urban perspective. Cities need to pay more attention to local circumstances to understand ageing, and its impact. They are especially well-equipped to address the issue, given their long experience of working with local communities and profound understanding of local problems.

One response to the increased demographic and social importance of older people within cities is the need to build what the World Health Organisation (WHO) (2007) term 'age-friendly communities'—that is, environments which provide support to people at different stages of the life course and which encourage participation in community life. Following this, the WHO suggests that:

It should be normal in an age-friendly city for the natural and built environment to anticipate users with different capacities instead of designing for the mythical 'average' (i.e. young) person. An age-friendly city emphasises enablement rather than disablement; it is friendly for all ages and not just 'elder-friendly (WHO 2007: 72).

The drive to create age-friendly cities may also be placed in the context of attempts to improve the quality of urban environments. This was reflected in new perspectives influencing urban development over the course of the 1990s and early 2000s—for example, ideas associated with 'sustainable' (Satterthwaite 1999) and 'harmonious cities' (UN-Habitat 2008). The former raised questions about managing urban growth in a manner able to meet the needs of future as well as current generations. The idea of 'harmonious' development emphasised values such as 'tolerance, fairness, social justice and good governance' (UN-Habitat 2008), these values being regarded as essential principles of urban planning. Such themes were also influential in the development of policies such as 'lifetime homes' and 'lifetime neighbourhoods' (Department of Community and Local Government 2008; Atlanta Regional Commission 2009), which emerged alongside recognition of the need for more systematic interventions to support population ageing at a community level. The key issue behind the 'lifetime' concept was an understanding that effective support for older people within neighbourhoods would require a range of interventions linking different parts of the urban system—from housing and the design of streets to transportation and improved accessibility to shops and services.

Despite progress in respect of policies, older people have faced a variety of problems in cities undergoing rapid economic and social change. The most important of these have included: spatial inequalities within cities (Wacquant 2008; Bridge and Watson 2011); the influence of economic globalisation and the rise of 'world cities' (Sassen 2012); and increasing inequality between cities affected by rapid industrialisation or de-industrialisation in the case of many medium-sized cities (Hall 2014). These aspects of urban development have affected neighbourhoods and communities in a variety of ways, with older people amongst those most affected by the changes involved. The next section of this chapter examines evidence for this, highlighting the impact on different groups within the older population, with a particular focus on issues relating to social inclusion and exclusion affecting older people living within cities.

Growing in Urban Neighbourhoods: Experiences of Inclusion and Exclusion

Promoting social inclusion and combating social exclusion emerged as important social policy and social work issues in Europe during the 1980s and 1990s, reflecting concerns about the social costs arising from long-term unemployment, the impact of poverty, and social divisions within urban communities (Scharf et al. 2005). While some research addressed such questions from a life-course perspective, with a particular focus on older people (Barnes et al. 2006), the dominant approach tended to be around children and families and younger adults. As a consequence, important sections of the population vulnerable to multiple disadvantages were under-represented in much of the research and practice literature (Levitas et al. 2007).

One group that may be especially susceptible to social exclusion comprises older people living in socially deprived inner-city neighbourhoods. Other vulnerable groups include those experiencing some degree of frailty (nearly half of community-dwelling people aged 70 plus are likely to be experiencing frailty to some extent, sometimes noticeably); and those with cognitive impairment associated with living with different forms of dementia (WHO 2015). The urban context, as represented by large metropolitan centres, presents a variety of environmental pressures, these arising from the closure of local services and amenities, crime-related problems, poor housing and social polarisation (Smith 2009). Such developments may increase the hazards and risks associated with later life (Fitzgerald and Caro 2014). Environmental perspectives in gerontology have made some progress in investigating these issues (Rowles and Bernard 2013). They have also been addressed in research examining social exclusion in old age (Smith 2009). However, the interconnections between place, urbanisation and social exclusion remain under-explored, especially in the context of changes affecting major urban areas (Phillipson 2010).

An important strand of the literature deals with the impact of social exclusion in the context of economic and social change *within* neighbourhoods. This reflects evidence suggesting that exclusion tends to be spatially concentrated in localities such as disadvantaged inner-city areas (Smith 2009). The research also highlights an overlap between socially excluded people and socially excluded places (Forrest 2008), with policies that target the neighbourhood a primary focus for promoting social inclusion (Rowles and Bernard 2013).

The significance of the neighbourhood dimension in later life reflects both the reality of long-term residence and the extended amount of time spent at home and in the immediate neighbourhood following retirement. The study of three Czech cities undertaken by Galcanova and Sykorova (2015) found that older people (65 and over) had been living in their apartments for an average of 30 years. In a study conducted in three neighbourhoods of Frankfurt, even longer periods of average length of residence were reported for people aged 70–89 years. On average, participants in the BEWOHNT study had lived for 59 years in the city of Frankfurt, for 45 years in their current neighbourhood, and for almost 38 years in their current home (Lofquist et al. 2013: 21).

Scharf et al. (2005) developed an approach to conceptualising and assessing exclusion that explicitly incorporates the neighbourhood dimension. They identified five forms of social exclusion relevant to the circumstances of older people living in deprived urban communities. These included exclusion from material resources, social relations, civic activities and basic services, as well as a dimension termed 'neighbourhood exclusion'. The latter may reflect negative views about the neighbourhood relating to physical decay, loss of amenities and certain types of social change linked with population turnover and rising crime rates.

Community studies involving older people suggest that they may be especially affected by processes associated with social exclusion. Research suggests that older people derive a strong sense of emotional attachment from both their home and the surrounding community (Phillipson et al. 2001; Rowles and Chaudhury 2005; Buffel et al. 2013). Indeed, Rowles (1978: 200) suggests that 'selective intensification of feelings about spaces' might represent 'a universal strategy employed by older people to facilitate maintaining a sense of identity within a changing environment'. While this may be possible in relatively secure and stable neighbourhoods, some residential settings impede the maintenance of identity in old age. The argument, which requires detailed empirical testing, is that this is much more likely in certain types of urban environments than in others, or in rural areas. It may, for example, especially be the case in the *zones of transition* marked by a rapid turnover of people and buildings, and in unpopular urban neighbourhoods characterised by low housing demand and abandonment by all but the poorest and least mobile residents (Newman 2003). Disadvantaged urban neighbourhoods, and the people who reside in them, may also be prone to 'institutional isolation' (Gans 1972) as services and agencies withdraw, resulting in restricted access to basic facilities such as grocery stores, telephones and banking (Scharf et al. 2002).

Urban areas also host a growing number of first-generation migrants who experience especially acute problems of poverty and poor housing. The study by Scharf et al. (2002) found that almost eight out of ten older Somali migrants and nearly seven out of ten older people of Pakistani origin found it very difficult to manage on their current incomes. Many of them had to cut back on essentials, including food, and had to limit their social activities. Similarly, Becker (2003: 135) highlighted the precariousness of the living conditions of older migrants living in inner-city neighbourhoods in Northern California. This study found that many elders belonging to minority ethnic groups lived in rooms without bathrooms or kitchens, and many others lived in overcrowded apartments. The neighbourhoods in which they lived were areas with a long history of illegal activities such as drug dealing, prostitution and gambling, these presenting particular challenges to creating a sense of home in old age (see further, Buffel et al. 2013).

Evidence from the Belgian Ageing Studies (De Donder et al. 2010) demonstrated that neighbourhoods with poor physical environments and limited access to services also increase feelings of insecurity. Conversely, older people who enjoy living in their neighbourhood and have the opportunity to have a say in what their neighbourhood looks like (e.g. through political participation) express fewer problems relating to lack of safety and security. Pain (2000: 365) makes the point here that fear of crime should be seen as 'inseparable from a range of social and economic problems concerned with housing, employment, environmental planning and social exclusion'.

Finally, implementing the age-friendly approach may encounter obstacles arising from policies associated with economic austerity (Walsh et al. 2015). There are significant pressures to reduce funding for the type of activities associated with the WHO (2007) model. Buffel et al. (2014) highlighted this in their assessment of age-friendly policies in Brussels and Manchester—both members of the WHO Global Network. In the case of the former, recessionary pressures meant that the council had been unable to increase public spending on community health and social care in line with increases in demand. A consensus had emerged that more investment was required to improve support to carers, as well as to develop more flexible and culturally sensitive services in response to the challenges posed by increasing diversity in the older population. In the case of Manchester, plans to promote age-friendly neighbourhoods have been affected by budget cuts which reduce public services such as libraries, information and advice centres, and day care facilities for groups such as older people. Threats to services may lead to a public perception that the 'age-friendly' brand is unrealistic and unlikely to be implemented given restrictions on public spending (see also, Tinker and Ginn 2015).

Developing a Critical Social Practice with Older People Living in Urban Environments

Given the challenges as well as the opportunities associated with urban environments: what responses might be expected from a critical social work practice, building on some of the central themes and issues developed through this volume? To address this question, this section will examine, first, current trends in social work with older people; second, the importance of developing social work practice with older people living in urban environments with high support needs; third, the potential for broadening social work practice to include community-based approaches; finally, running through all these areas, will be an argument about developing citizenship and social justice as key dimensions for a critical social work practice with older people.

Social Work with Older People

What are the current trends that can be identified in terms of social work practice with older people? The international definition of social work highlights the importance of working to achieve social change and cohesion, underpinned by commitments to social justice and empowerment for individuals and groups (IFSW 2014). Combined with a focus on ecological perspectives (defined as the interaction between people and their environment), in their policy on global population ageing the International Federation of Social Work (IFSW) suggest that social workers are well-placed to collaborate with older adults in creating and advocating for age-friendly policies and programmes.

But differences in the way that social work in general and, specifically, social work with older people is defined and operationalised, result in variations in the balance between individual and collective approaches to practice. In the Global North, social work with older people has tended to prioritise individual practice with an attendant focus on administrative and technical approaches (see e.g. Lymbery 2010). Although the notion of gerontological social work is recognised in countries such as Australia and the USA, there is variability in the extent to which the term is used to convey a specialist area of work. For example, in response to the marginalisation of social work with older people—and, by implication, the low priority given to older people using social work services—investment by the John A. Hartford Foundation in North America has, among other achievements, led to changes in the curriculum to: first, prioritise the visibility of ageing in the social work practice; second, improve gerontological social work research capacity; and, third, develop practice learning opportunities in gerontological settings. By contrast, in the case of England, social work with older people has been largely amalgamated into generic adult services and, to a significant extent, submerged within the amorphous term 'social care'. Notwithstanding such pressures, social work might still make a significant contribution to the age-friendly approach—a view illustrated in the examples discussed below.

Developing an Age-Friendly Practice

This chapter has already highlighted the emotional attachment that older people are likely to have to their homes and immediate community, reinforced by long periods of residence (Buffel et al. 2013 pp. 89–109). That older people identify a wish to 'age in place' is well-rehearsed and would appear consistent with welfare arrangements underpinned by narratives of independence, active ageing and self-responsibility. In reality, however, this approach creates challenges for older people living with deteriorating or uncertain long-term conditions, especially for those residing in deprived urban environments. Writing from a Canadian perspective, but reflecting on trends in other countries, Aronson and Smith (2010: 530) comment on the 'dramatic offloading' of public services and the growth of structures focused on targeting, gatekeeping and the commodification of care. In this context, the concept of need is inextricably entwined with individual eligibility for welfare services defined by evidence of personal risk, safety, and threats to life and limb. Care is, therefore, predominantly associated with meeting needs associated with the failing or frail body (e.g. bodily hygiene, managing continence), or to safety (e.g. surveillance and monitoring of people living with cognitive impairment). This care is given at the expense of working to meet needs emanating from other aspects of personhood—such as sustaining or developing valued social relationships, citizenship, alleviating poverty or accessing local resources. Ageing in place with care which has little or no regard for an older person's social relationships, networks and occupational identity can mean a lived experience characterised by basic survival which accentuates and reinforces social exclusion and, at its worst, constitutes a form of 'house arrest' (Phillipson 2004: 966).

There is clearly a case for social work assessment as a key aspect of working with older people with complex and changing needs (Ray et al. 2009) and for a continued social work presence for those older people who lack other forms of long-term support (Lymbery 2013). Moreover, this requires the development of a practice which harnesses the power of communities to provide different types of support to older people. One such example has been the development of Naturally Occurring Retirement Communities (NORCs). These were initially developed by social workers (Vladeck and Altman 2015) with the aim of promoting ageing in place as a viable option for older people that was focused on improving quality of life. The NORC concept began in New York City, in a neighbourhood with a concentration of older people with significant levels of functional impairment. This group faced significant problems living in homes unsuitable for complex and co-existing physical and cognitive impairments (Greenfield et al. 2013). The NORC model aims to provide a range of core resources and support (formal services and voluntary) including social work, health care, mental health services, activities and financial advice, which help older people to remain in their own homes as a positive experience. The model develops involvement and partnerships from a variety of stakeholders (e.g. building owners, service providers) and includes older people as leaders in shaping the development of the project and participating as volunteers. Taking a broader perspective, the NORC model aims to be responsive to local need and to spearhead community-wide age-friendly developments, as well as being a vehicle for wider innovation to promote quality of life amongst older people (Vladeck 2014). Evaluations of the NORC model (e.g. Anetzberger 2010; Bedney et al. 2010) indicate that outcomes for older participants include: a reduction in social isolation, the fostering of links between older people and services, and a self-reported increase in older people's confidence in their ability to remain at home.

Greenfield et al. (2013), in a survey of programme leaders for 62 NORC projects, identified similar benefits but pointed to a number of challenges in the sustainability of the model as it was originally conceived. NORCs were more likely to be dependent on a single source of government funding and their long-term sustainability was therefore vulnerable to cuts in funding. In addition, a key dimension of NORCs was to support the active collaboration of older people as leaders, partners and volunteers; this was a challenge for some older people with higher support needs. Similar findings have been reported in evaluations of older people's participation and leadership in retirement communities in England (Scharf et al. 2013), which points to the need for a more nuanced definition of citizenship embracing diversity in abilities, motivation and resources amongst different groups of older people (see pp. 000–00).

Changing Attitudes Towards Older People

A second example relates to the development of an '*ageing studies certificate*' targeted at older people living in the city of Manchester in North West England. As part of the WHO's Global Network of Age Friendly Cities (GNAFC) Manchester's age-friendly strategy included the development of opportunities for older residents to engage with the city and to have a voice in shaping their neighbourhoods, as well as to supporting the city's aim to become an age-inclusive city (McGarry and Morris 2011; Buffel et al. 2014). The course was initially developed and presented in 2011 by academics from social work and social gerontology with 20 older people from Manchester city with diverse health profiles, interests and aspirations. Over eight weeks, the course aimed to develop discussion, debate and mutual learning on critical themes including: policies and practices for an age-friendly city; rights, citizenship and participation; ageism and age-based discrimination; life course perspectives and ageing; health and well-being; and mental health and well-being.

Participants highlighted a number of benefits including: involving participants as much or as little as people wanted; considering ways in which information could be applied to personal and wider contexts; exploring political, social and cultural influences on the way ageing is constructed, opportunities for social contact—meeting new people and making new relationships; vigorous debate and opportunities for utilising personal experience and strengths and for challenging myths and assumptions about ageing. In consultation with participants from the original presentation, the course was subsequently refined and developed to include participants from a diverse inter-disciplinary workforce. An evaluation of the impact of the course suggested a number of benefits including: the value of learning with and from a cross-sector group representing a wide range of disciplines and interests; evidence of new, inter-disciplinary collaborations developed as a result of taking part in the course; increased awareness of the ageing agenda and particularly social, political and cultural influences on ageing; and the importance of developing a more positive image of ageing, underpinned by recognition of the diversity of ageing experiences (Revell and Stockwell 2013).

Age-Friendly Practice and Citizenship

While the above examples illustrate how social work may be involved in supporting and developing age-friendly cities, social work perspectives can be influential in other kinds of ways. These might include considering how social work (in partnership with user groups, families and carers) can continue to encourage and support the visibility and participation of older people with high support needs, especially those people living in environments traditionally excluded from mainstream debates about what constitutes age-friendly practice. Older people living in care/nursing home settings illustrate the importance of a rights-based commitment to practice. This can result in significant improvements in older people's ability to influence decisions which directly affect the quality of their lives. Research has demonstrated that social workers taking such an approach to practice with older people diagnosed with dementia were more successful in enabling them to articulate their preferences and advocate for them to retain their chosen lifestyles (McDonald 2010). Social work practice can also highlight the denial of rights and inequalities that older people may experience in collective care settings. Citing evidence that many older people living in care homes are lonely and depressed, have poor access to meaningful activity and problems accessing health care standards, the National Institute for Care and Clinical Excellence (NICE 2013) have published evidence-based standards for promoting the mental health and wellbeing of older people living in care homes in England. Social workers are well-placed to argue for the implementation of these standards and to assess progress towards their achievement via individual work with older people in care planning and review, collaboration with care home staff, regulatory bodies and commissioners. The relevance of the debates on age-friendly cities has yet to reach into care home settings, but it merits attention, not least because appropriate access to care is a necessary element of support for older people in urban environments.

Finally, social work can make a distinctive contribution to age-friendly work given its emphasis on rights and citizenship. Bartlett and O'Connor (2010: 37) offer a definition of what they term 'social citizenship' in their work on developing policy and practice in dementia: 'Social citizenship can be defined as a relationship, practice or status in which a person with dementia is entitled to experience freedom from discrimination, and to have opportunities to grow and participate in life to the fullest extent possible. It involves justice, recognition of social positions and the upholding of personhood, rights and a fluid degree of responsibility for shaping events at a personal and societal level.'

The approach by Bartlett and O'Connor (2010) does not assume a fixed or pre-determined definition of citizenship, rather, one which is underpinned and informed by four key principles: active participation is maximised and valued; the potential for growth and positivity is recognised and promoted; an understanding of the fundamental relationships between individual experience and broader social, political and cultural influences and structures; and the importance of solidarity with people living with dementia and the value of community building. The reconceptualisation of citizenship along these lines has fundamental implications for both social work as practice and social work as an academic discipline. Older people whose rights to citizenship are threatened by social exclusion, impairment and the limited interventions designed to 'protect' them are most likely to benefit from a social work practice which is able to respond creatively to their circumstances (Lymbery 2003) and which consciously engages with the socio-political and structural forces which influence their circumstances. A multidimensional approach to practice (Bartlett and O'Connor 2010: 91) highlights the value of community-based interventions, including revealing oppressive practice and policies, and socio-political interventions, including forming alliances with user organisations and working to remove barriers to participation. Individual experience and interpersonal relationships form an essential part of a multi-dimensional approach but, if social workers are to influence the ramifications of social, political, economic and cultural factors and their influence on ageing in the city, then they must be able to work effectively across these domains. This is in direct contrast to the contemporary policy emphasis on the individual and self-responsibility in many Western countries. Lloyd et al., (2014), for example, has argued that new perspectives on practice with older people might realistically only be found outside of the statutory system within older people's grass roots projects and organisations.

Commenting on the catastrophic implications of austerity for social work in southern European countries, Ioakimidis et al. (2014) note that, at a time when social work is arguably needed most, state social work has been marginalised and cut to the point of extinction along with agencies providing vital sources of support and care to older citizens. The authors argue that social workers in Greece, Spain and Portugal are, in response to these threats, working to reclaim the political role of social work towards critical and radical approaches characterised by the development of grassroots alliances, political argument and the representation of service users and social workers in the struggle for social justice. The struggle for social work here is to galvanise communities to respond to meeting basic human needs.

This section began by highlighting international differences in approaches to social work practice with older people. But, despite some variation in focus, there is an overarching need for social work to engage more fully with collective and community approaches to practice with older people living in the city if it is to realise its aspirations for social justice and the empowerment of different groups of older people.

Conclusion: Planning Cities for All Ages—The Role of a Critical Social Work Practice

Developing cities which meet the interests of all generations remains an important goal for economic and social policy. The future of communities across the world will, in large part, be determined by the response made to achieving a higher quality of life for their older citizens. A crucial part of this response must lie in creating supportive environments providing access to a range of facilities and services. However, the policy and social work practice agenda will need to develop significantly if their part in its progress is to be realised.

First, the issues raised by developing age-friendly communities within complex urban environments will require a more coherent recognition of the implications of social work in an urban context. Geldof (2011: 28) has argued that the role of the city is often minimised 'as a kind of "urban décor" for social work or social work research. As this book demonstrates, a range of factors are affecting the lives of people living in urban areas, these including: changes arising from international migration; concerns about the future sustainability of resources under particular pressure in urban environments, higher concentrations of people with complex needs; and the spatial segregation of vulnerable people with multiple social problems. These developments underline the need for an urban social work to respond consciously to these challenges.

Second, areas of the social work profession most profoundly affected by managerialist welfare agendas need to find ways to reconnect with collective and community approaches to practice and to forming alliances with older peoples' networks and user groups (e.g. Lymbery 2013). Linked with this, it is vital that, if social work is to participate actively in the development of age-friendly cities, it must engage not only with the physical and mental health problems older people may be at risk of experiencing, but also the influence of the socio-political, economic and environmental contexts on the experience of older people. While the value base of social work does appear to lend itself to supporting age-friendly developments, there is little international evidence to support the existence of a coherent or collective engagement of social work with the age-friendly movement. Neither is there compelling evidence of a social work identity, regardless of the context in which it operates, which includes a core commitment to forging alliances and partnerships with older people and other professional and community groups, in order collectively to challenge discriminatory policies and practices and to campaign for policies which may be of direct benefit to older citizens.

Finally, incorporating issues about ageing in urban environments with the wider debate concerning spatial justice is also essential. Here, we would underline the relevance of Soja's (2010: 19) argument that the:

'geographies in which we live can have both positive and negative effects on our lives'. He writes:

> They are not just dead background or a neutral physical stage for the human drama but are filled with material and imagined forces that can hurt us or help us in nearly everything we do, individually and collectively.

He concludes:

> This is a vitally important part of the new spatial consciousness, making us aware that the geographies in which we live can intensify and sustain our exploitation as workers, support oppressive forms of cultural and political domination based on race, gender, and nationality, and aggravate all forms of discrimination and injustice.

Ensuring spatial justice for older people is now a crucial part of this debate, with developing an integrated approach to demographic and urban change representing a key task for public policy, research and practice.

Acknowledgement The authors are grateful for the assistance of Samuèle Rémillard-Boilard in the preparation of this chapter.

References

Anetzberger, G. J. (2010). Community options of greater Cleveland, Ohio: Preliminary evaluations of naturally occurring retirement community program. *Clinical Gerontologist, 33*, 1–15. doi:10.1080/07317110802478032.

Aronson, J. and Smith, K. (2010) Managing restructured social services: expanding the social? *British Journal of Social Work,* 40 (2), 530–547.

Atlanta Regional Commission. (2009). Lifelong communities: A framework for planning. http://www.atlantaregional.com/aging- sources/lifelongcommunities/lifelongcommunities. Accessed 28 Jan 2015.

Barnes, M., Blom, A., Cox, K., Lessof, C., & Walker, A. (2006). *The social exclusion of older people: Evidence from the first wave of the English Longitudinal Study of Ageing (ELSA)*. London: Office of the Deputy Prime Minister, Social Exclusion Unit.

Bartlett, R., & O'Connor, D. (2010). *Broadening the dementia debate: Towards social citizenship*. Bristol: Policy Press.

Becker, G. (2003). Meanings of place and displacement in three groups of older immigrants. *Journal of Aging Studies, 17*, 129–149.

Bedney, B. J., Goldberg, R. B., & Josephson, K. (2010). Aging in place in naturally occurring retirement communities: Transforming aging through supportive service programs. *Journal of Housing for the Elderly, 24*, 304–321.

Bridge, G. Watons, S. (2011) *The Blackwell Companion to the City,* Chichester: Wiley-Blackwell.

Buffel, T., Phillipson, C., & Scharf, T. (2013). Experiences of neighbourhood exclusion and inclusion among older people living in deprived inner-city areas in Belgium and England. *Ageing & Society, 33*(Special Issue 01), 89–109.

Buffel, T., McGarry, P., Phillipson, C., De Donder, L., Dury, S., De Witte, N., & Smetocran, A.-S. (2014). Developing age-friendly cities: Case studies from Brussels and Manchester and implications for policy and practice. *Journal of Aging and Social Policy, 26*, 52–72.

De Donder, L., Buffel, T., De Witte, N., Dury, S., & Verté, D. (2010). Social capital and feelings of unsafety in later life. In L. De Donder, *Feelings of unsafety in later life.* Brussels: VUB Press.

Fitzgerald, K. G., & Caro, F. (2014). An overview of age-friendly cities and communities around the world. *Journal of Aging and Social Policy, 26*, 1–18.

Forrest, R. (2008). Who cares about neighbourhoods? *International Social Science Journal, 59*, 129–141.

Galcanova, L., & Sykorova, D. (2015). Socio-spatial aspects of ageing in an urban context: An example from three Czech Republic cities. *Ageing and Society, 35*(6), 1200–1220.

Gans, H. (1972). *People and plans: Essays on urban problems and solutions.* London: Routledge.

Geldof, D. (2011). New challenges for urban social work and urban social work research. *European Journal of Social Work, 14*(1), 27–39. doi:10.1080/13691 457/2010.51621.

Greenfield, E. A., Scharlach, A. E., Lehning, A. J., Davitt, J. K., & Graham, C. L. (2013). A tale of two community initiatives for promoting aging in place: Similarities and differences in the national implementation of NORC programs and villages. *The Gerontologist, 53*(6), 928–938.

Hall, P. (2014). *Good cities, better lives.* London: Routledge.

IFSW (International Federation of Social Work). (2014). Global definition of social work. http://ifsw.org/get-involved/global-definition-of-social-work/.

Ioakimidis, V., Santos, C. C., & Martinez Herrero, I. (2014). Reconceptualising social work in times of crisis: An examination of the cases of Greece, Spain and Portugal. *International Social Work, 57*(4), 285–300.

Isaacs, B., Livingstone, M., & Neville, Y. (1972). *Survival of the unfittest*. London: Routledge & Kegan Paul.

Katz, B., Altman, A., & Wagner, J. (2008). An agenda for the urban age. In R. Burdett & D. Sudjic (Eds.), *The endless city* (pp. 474–481). London: Phaidon.

Klinenberg, E. (2002). *Heat wave: A social autopsy of disaster in Chicago*. Chicago: University of Chicago Press.

Levitas, R. A., Pantazis, C., Fahmy, E., Gordon, D., Lloyd, E. H. R. R., & Patsios, D. (2007). *The multi-dimensional analysis of social exclusion*. London: Department for Communities and Local Government (DCLG), Cabinet Office, Social Exclusion Task Force.

Lloyd, L., Tanner, D., Ray, M., Richards, S., Milne, A., Phillips, J., Beech, C., & Sullivan, M. P. (2014). Look after yourself: Active ageing, individual responsibility and the decline of social work with older people in the UK. *European Journal of Social Work, 17*(3), 322–335. doi:10.1080/13691457.2013.829805.

Lymbery, M. (2003). Negotiating the contradictions between competence and creativity in social work education. *Journal of Social Work, 3*(1), 99–117.

Lymbery, M. (2010). A new vision for adult social care? Continuities and change in the care of older people. *Critical Social Policy, 30*(1), 5–26. doi:10.1177/0261018309350806.

Lymbery, M. (2013). Austerity, personalization and older people: The prospects for creative social work practice in England. *European Journal of Social Work, 17*(3), doi:10.1080/13691457.2013.830594.

McDonald, A. (2010). The impact of the 2005 Mental Capacity Act on social workers' decision-making and approaches to the assessment of risk. *British Journal of Social Work, 40*(4), 1229–1246.

McGarry, P., & Morris, J. (2011). A great place to grow older: A case study of how Manchester is developing an age friendly city. *Working with older people, 15*(1), 38–46.

Mumford, L. (1956). For older people—Not segregation but integration. *Architectural Record, 119*, 109–116.

Newman, K. (2003). *A different shade of gray*. New York: New Press.

NICE (National Institute of Care and Clinical Excellence). (2013). *Mental well-being of older people in care homes (QS 50)*. London: NICE. https://www.nice.org.uk/guidance/qs50.

OECD. (2015). *Ageing in cities*. Paris: OECD Publishing. http://dx.doi.org/10.1787/9789264231160-en.

Lofquist, C., Granbom, M., Himmelsbach, I., Iwarsson, S., Haak, M., & Oswald, F. (2013). Voices on relocation and ageing in place in very old age: A complex and ambivalent matter. *The Gerontologist, 53*(6), 919–27. doi:1093/geront/gnt34.

Pain, R. (2000). Place, social relations and the fear of crime: A review. *Progress in Human Geography, 24*(3), 365–387.

Phillipson, C. (2010). Growing old in the 'century of the city'. In D. Dannefer & C. Phillipson (Eds.), *The Sage handbook of social gerontology* (pp. 597–606). London: Sage.

Phillipson, C. (2004). Urbanisation and ageing: Towards a new environmental gerontology. *Ageing and Society, 24*, 963–972.

Phillipson, C., Bernard, M., Phillips, J., & Ogg, J. (2001). *The family and community life of older people*. London: Routledge.

Portacolone, E. (2013). Precariousness among older adults living alone in the United States. *Journal of Aging Studies, 27*, 166–174.

Ray, M., Bernard, M., & Phillips, J. (2009). *Critical issues in social work with older people*. Basingstoke: Palgrave Macmillan.

Ray, M., Milne, A., Beech, C., Richards, S., Sullivan, M. P., Tanner, D., Lloyd, L. & Phillips, J. (2014). Gerontological social work: Reflections on its role, purpose and value. *British Journal of Social Work Advance Access*, published 16 January 2014, doi:10.1093/bjsw/bct195.

Revell, A., & Stockwell, S. (2013). *Ageing studies certificate: Evaluation report*. Unpublished report. Manchester, Valuing Older People/Keele University.

Richards, S., Sullivan, M. P, Tanner, D., Beech, C., Milne, A., Ray, M., Phillips, J. & Lloyd, L. (2013). On the edge of a new frontier: Is gerontological social work in the UK ready to meet 21st century challenges? *British Journal of Social Work*, online version 10 May 2013.

Rowles, G. (1978). *Prisoners of space? Exploring the geographical experience of older people*. Colorado: Westview Press.

Rowles, G., & Bernard, M. (Eds.). (2013). *Environmental gerontology: Making meaningful places in old age*. New York: Springer Publishing Company.

Rowles, G., & Chaudhury, H. (Eds.). (2005). *Home and identity in later life: International perspectives*. New York: Springer Publishing Company.

Rubinstein, R. L., & Parmelee, P. A. (1992). Attachment to place and the representation of the life course by the elderly. In I. Altman & S. M. Low (Eds.), *Handbook of the sociology of aging: Place attachment* (pp. 139–164). New York: Plenum Press.

Sassen, S. (2012). *Cities in a world economy*. London: Sage.

Satterthwaite, D. (Ed.). (1999). *The Earthscan reader on sustainable cities*. London: Earthscan.

Scharf, T., Phillipson, C., Smith, A., & Kingston, P. (2002). *Growing older in socially deprived areas: Social exclusion in later life*. London: Help the Aged.

Scharf, T., Phillipson, C., & Smith, A. (2005). *Multiple exclusion and quality of life amongst excluded older people in disadvantaged neighbourhoods*. London: OPDM and Social Exclusion Unit.

Scharf, T., Liddle, J., Bartlam, B., Bernard, M., & Sim, J. (2013). Assessing the age-friendliness of purpose-built retirement communities. *Irish Journal of Medical Science, 182*, S211.

Sheldon, S. (1948). *The social medicine of old age*. Oxford: Oxford University Press.

Smith, A. (2009). *Ageing in urban neighbourhoods: Place attachment and social exclusion*. Bristol: Policy Press.

Soja, E. (2010). Spatializing the urban. City, 14(6), 629–653

Tinker, A., & Ginn, J. (2015). An age friendly London? Paper presentation at: The Compassionate Care Conference, 12.2.15, London, Institute of Gerontology, Kings College.

Townsend, P. (1957). *The family life of old people*. London: Routledge & Kegan Paul.

UN-HABITAT. (2008). *State of the world's cities 2008/2009*. London: Earthscan.

Vladeck, F. (2014). *A good place to grow old: New York's model for NORC supportive service programs*. New York: United Hospital Funds.

Vladeck, F., & Altman, A. (2015). *The future of the NORC-supportive service model*. Public Policy and Aging Report, The Gerontological Society of America. doi:10.1093/ppar/pro050.

Wacquant, L. (2008). *Urban outcasts: A comparative sociology of advanced marginality*. Cambridge: Polity.

Walsh, K., Carney, G., & Ní Léime, Á. (Eds.). (2015). *Ageing through austerity: Critical perspectives from Ireland*. Bristol: Policy Press.

WHO (World Health Organization). (2007). *Global age-friendly cities: A guide*. Geneva: WHO.

WHO (World Health Organization). (2015). *World report on ageing and health*. Geneva: WHO. http://apps.who.int/iris/bitstream/10665/186463/1/9789240694811_eng.pdf?ua=1&ua=1.

7

Disabling Cities and Repositioning Social Work

Michael J. Prince

Introduction

For people with disabilities, the history of urbanization involves a history of institutional segregation, sterilization, charitable responses to needs, stigma and prejudice, and the medicalization of conditions and identities. As a shift from agricultural to industrial labour, urbanization fundamentally altered the nature of paid work, family relationships and social networks, producing new impairments associated with factory work, and, from the logic of capitalism, raising issues of the employability or the incapacity of people with impairments.

This chapter focuses on the experiences of disabled people living in urban social spaces. More specifically, it explores the relationship between modern cities, people with disabilities and social work practices. How do cities affect the living conditions and social relations of people with

M.J. Prince (✉)
Faculty of Human and Social Development, University of Victoria, Victoria, BC, Canada

© The Editor(s) (if applicable) and The Author(s) 2016
C. Williams (ed.), *Social Work and the City*,
DOI 10.1057/978-1-137-51623-7_7

disabilities? How do people with disabilities and their families experience urban life? What does disability reveal about the character of cities and urbanism, and about the profession of social work? And how does social work, as a field of diverse practices, connect with people with disabilities?

Disablement is an integral aspect of the urban condition with experiences of inclusion and oppression; so, too, social work is an urban phenomenon (Wilensky and Lebeaux 1958: 180; Hallahan 2010). The chapter will show that cities construct, enable and constrain opportunities for citizens with physical and mental disabilities. Through city design, land use and employment patterns, urban society erects obstacles and imposes barriers on people living with impairments, thus limiting, isolating and excluding them from spaces of general public interactions and shared activities (Gleeson 1999: 137). Where and how social workers conduct their practice people with disabilities has ramifications for issues of mobility and accessibility, as well as for human rights and dignity. Enabling cities must be part of the agenda of promoting the full citizenship of people with disabilities, a project to which progressive and critical social work can make an important contribution. In what follows, cities and urban life are discussed in fairly general terms. Of course, cities vary greatly in geographic and population size, their history, economic base, political system and demographic mix, among other characteristics. A common theme across the diversity of modern urban centres, and the underlying premise of this chapter, is that all cities are disabling cities; that for people with disabilities, city life is marked by much exclusion and some inclusion; and that disability organizations constitute a social movement in pursuit of equality and rights of citizenship.

A statement on terminology is in order. Kathryn Church and her colleagues cogently outline a basic conceptual issue in this field of inquiry and action: 'People with disabilities? Or disabled people? There are ongoing and unresolved debates about ways to talk about disability. It is common practice to use what is called 'people first' language. This is the result of arguments made by some disability scholars/activists that 'we are people first, and disabled only incidentally'. The strategy here is to use language to dislodge bodily difference, 'impairment' and/or limitation as a 'master status' in defining how people are perceived and treated. We are comfortable with this terminology but we are also aware of arguments made recently by other scholars/activists that 'disability' is not only such a primary, but also such a valued aspect of identity (and also of social perception) that it is not possible, or even advantageous, to push it to the periphery. From this perspective, 'disabled' does not signify a 'damaged' identity. Instead, 'it is a differently legitimate form of personhood that can be fully incorporated into a valued self' (Church et al. 2007: 22). Mostly, I use the expression 'people with disabilities', the phrase widely used within the American, Australian and Canadian disability movements, recognizing that some authors and advocates, in these countries and especially in the United Kingdom, prefer the term 'disabled people'.

The first section introduces the concept of disability and ableism, and examines how people with disabilities have been viewed traditionally and can be understood in a more positive and respectful way. Ableism—discriminatory assumptions and actions toward individuals or groups based on their disabilities—persists in public opinion across societies. Often, people with mental illnesses are feared; people with learning disabilities are misunderstood; people with developmental disabilities are assumed to be incompetent to make decisions about their lives. The second section considers how disabled people figure in accounts of urbanism (ways of thinking about urban society) and describes the picture of city life for many people with disabilities. The third section explores the association between social work and people with disabilities. The fourth section examines the character of contemporary disability activism and the final section makes some general conclusions about the relationship between modern cities, people with disabilities and social work practices. Progressive disability politics and social work practice are about choices over whether the priority in policy and practice should relate to body structures and functions, daily activities and social activities, or environmental and cultural factors requiring adaptation and transformation.

Social and Cultural Constructions of Disability

Disability is the subject of assorted perspectives, interests and debates. A functional view of disability—expressed in personal and professional assessments of having difficulty with daily living activities, or having a physical or mental condition or a health problem that reduces the kind of activity that an individual can do—is a dominant perspective of disability. Such difficulties and limitations restrict a person's ability to participate fully in society. This is a conventional definition of who is a person with a disability and what makes him or her disabled. It is rooted in biological and medical ways of understanding disablements.

Disability is heterogeneous in character and so the term signifies people with developmental or intellectual, mental health, physical, visual or sensory conditions. As the United Nations Convention on the Rights of Persons with Disabilities (CRPD) states, disability includes 'physical, mental, intellectual or sensory impairments which in interaction with various barriers may hinder their full and effective participation in society on an equal basis' (UN 2006: 4). A theme underpinning this chapter is that the diversity and the severity of disability must be better recognized in public policy design. Definitions of disability in public programs in most countries tend to incorporate medicalized dichotomies that a person is either able-bodied or disabled. Although definitions do vary among programs, the general effect, because of a shared medical orientation, is to individualize and pathologize a person's condition, to emphasize the inability to work rather than focus on work capacity, to ignore fluctuating or episodic conditions and, consequently, to exclude some people from qualifying for specific programs (Prince 2009).

Being disabled is not some essential, separate state of being. For its observable social meaning and its personal and political significance, disability is co-constructed with ability—as abnormal is correlated with normal, exclusion with inclusion. Disability, in other terms, is produced through everyday interactions with other embodied individuals in specific localities and built environments, and particular economies, governmental arrangements and cultural contexts. Here, disability is part of the fabric of society, something that all individuals experience in one way or another and from which everyone can learn. Attention focuses especially on attitudes, beliefs, body identities and social values, as well as on issues of human rights, prejudice and stigma. Moreover, disability is an assemblage of socio-economic, cultural and political disadvantages resulting from an individual's exclusion by society. Disability exists or occurs when a person with impairment encounters barriers to performing everyday activities of living, barriers to participating in the societal mainstream, and/or barriers to exercising his or her human rights and fundamental freedoms. In this perspective, disability is understood as a social process more than as some individual condition.

A significant disjuncture exists between this socio-political perspective and much of public policy and service provision in liberal democratic welfare states. Most programs and delivery systems embody aspects of other perspectives on disability: a bio-medical, charitable and worthy poor welfare viewpoint. Traditionally, and still today, most public policy on disability focuses on a person's functional limitations due to disease, injury, or chronic illness as the cause or a major explanation for relatively low levels of formal educational attainment, employment and income. An image of people with disabilities still common is that of a person who suffers from an affliction, accidental or biological, and thus to be pitied or feared.

Ableism captures many aspects of the cultural dimension of stratification—the process of being 'defined from the outside, positioned, and placed, by a network of dominant meanings' (Young 1990: 59). People with disabilities constitute one of the social groups 'culturally oppressed by being defined as the Other, the different and the deviant', thus rendering one's own experience, perspective, and aspirations marginal, if not invisible (p. 88). At a systemic or personal level, ableism can encompass silencing, segregation or exclusion, marginalization, denial, neglect, violence and abuse, and poverty-based on one disability or more. Power, prestige and privilege in society—all features central to social stratification—are distributed based on prevailing notions of ability and normalcy, thus downgrading the status of persons with disabilities. Not surprisingly, the modern disability movement engages in the politics of recognition, which 'questions certain everyday symbols, practices, and ways of speaking, making them the subject of public discussion, and explicitly matters of choice and decision' (p. 86). Notice the shift in language since the mid-1980s, in some jurisdictions, from mentally retarded, to mentally handicapped, to people with developmental/intellectual disabilities.

Disabilities and Cities: Spatial Exclusions and Inclusions

When it is said that disability is spatially constructed, we need to ask some basic yet important questions: Who are the builders or manufacturers of disablement? On what sites and spaces does the construction take place, and with what tools and materials? And, whose construction of disability prevails and whose does not?

Disability in cities links closely to the constitution of urban power and the composition of the urban landscape. Briefly, the constitution of urban power encompasses the roles and relations between formal governmental structures and governance processes, the political economy of development, and myriad organized interests, social movements, community groups and human service professions such as social work (Valverde 2012). In turn, the composition of a city landscape includes patterns of settlement (e.g. migration, segregation, gentrification and densification), physical design and layout, and infrastructure (e.g. modes of transportation, housing options, recreation facilities, education and other social amenities). In looking at the industrial city, Brendan Gleeson conceives of the social space of disability as 'a dynamic, restless landscape marked by … inclusionary and … exclusionary pressures on impaired bodies' (1999: 125).

Richard Scotch writes that 'as communities vary in their inclusiveness and support, impairments may become more or less salient to individual experience and life chances' (2011: xvi). Gleeson states further, there are 'two main urban dimensions of disability oppression: physical inaccessibility and socio-spatial exclusion in institutionalised forms of social care' (1999: 137). Physical inaccessibility relates to buildings, sidewalks and streets, inadequate transit, signage and public spaces, while exclusion occurs in the domains of schools and colleges, training and employment, cultural events and media representations, voting and other political processes. Unemployment, lower levels of educational attainment, social isolation, poverty and welfare dependency are frequent outcomes of this oppression. Signs of physical inclusion in cities for at least some people with disabilities include curb cuts, wheelchair ramps, automatic door openers, handicapped parking spaces, Braille signs and accessible toilets. Signs of exclusion are people with mental conditions who are homeless and live on the streets; those disabled who live in low-income housing shelters, or who attend special education programs at a local school, or those who participate in segregated recreation activities at a community centre.

Even in large and densely populated cities, freedom of association and the chance for everyday contact with people other than caregivers or paid service providers is not always easy for persons with disabilities. Widespread barriers to accessibility limit mobility and thus limit interactions, resulting in social distance and isolation, and restricting the scope and nature of experiences in city life. In urban settings, 'there is constant association with strangers' (Wilensky and Lebeaux 1958: 117), which means people are commonly judged 'by superficial appearances, by how they look and speak'; judgements which derive from community beliefs and norms. Established norms and common stereotypes about disablement devalue people with disabilities in a variety of social settings. Parker suggests that people with disabilities are identified as Other, as different from the community norms, as those:

> negatively regarded by mainstream, society often find that their exclusion from social, economic and political life is more intensified in an urban environment that ... is designed by and for the holders of economic and political power (2011: 122).

Urban life is a highly organized life. Certainly cities are places of large-scale complex organizations and networks of groups in each of the public, private and voluntary sectors of urban society. Complex formal organizations tend, of course, to be hierarchical forms of administration, often with standardized and differentiated systems of service provision; features of bureaucracy that present problems for people with disabilities, and other marginalized groups, frustrating their efforts to 'fit in' and to be able to comprehend and navigate the seemingly countless agencies, departments, mandates, human service workers, programs and rules.

City life is highly organized in four respects. First, there are the formal systems of the welfare state and its assemblage of services and benefits, yet also surveillance and controls (Valverde 2012). Welfare state activities include mental health, education, rehabilitation, corrections, public housing, employment and veterans' programs. Second, there are voluntary organizations and charities, frequently with social work practitioners, that serve people with disabilities and many others. These may include faith-based social services and foundations, and community agencies for children and families, for immigrants and newcomers, for older people and others with special needs. Then, third, there are the interest group and advocacy organizations of and for people with disabilities, often organized by type of impairment or condition. These disability organizations provide important spaces for making connections and enabling participation by the disabled in urban politics and policy. Finally, there is the street community with networks of exchange and support of varying structures, including homeless shelters, as well as panhandling, criminal activity and public begging. A notable number of people existing on city streets have psychiatric conditions or other mental health issues. Commenting on the American situation in the aftermath of the de-institutionalization, 2001–2014, of people with intellectual disabilities and mental disabilities, a community consultant notes that the increasing number of people with mental health issues on streets is due to assorted factors:

> more restrictive criteria for involuntary commitment, the limited availability of effective inpatient care, a paucity of effective community-based services, and a lack of community support programs, as well as, more recently, the impact of trauma for veterans of the war in Iraq [and Afghanistan] (Borg 2010: 139).

For many homeless and street-involved people, support networks are limited, as are emergency shelter and food provisioning services in many cities.

A shift toward greater inequality in the distribution of income and wealth is apparent in many industrialized countries. With this growing inequality has come a stagnant or shrinking middle class, a widening gap between the higher-income and lower-income groups, and a mounting sense of insecurity and unfairness. In this troubling context of urban life, the disabled are one of the most disadvantaged and vulnerable groups.

Among people with disabilities who are employed, a sizable number occupy rather limited occupational worlds and career pathways, facing few opportunities for upward mobility and relatively high rates of perceived discrimination. For many individuals with disabilities, especially those with severe impairments, unemployment is a prevalent feature in their lives. Not actively engaged in the labour force results in the lack of social contacts at a workplace and, in some cases, the benefits provided by employers and or unions. Persistence of barriers to access, ongoing unmet needs for basic services, and obstacles to real jobs for real pay account, in large measure, for the activism of individuals with disability and their families, and the politicization of these issues and of traditional ways of providing services to people with disabilities. Cities become a primary focus of disability activism with independent living or community living groups engaging with local governments and urban authorities over issues of accessibility, whether of buildings, local parks, buses and transit systems, housing projects or schools.

Social Work and Disability: Troubled Yet Shifting Relations

According to Bigby and Frawley, 'Social work more than any other profession occupies the space between citizens and the state located in the organizational structures that allocate and ration collective resources' (2010: 95). Most of these organizations and most of the resources social workers distribute and regulate to most individuals and families take place in cities. In this sense, social work is spatial work. Within the field of disability supports, services and systems, social workers hold positions that 'undertake assessment and planning functions, such as case or case managers'. Social workers 'perform functions such as person-centred plan facilitation, guardian of last resort, advocacy, carer support, individual brokerage, or casework' (Bigby and Frawley 2010: 59). These and other functions take place in family support and respite services, day support programs, pre-employment services, legal aid and advocacy, group homes and residential services, special education and recreation, income security programs, mental health, and child and youth welfare. However, as Stainton and colleagues point out:

> the role of social work in working with people with disabilities is becoming diminished in many jurisdictions, which may be compounded by the marginalised place of disability in social work curricula (Stainton et al. 2010: 2).

More than 30 years ago, a disability scholar remarking on UK experience noted 'a number of studies which have discussed social work in relation to disabled people—none is complementary to social work' (Oliver 1983: 12). Criticisms ranged from a lack of access to social workers, limited qualifications and lack of knowledge by social workers about the needs and lived experiences of disabled people, and a primary focus often on the person's functional limitations rather than on societal barriers. People with disabilities encountered provider-led support rather than person-centred, on a discretionary basis rather than rights-based, with limited, if any, choices; all resulting in felt stigma and an identity of dependency (Oliver 1983: 27–30; Oliver and Barnes 1998: 99).

These issues and challenges for social work and disabled people have definitely not disappeared; in some respects, they have not diminished significantly. Professional practices and personal attitudes may unintentionally stereotype, separate and stigmatize individuals with disabilities and their families. As two American social work scholars explain, 'Human service workers are susceptible to adopting society's ableist attitudes without conscious awareness. Ableism can lead workers to underestimate their capabilities and to restrict the self-determination of people with disabilities with whom they work' (Mackelprang and Salsgiver 1999: 4). Traditional practices still prevail: a social worker (and other human service workers) may relate to a person with a mental health condition as a patient and expect the individual to simply comply with bio-medical care plans determined by professionals; a social worker may connect to a person with a physical disability as a client who is ill or incapacitated and who should receive rehabilitation or other treatment; a social worker may interact with a person with a learning difficulty or intellectual disability and see that individual as a person with special needs and behavioural deficits who requires remedial assistance and protection (Mackelprang and Salsgiver 1999).

Stainton and colleagues emphasize that:

> the relationship between people with disabilities and social work and policy has not always been a positive one: a mix of charity at best and incarceration at worst, a trend that has continued to some degree into the present day (Stainton et al. 2010: 1).

A Canadian social work scholar writes of the 'disability gap' in social work education and professional practice, noting that:

> 'Despite shifts in the construction and translation of knowledge dedicated to human diversity across the social sciences, the profession of social work has yet to fully embrace the significance of disability.' She adds: 'social work education continues to rely on medical, rehabilitation, and psychosocial perspectives in theorizing disability' (Vick 2012: 55).

In many jurisdictions, social work remains implicated in the production of exclusion and client-hood through the provision of segregated day programs, sheltered workshops, and large residential institutions. In this context, 'it is easy to understand that people with disabilities and their families have a mix of reactions to social work. These can range from valued supporter, ally, and advocate to paternalistic interventionist, assumed expert, and gate-keeper to flawed service systems' (Stainton et al. 2010: 1).

There are positive similarities between social work and the disability movement. Social work and disability rights perspectives share a number of broad values. These include: 'respect for individual rights, dignity and autonomy, a commitment to realize people's optimal capacity and well-being, and to bring about social change to discriminatory and unjust social relations' (Bigby and Frawley 2010: 60). Likewise, in this era of disability rights (Beaulaurier and Taylor 2001; Prince 2009), a close affinity exists between the value commitments and mission of social work and the moral demands and equality of planning and of the Convention on the Rights for People with Disabilities (Kim 2010). Moreover, the International Federation of Social Workers (IFSW), an association with members from 116 countries, recently gave robust expression, through a policy statement of global solidarity between the social work profession and the worldwide disability movement (IFSW 2012). Australian social work professor Lesley Chenoweth usefully itemises examples of how social work and disability converge in theoretical and practical terms:

> systems and ecological models [of social work] are critical for understanding the experience of people with an intellectual disability in families, communities and service systems especially if we are aiming for inclusion in community. The current person-centred planning approaches in disability have strong resonances with strengths-based and narrative approaches of social work. Developing community capacity to welcome and include people with an intellectual disability relies on social work's commitment community development frameworks (Chenoweth 2010: xi).

Bigby and Frawley additionally highlight overlaps in approaches to self-determination, noting that the advocacy principles of the disability community—encapsulated in the slogan 'Nothing About Us Without Us'— 'are aligned with social work principles, in particular in relation to supporting people to make their own decisions and be engaged in creating change that will positively affect their own lives and the lives of others through policy and practice reform' (Bigby and Frawley 2010: 177).

What can be done in our world of disabling cities to move towards an enabling urban social work profession? Drawing on critical social work orientations, such as anti-oppressive theory and newer theories of disability (Hiranandani 2005), provides a basis for critiquing the ways in which social work has disadvantaged people with disabilities and to identify the privileged status of social work in relation to this marginalized group in societies. Alongside sexism, racism and classism, critical social work education needs routinely to highlight ableism and disability oppression as a form of cultural imperialism, to use Young's term (Young 1990), interrogating disabling beliefs and challenging the cultural devaluation of people with physical, mental, intellectual or sensory impairments. While urban theorists of past generations warned of lonely crowds and current theorists frequently promote a vision of diverse civic publics, the reality in cities is all too often of the excluded Others. As the social model of disability underlines, cities are full of structural and attitudinal barriers to participation by people with impairments. Nonetheless, another theme is that there are possibilities for making cities more inclusive and partici-patory places. Social differences among people are general and desirable realities of community living in urban societies.

Theoretical and empirical works by human geographers offer invalu-able insights for social work educators and practitioners. This includes ground-breaking work on documenting disabling environments (Imrie 1996, 2000) and appreciating the geographies of disability (Gleeson 1998, 1999) alongside the interplay of space, power and the exclusion of disabled people (Kitchin 1998). The 'disabling city'—the urban setting that restricts, ignores and excludes people with disabilities from regular participation in everyday activities. The social construction of disability draws attention to the importance of supports in the built environment, attitudes of city residents, and the actions and inactions of policy makers in shaping how much a person with a disability has difficulty in living, working, playing, studying and generally moving about a city. As plan-ners and geographers point out, realizing accessibilities in cities involve personal costs along with public sector and private sector investments in time, travel, finances and other resources.

Social work is responding by supporting people with disabilities in their struggles and campaigns for economic and social justice, and by insisting on respectful and empowering practices. Patterns of civic exclusion need interrogating, whether those practices deal with panhan-dling, homelessness, group homes, or the personal understandings and responses to people with particular disabilities.

Much more can and should be done by social work in promoting inclusive and democratic social spaces in cities. 'As professionals,' says Vick, 'we can take practical and political action to eradicate discrimina-tion, and support more just and equitable policies that shape the lives of all persons with disabilities' (2012: 56). Whether in counselling and case work, group work or community development work, Vick calls on social workers to 'believe in the embodied experience of all people', defend human rights and dignity, and 'cultivate a professional sensitivity to the diverse expression of disability' (2012: 55). This diverse expression consists of disabilities that are prolonged and many others that are episodic; disabilities both visible and hidden to onlookers; impairments that range from mild to very severe in their limitations; disabilities that are physical or cognitive in etiology; those which are well-established conditions and others that are hotly contested by medical science; and disabilities acquired at birth and those obtained later in life. With intersectional analyses, understanding this complex diversity goes further when disability is examined both in discourse and in policy in relation to social categories of age, class, ethnicity, gender, locality, race and sexuality (Oliver and Sapey 2006; Prince 2009; Hallahan 2010). An intersectional approach helps avoid essentializing disability and also acknowledges the phenomenon of social stratification with disability as a factor caught up in the structure of inequalities in urban societies.

Beyond having sympathy for people with different disabilities or developing greater sensitivity to disability issues, social workers must practice solidarity with all people with disabilities. A large challenge, to be sure, this entails 'new models of understanding, collaboration, and research' (Stainton et al. 2010: 1). It further requires social workers working alongside disability self-advocates, families, local groups and urban-based disability movement organizations. This solidarity means that social work practice must take action in supporting an agenda of reform that, in partnership with people with disabilities and disability organizations, promotes supported decision making, individualized funding (also known as 'direct payments'), integrated and individualized supports (Borg 2010; Prince 2011), inclusive employment opportunities (Shankar et al. 2011), public policies and laws on accessibility across public and private domains of life, reasonable accommodation, and universal or inclusive design (Prince 2009). In all this, social workers need to participate with disability activists and their associations in monitoring state responsibilities and obligations.

Disability Activism Today

Three forms of struggle for social change and social justice define contemporary disability activism: the comparatively new politics of cultural recognition and identity interacting with the long-established politics of redistribution of material goods, and a politics of representation that combines conventional and alternative modes of decision making. Analytically, these three types of political struggle correspond to distinct institutional domains: the politics of recognition to the cultural order of society, the politics of redistribution to the market economy and welfare state (including the role of social workers and other human service professionals as interpreters and implementers of public policies), and the politics of representation to the political system and civil society. Fundamental obstacles to full participation by persons with disabilities include their non-recognition as full persons in prevailing cultural value patterns; the mal-distribution of resources in the form of income, employment, housing and other material resources; and their misrepresentation or marginal voice in elections, policy development and decision making processes.

As a social movement, disability groups emphasize a form of identity politics in reference to altering self-conceptions and societal conceptions of people with disabilities from passive, deviant and powerless to positive, self-created conceptions for themselves. As one social policy/disability advocate remarks: 'In the struggle for equality, the institutional forms of domination that affect the lives of the disabled cannot be separated from the cultural ones'. It should come as no surprise to anyone familiar with civil rights movement history, that 'the same dynamics that all historically oppressed groups play out continue within the policies and interventions aimed at individuals with mental and physical disabilities' (Borg 2010: 139). However, the cultural struggles of the disability movement are not to the exclusion of material issues of employment, accessible education and income security, or of governmental issues of public participation in policy making. A politics of socio-economic redistribution is at the core of disability activism complemented by a cultural politics of recognition and a democratic politics of representation, the latter of which involves claims for more accessible, empowering and accountable policy making structures and processes. Similar to many urban social movements, the disability rights movement makes claims to:

'the right of the city,' claims for 'affordable housing ... access to decently paid employment, public services such as education, health and welfare, or to a safe and pleasant environment' (Parker 2011: 68).

At the same time, as part of a new urban entrepreneurialism, the case for promoting the status of people with disabilities rests on market logic, viewing them and their families as valuable customers, as tourists with disposable incomes for leisure and entertainment, and as a potential pool of loyal workers in private businesses, community agencies or social enterprises.

Active in claiming a self-defined identity in place of that previously dominant in society, disability movement organizations question traditional state practices and professional controls. Challenging a purely biomedical perspective on disability, activists are promoting a socio-political model with a focus on the interaction between individuals and the larger environment. The psychiatric survivors' movement calls for drug-free treatments and greater use of peer counselling, while the 'mad movement' is promoting dignity and self-respect around bipolar disorder and schizophrenia. The movement conveys strong interest in social reform, and in public services and programs generally (François et al. 2013). 'For social work', as Stainton and colleagues notice:

> these demands for social justice and self-determination align directly with core social work values and suggest that ethical practice should place social workers squarely in line with the disability movement in their struggle for meaningful equality (Stainton et al. 2010: 1).

Conclusion: Toward an Enabling Urban Social Work

This chapter has explored the relationship between cities, people with disabilities and social work. People with disabilities are a varied category of individuals with physical, mental, intellectual or sensory impairments. Urban contexts reveal disability to be a diverse social phenomenon and everyday existence, and social work as a profession and set of practices with mixed implications for disabled people. Both disability and social work appear as socio-spatial encounters with intertwined histories and contemporary relationships. In evocative imagery, Wilensky and Lebeaux once described 'central cities [as] holding a large bag full of well-developed social problems' (1958: 177). This picture of urban life still applies, and in a truly global manner. As Parker notes, 'cities tend to concentrate poorer populations and exhibit greater income inequalities and class variation than suburban and rural societies' (2011: 73). Unemployment, poverty and welfare are prevalent realties in the lives of most people with disabilities. The large bag of social problems in cities extends further than poverty and income inequalities to include issues of embodied politics: to ableism and inaccessibility, and to fundamental understandings of human capacity and dignity. Cities are, and will continue to be, associated with obstacles and exclusions for disabled citizens because of the inertia of existing infrastructure in city landscapes and the massive scale of work involved in making our built environments genuinely inclusive, never mind the ever-present NIMBY (not in my backyard) politics in urban social policy making. Also, obstacles against people with disability persist because of entrenched asymmetries in the relations of power in urban governance and in liberal democratic capitalist societies more generally. A further reason for the persistence of obstacles is that established cultural beliefs and practices regarding ability and disability continue to focus on the individual or immediate family and, consequently, de-emphasize systemic barriers and societal solutions. All is not dark and bleak, however.

Possibilities for change are in evidence for improving the lives of people with disabilities, in making cities less disabling and more inclusive, and in social workers acting in effective solidarity with people with disabilities. A participant in the community mental health movement in New York City criticizes the tendency to pathologize and individualize psychiatric disabilities, and argues instead for compassion and responsive community responses: 'at the core of all these *human responses* to suffering that need remedy is a deep sense of empathy with the struggles of existing at this time in this society, in a state of perpetual dread over the immense social problems that infect those around us, and that seem (and often are) insurmountable' (Borg 2010: 136, emphasis in original). Along these lines, promising developments include ratification of the United Nations Convention by most countries, the introduction of accessibility laws in some national and sub-national jurisdictions, and the formation of accessibility committees or inclusive design panels in certain city governments.

Other encouraging trends are the mobilization of people with disabilities and their families through self-governing entities, disability-specific organizations and cross-disability associations advocating for recognition, for benefits and supports, and for a voice in public policies and laws that affect them. And, in some cities and service sectors, there are signs of transformation in the traditional systems of special education classes, day programs and sheltered workshops for people with disabilities, towards new structures and practices of participation; for example, in supported employment, family-based governance arrangements, inclusive education and social enterprises. By way of these developments, social work is necessarily shifting and repositioning itself, although not completely away from being urban service providers and street-level public servants. These roles and others undertaken by social workers will, however, be infused more thoroughly with a rights-based approach—an approach that challenges urban practices of exclusion and ableism, and that champions cultural and structural change to advance the equality of all people with disabilities.

References

Beaulaurier, R. L., & Taylor, S. H. (2001). Social work practice with people with disabilities in the era of disability rights. *Social Work in Health Care, 32*(4), 67–91.

Bigby, C., & Frawley, P. (2010). *Social work practice and intellectual disability*. London/New York: Palgrave Macmillan.

Borg, M. B. (2010). Disability, social policy and the burden of disease: Creating an 'assertive' community mental health system in New York. *Psychology, 1*, 134–142.

Chenoweth, L. (2010). Foreword. In C. Bigby & P. Frawley (Eds.), *Social work practice and intellectual disability*. London/New York: Palgrave Macmillan.

Church, K., Frazee, C., Panitch, M., Luciani, T., & Bowman, V. (2007). *Doing disability at the bank: Discovering the work of learning/teaching done by disabled bank employees*. Toronto: RBC Foundation Institute for Disability Studies, Ryerson University.

François, B. A., Menzies, R., & Reaume, G. (Eds.). (2013). *Mad matters: A critical reader in Canadian mad studies*. Toronto: Canadian Scholars' Press.

Gleeson, B. (1998). Justice and the disabling city. In R. Fincher & J. M. Jacobs (Eds.), *Cities of difference* (pp. 89–119). London/New York: Guilford Press.

Gleeson, B. (1999). *Geographies of disability*. London/New York: Routledge.

Hallahan, L. (2010). Legitimising social work disability policy practice: Pain or praxis? *Australian Social Work, 63*, 117–132.

Hiranandani, V. (2005). Towards a critical theory of disability in social work. *Critical Social Work, 6*(1). http://www1.uwindsor.ca/criticalsocialwork. Accessed 24 Apr 2015.

IFSW (International Federation of Social Workers). (2012). People with disabilities. http://ifsw.org/policies/people-with-disabilities. Accessed 16 Apr 2015.

Imrie, R. F. (1996). *Disability and the city: International perspectives*. London: Sage.

Imrie, R. F. (2000). Disabling environments and the geography of access policies and practices. *Disability & Society, 15*, 5–24.

Kim, H. S. (2010). UN disability rights convention and implications for social work practice. *Australian Social Work, 63*, 103–116.

Kitchin, R. (1998). 'Out of place', 'Knowing one's place': Space, power and the exclusion of disabled people. *Disability & Society, 13*, 343–356.

Mackelprang, R. W., & Salsgiver, R. O. (1999). *Disability: A diversity model approach in human service practice*. Pacific Grove: Brooks Cole.

Oliver, M. (1983). *Social work with disabled people*. Basingstoke: Macmillan.

Oliver, M., & Barnes, C. (1998). *Disabled people and social policy: From exclusion to inclusion*. London: Longman.

Oliver, M., & Sapey, B. (2006). *Social work with disabled people* (3rd ed.). Basingstoke: Palgrave Macmillan.

Parker, S. (2011). *Cities, politics and power*. London/New York: Routledge.

Prince, M. J. (2009). *Absent citizens: Disability politics and policy in Canada*. Toronto/Buffalo/London: University of Toronto Press.

Prince, M. J. (2011). Integrated and individualized service provision for people with disabilities: Promising practices in liberal welfare states. *Journal of Comparative Policy Analysis, 13*, 545–560.

Scotch, R. K. (2011). Introduction: Disability and community. In A. C. Carey & R. K. Scotch (Eds.), *Disability and community: Research in social science and disability* (Vol. 6). Bingley: Emerald Group.

Shankar, J., Barlow, C. A., & Khalema, E. (2011). Work, employment, and mental illness: Expanding the domain of Canadian social work. *Journal of Social Work in Disability & Rehabilitation, 10*, 263–283.

Stainton, T., Chenoweth, L., & Bigby, C. (2010). Social work and disability: An uneasy relationship. *Australian Social Work, 63*, 1–3.

UN (United Nations). (2006). Convention on the rights of persons with disabilities and optional protocol. http://www.un.org/disabilities/documents/convention/convoptprot-e.pdf. Accessed 25 Apr 2015.

Valverde, M. (2012). *Everyday law on the street: City governance in an age of diversity*. Chicago: University of Chicago Press.

Vick, A. (2012). Theorizing episodic disabilities: The case for an embodied politics. *Canadian Social Work Review, 29*, 41–60.

Wilensky, H. L., & Lebeaux, C. N. (1958). *Industrial society and social welfare*. New York: Russell Sage.

Young, I. M. (1990). *Justice and the politics of difference*. Princeton: Princeton University Press.

8

Care, Austerity and Resistance

Donna Baines

Introduction

The Organisation for Economic Cooperation and Development (OECD) recognizes a worldwide 'care deficit' (OECD 2011; see also Ehrenreich and Hochschild 2004). This deficit emanates from a number of sources including the further retraction of the welfare state under policies of austerity, contracted-out and 'personalisation' services that pay poorly and fail to cover all care needs, a growing number of women involved in paid employment outside the home (resulting in women being less available to undertake unpaid care work in the home), and the growing proportion of the population who are aged and in need of care (Folbre 2006a, b; Cohen 2013; Baines and Daly 2015).

Cities have often proven to be places that attract those in need of care and provide innovative solutions to many care needs (Harvey 1989, 2010; Peck 2012). The solutions range from publically funded and operated

D. Baines (✉)
University of Sydney, Sydney, NSW, Australia

193

services aimed at equal access and redistribution to store-front services for those who exist somewhat outside the formal 'system'. Such services, among others, comprise:

- Services for people who are homeless, use alcohol or drugs harmfully, or have mental health problems—for example, soup kitchens, mobile crisis and health care units, drop-in centres and church basement hostels;
- Social movements that provide services for members and the larger community—for example, unions providing employment and counselling services following mass lay-offs, or the immigrant rights movement providing child care services for the children of people on temporary work visas;
- 'Under-the-table' or 'grey economy' care, such as care givers working without formal citizenship, generally working for cash—for example, 'undocumented' nannies/au pairs or live-in caregivers for dependent adults.

This plethora of care services incorporates the diverse populations who comprise modern metropolises and reflect the complexity of global care chains (Williams 2008; Sassen 2012). Whether 'legal' or 'illegal', one thing these workers share in common is that they expend significant amounts of their time and energy on the care of others.

Feminist and care ethicists such as Gray (2010: 1807) argue that 'compassion or care or any other virtuous attitude does not happen automatically. It is not a natural human response, but a learned and increasingly inculcated moral attitude gained through socialization.' In other words, care does not happen in a vacuum, social conditions need to be fostered in which is 'good to be good' (Noddings 1984; Orme 2002; Weinberg 2010). Cities sometimes form complex contexts in which virtuous attitudes flourish, often alongside or in opposition to more oppressive and harmful practices (Harvey 2011). In short, due to their population density, diversity and history of progressive struggle, as well as the presence of those with the capacity and willingness to pay privately for care, cities are incubators for highly collective and social behaviour; conversely, these circumstances also exacerbate problems.

This chapter will argue that social work is part of a group of jobs that are bound by the tasks they undertake to patch up people's lives, psyches and bodies so that they can go on to another day and, maybe, make their lives and the lives of those around them better. Though care can be, and often is, a solitary, privatised undertaking, it can also be collectivised under government models of equity and redistribution, or as part of social reform efforts and movements for social change. Social workers—in particular, among care workers[1]—have a history of collectivism from early times,[2] including the community-based settlement houses which sought community-wide solutions to individual difficulties (such as Hull House, established in 1889 in Chicago); radical social work organisations (such as the Rank and File in the USA, the League for Social Reconstruction in Canada, and similar efforts in Australia and the UK) that sought the fundamental restructuring of society in more equitable ways; and close ties to social movements in the new left activism of the 1970s (Ferguson et al. 2005; Carniol 2010; Baines 2011; Lundy 2011). These ties thinned out after the mid-1980s as social movements encountered neoliberalism and the demise of social conditions that supported mobilized publics as a healthy part of the political landscape (Harvey 1989; Carniol 2010). Restructured alongside the welfare state, social workers found it increasingly difficult to undertake advocacy, community organizing, or policy critique as their jobs narrowed and became more tightly scripted and monitored (McDonald 2006; Carey 2008; Baines 2010; Beddoe 2010).

The post-1980s, as well as recent experience, confirms that it has been difficult to sustain and build social causes and movements under the conditions of neoliberalism and, at the same time, that it has been increasingly difficult to meet care needs (Armstrong and Armstrong 2004; Lundy 2011). In the era following the 2008 global financial crisis, governments in the industrialized countries introduced policies associated

---

[1] Social workers are relatively privileged, professionalized care workers, with specialized knowledge, skills and credentials, and with a code of ethics that explicitly recognizes social justice as part of their mandate.

[2] Social work is a highly contested field with mixed historical origins reflecting larger ideological differences about social obligation and care. These divisions are still in place, leading to competing schools of logic assigning responsibility for making changes for individuals, collective society or both (see Carniol 2010 or Lavalette 2011).

with austerity that intensified the care crisis (Albo and Evans 2011; Peck 2012). Under austerity, government stimulus and direct provision of services were seen to be harmful; balanced budgets and zero deficits were often mandated in new binding legislation; social spending and social programs were radically cutback; public sector workforces were sharply reduced; and the private sector was valorized as the solution to sluggish economies and all social and environmental problems (Albo and Evans 2011; Clarke and Newman 2012). These policies and the ideology accompanying them remade care as a private responsibility, rather than as a social project of equity and redistribution (Charlesworth 2012; Baines and McBride 2014; Cohen 2013). In the process, it remade social workers and care workers employed in the formal economy as conduits of neoliberalism, offering reduced and increasingly standardized service to increasingly desperate and neglected service users.[3] Providing services at the 'leading and bleeding edge' of 'austerity's extreme economy' (Peck 2012: 2), social workers and other care workers simultaneously used the opportunities available to them to provide quality care where possible and, in small, individual and larger, collective ways, to resist austerity and to mend the holes in the social fabric of the city (Baines and Van den Broek 2016).[4]

This chapter views the care endeavour as a site of innovation and struggle in the city, as well as a potential site for growing solidarity and social change. The chapter first explores what is happening in terms of care work in the city in the context of neoliberalism and austerity. It does so by analyzing the conditions of three kinds of care workers: paid workers in the formal economy (such as social workers in public, non-profit and private agencies), paid workers in the informal or 'grey economy' (such as nannies/au pairs and in-home care workers without citizenship rights in the country in which they are employed), and unpaid workers in both sites (such as those compelled to volunteer, those who volunteer from free will, resisters, family and community members). This section will also discuss national and international policy frameworks shaping care

---

[3] 'Service user' is the term currently preferred in social service work. It is used in this chapter as a generic term for those seeking services from state-run or contracted-out services, including health, long-term care, voluntary services, social work and so on.

[4] Thanks to Charlotte Williams for suggesting this phrase.

work, impacts on the work and workers, and forms of resistance common across all these sites. The final section of the chapter will discuss what social work can do, and is doing, in this context of transition, struggle and adaptation. The chapter takes as a starting point the fact that cities are crucibles of changing social relations, social organization and resistance, and adopts a gendered, labour-based and place-based perspective to explore care as an urban, highly gendered, increasingly racialized, and wholly classed phenomenon.

Formal, Informal and Unpaid Care Work in the Context of Austerity

In 2001, Pierson (see also, Pierson 2002) argued that the governments of affluent countries had been pursuing policies of 'permanent austerity' for some time and would likely intensify this approach. Pierson's words were doubly confirmed after the 2008 financial crisis, when even countries that had not experienced recession (such as Canada and Australia) introduced policies aimed at significant reductions in welfare state provisions, restructuring of labour markets and cutbacks in most areas of government spending (with the exception of the military, see Albo and Evans 2011). The terms 'austerity' and 'austere' are used here to denote this policy direction and the neoliberal ideology accompanying it, rather than a specific moment in time. To recap, this section will discuss formal, informal and unpaid care work in relation to policy frameworks, managerialism (where it exists), impacts on the work and workers, and resistance. Though care economies interweave in multiple ways, for the purpose of this chapter they will be delineated as: the formal care economy—comprising services provided by the state, private and non profit sectors; the informal care economy—care transactions for which cash is generally paid and employers do not contribute to taxes, or necessarily comply with minimum employment standards; and the unpaid care economy—unwaged care work provided by family members (usually women), volunteers, and care workers in their own time.

Care Work in the Formal Economy

From the 1980s, governments in the richer countries promoted policies of contracting public sector service out to the private and non-profit sectors in order to reduce costs and social obligation (Evans et al. 2005; Clarke and Newman 2012; Baines and McBride 2014). In order to receive government contracts, agencies were required to adopt New Public Management, private sector compatible practices emphasizing competitive performance management, outcome metrics, efficiencies and risk management (Evans et al. 2005; Davies 2011). With an eye to cost savings, work practices have been increasingly standardized; this has reduced professional discretion and skill sets, and increased workloads. This tendency to deskill through the standardization and degradation of the work has been observed and analyzed across a range of care workers including social work (McDonald 2006; Smith 2007; Carey 2009; Harris 2014) aged care (Armstrong and Armstrong 2004, 2008; Cunningham 2008; Daly and Szehebeley 2012; Armstrong and Braedley 2013), and nursing (Zeytinoglu et al. 2011; Armstrong et al. 2008; Grant 2004). Within this restructuring whirlwind, higher-skilled, credentialed professionals are being replaced by lower-skilled quasi professional and generic workers, or even volunteers (Baines 2004; Carniol 2010).

Many have noted a simultaneous polarization of employment with top jobs providing greater autonomy, variation of task and possibility for advancement, while the majority of care jobs are increasingly deskilled, tightly scripted, low-paid and precarious (McDonald 2006; Carey 2008; Cunningham 2015). Skills associated with more collectivist and social justice traditions are likely to be reduced or removed under outcome metrics, as these altruistic practices are generally open-ended, relationship-based and difficult to quantify (Armstrong et al. 2008; Ross 2011; Smith 2011). Many care workers and managers resent the loss of community-engagement skills and professional autonomy, as well as the increased caseloads, the higher intensity and accelerated pace of work accompanying standardized outcome metrics. As will be discussed below, many are willing to resist (Carey 2008; Noble and Irwin 2009; Carniol 2010; Aronson and Smith 2011).

Cutbacks in public services and income supports have left growing numbers of service users in deeply difficult circumstances, meaning that the kinds of issues that bring them to care services are generally more complex and intense than previous eras and do not lend themselves to short-term, easy solutions. This adds to intensified workloads in a context of falling staffing levels and resources. In many cases, care workers feel trapped between the demands of progressively more distressed service users and the demands of employers—and the state as the funder behind the employer—for rapid turn-around, fast-paced care work and growing documentation to confirm that fast-paced care has occurred (McDonald 2006; Cunningham and James 2009; Daly and Szebeheley 2012). Hall (2004) captures this dilemma in his observation that 'recent service user experience is characterised by unmet needs, an absence of individualised care, lack of therapeutic interventions and loss of power in decision making (p. 541)'. Thwarted rights and stunted care suggest neglect at the systemic level (though under-funding and metrics detract from care provision); this is experienced at the individual level where workers are constantly and systemically—not arbitrarily—rushed and compelled to provide thin, technical, tightly quantified care to those in need. Under the set of policies currently known as 'austerity', which ensure a deeper contraction of the welfare state and growing reliance on the private sector, these kinds of tensions are being intensified and can be expected to continue to as governments pursue this unrelenting course of privatization and dissolution of the social (Clarke and Newman 2012; Baines and McBride 2014).

Care workers note that, within this context, *ethical care* is an increasingly exhausting and elusive pursuit. Colley (2012) argues that many public sector workers have found it very difficult to live with the contradictions between good, ethical practice and the technical, alienating way they are compelled work under managerialism. An increasingly common response to these ethical dilemmas has been to leave the profession entirely (see also Zeytinoglu et al. 2011). Social workers and other care workers experience similar tensions as Gray (2010) notes, 'in the harsh, risk-aversive, managerial environments of contemporary practice, it becomes increasingly difficult to maintain an ethical perspective' (p. 1796). Webster (2010) concurs, observing that the re-emergence of a Taylorist scientific model has contributed to questionable ethics and a general deskilling of social work practice under the guise of new managerial effectiveness, efficiency and economy (p. 29).

Many care workers, including social workers, use their remaining autonomy to resist informally through unpaid care work and personal touches, and formally through union and community activism. In the case of the former, many care workers intentionally undertake unpaid hours of work in their workplaces and work beyond their mandates to provide care on-the-fly and unpaid for care to those on their caseloads (Baines and Daly 2015; Cunningham 2015). They accord this form of self-exploitation with oppositional meanings, which helps care workers to feel that they are part of a moral project of making the world a better place (Charlesworth 2012). As a social worker quipped in a recent study of non-profit social services, 'the wages are terrible here anyway so why not work even more hours for no pay if it means you can keep a program afloat or keep someone from having to put their kids to bed hungry' (Baines and Daly 2015). Some workers spoke about the importance of resisting government agendas; one senior community worker reflected the sentiments of many when she noted, 'we don't count our hours closely here. If we did, we'd probably all cry. Given our current government, we can't change much, but we can try to make things less awful for some people' (Baines and Daly 2015). Workers were aware that unpaid work was a form of self-exploitation but argued that this compromise made society seem less cruel—which, these days, is an act of resistance itself. Unpaid care work also contributes to the development of shared oppositional identities and practices, as an aged care worker observed, 'everyone who works here is very progressive. We always talk about everything and learn from each other' (Baines 2016).

Care workers also intentionally use their unions to challenge injustices within the workplace and in the larger community. For example, in one social service workplace, unionized workers voted in favour of strike action when management continuously refused to provide improved conditions for part-time workers, despite agency policy briefs condemning growing precarity and poverty in the larger society (Baines et al. 2014). This schism between external and internal policy was unacceptable to the social service workforce and they ended up on a ten-day strike.

Similarly, many care workers want a louder voice in agency policies and practices. As the local union president in a social agency noted:

> Wages and working conditions are always important to our members, but people really want a voice in how decisions get made. We have expertise in our program areas, we know our clients and communities, and we want some say in how things get done. (Baines 2010)

Care workers also link their commitment to service users with unions and social justice causes in the larger community. Commenting on her willingness to try to create change outside and inside the workplace, one union activist argued:

> Our work doesn't stop at the end of the day or at the door of the agency. We bring the world in with us to work and the world walks through those doors everyday looking for help and assistance. It's only natural that we would get involved in activist work in this city—heck, activist work in this world,'cause it sure never needed it more. (Baines 2010)

Formal care work is also increasingly undertaken outside of agencies or institutions—usually in private homes in the form of home care, or as part of personalisation plans in which government monies are provided to individuals to employ their own care work staff privately. Aronson and Neysmith (2006) note that, under cost rationalization, home care workers are rarely allotted sufficient time to undertake even short conversations or relationship-building with service users before proceeding directly with care tasks that are almost impossible to complete in the time allotted. Workers feel this strips the humanity from their work and diminishes the dignity of people for whom they often perform intimate care. As other care workers, home care workers undertake unpaid work in order to sustain their own integrity and the self-respect of service users (Aronson and Neysmith 2006; Denton et al. 2006).

As noted above, in-home care for people with disabilities is also increasingly paid for under government-funded personalization programmes. Cunningham (2015) observes that personalization payments are rarely adequate to cover the full cost of the service users' needs and wants. This places front-line caregivers, rather than the state or employers, in the position of directly and often repeatedly trying to negotiate and meet service users' demands within tight budget allotments and heavy workloads. This generally leaves both parties feeling powerless and frustrated: the exception to this is males with professional skills and physical disabilities, who tend to do well in these situations. Workers in this situation are almost always unprotected by occupational health, minimum standards or fair wage protections, and often work unpaid hours out of care and/or fear for their employment (Rubery and Urwin 2011; Cunnningham 2015). Workers also complain that they work split shifts, early in the morning when people want to get up and late at night when people want to be put to bed, with no paid work in between. These unsocial hours make finding other employment and making home life very difficult, as it places financial, emotional and familial stress on marginally employed workers. In addition, job turn-over in this kind of work is quite high, suggesting significant insecurity and employers who are difficult or irresponsible. Rubery and Urwin (2011) argue that care workers need a standard employment relationship with employers in which they can expect full-time, permanent employment, as well as full employment protections and benefits. Without this, they argue that workers will continue to move in and out of the sector as better opportunities present themselves and that the quality of care will be inconsistent for people in high need of services. As personalization is a fairly new programme in most jurisdictions, much more research is required to understand the full impacts of these policies on all parties.

A growing population of formal economy care workers comprises au pairs, nannies and other caregivers on temporary visas. This group of care workers is often seen as the ultimate 'flexible' workforce created through immigration policy that favours a disposable workforce that has no rights (Williams 2012; Da Roit and Weicht 2013). Temporary care giver visas tend to stipulate the start and end dates of employment, that workers may not move from one employer to another, and that workers are not allowed to apply for citizenship (Ehrenreich and Hochschild 2004). The overwhelming majority of these workers are racialized women who work and live in their employer's home. They are rarely protected by minimum wage, occupational health or employment standards, and are sent home if they are ill or injured, or if their employer terminates their contract.

Temporary visa care workers are also increasingly employed by private individuals and families to supplement care in aged care homes and other residential care settings (Daly et al. 2015). As private employees of families and individuals, these workers have few protections and little recourse if employers are unfair, abusive or exploitive. Together, these care workers form a group of largely unseen women working at the edges of the formal care economy with few rights or protections (Shutes and Chiatti 2012). A growing body of literature exists on this phenomenon and on the actions of the workers themselves, in conjunction with unions, immigrant rights and feminist groups, to extend the rights of citizenship to these workers (McGregor 2007; Sassen 2012; Williams 2012; Bauer and Osterle 2013). This social activism is an example of the way that the possibility for shared concerns about care and care work across large numbers of people permits collective efforts for social change. In this example, and many others, people in cities gather together around causes that are often unseen by the majority of the population. Activists draw these issues out of the shadows into the public eye and demand the extension of rights, fair treatment and entitlement to those on the margins of the law and society (Sharma 2006). Given that the care deficit is not likely to be easily resolved, this kind of activism around legal and illegal care givers is likely to continue to be part of the urban landscape.

Care Work in the Informal Economy

Though some of the gaps in the formal care economy are filled by those either working on temporary visas or in the employ of personalization monies, individuals who can afford it also turn to the informal or grey economy to pay care workers in cash, outside of the formal economy, in order to save costs on wages, taxes and government required workplace protections (Sassen 2012; Elgin and Oyvat 2012). Just as the city is a draw for those in need of care, it is also a draw for those needing employment and willing to undertake precarious care work—particularly women from countries where fair-waged employment is difficult to find.

The exchange rates on most first-world currencies mean that even low-paid, 'illegal' care workers can manage to send remittances home to support family members. Most of these care workers are racialized women without formal citizenship rights, who fear identification by immigration authorities and subsequent deportation. These factors mean that these workers are a highly exploitable and compliant workforce (McGregor 2007; Bauer and Osterle 2013). Sassen (2008) calls these care workers 'modern day servants', as their low-waged care of others permits higher-waged workers to live lives of greater luxury and privilege (p. 481).

The informal care economy involves a myriad of forms of work: some blended with the formal economy; some people holding citizenship, but willing to work in the 'underground' care economy; and some, such as workers without citizenship or visas, working wholly in the underground care economy (Oyvat & Elgin 2012; Sassen 2008). For example, it is not uncommon to find women with citizenship or on temporary visas employed both as care workers within the formal economy and, simultaneously, within the informal economy, performing a certain additional number of hours per day 'under the table' for cash (McGregor 2007). Other workers may be legally employed in a non-care work job and work additional hours as a care worker in the underground economy in order to supplement their incomes. These categories of workers have one foot in both the formal and the informal economy, and are an increasingly important element in global care chains (Ehrenreich and Hochschild 2004; Elgin and Oyvat 2012). Other care givers in the grey economy are legally employed on temporary visas for a certain family for a certain number of hours per day and then work 'under the underground table' for other family members, or for other employers for additional cash (though they may just as likely work two shifts and receive no additional pay).

Together, these groups of women form a quiet and largely unseen army of care givers, putting people to bed and getting them up the next day, cleaning their bodies and their houses, doing their laundry, caring for their children and dependents. Daly et al. (2015) calls these 'invisible' women and investigates the many ways that formal institutions tolerate, or even appreciate, the presence of additional hands to provide care in the context of austerity-inspired cutbacks and work intensification inspired by New Public Management. More research is needed to understand the complex overlap of in-home/institutional, paid/under-paid/unpaid and formal/informal care economies in the many contexts of care work in the contemporary urban landscape, as well as the everyday conditions and lives of these officially unnoticed but very present and exploited care givers.

Research and activism with this particular group of care workers is difficult because of their fear of immigration and other authorities; hence, little is known about how they live their everyday lives, caring for and about those who choose to eschew the formal care market and, instead, contribute to the growing underground care economy. The informal economy can, and does, operate in non-urban environments but seems to flourish in the density of cities (Trinci 2006; Elgin and Oyvat 2012). In the case of care work, the informal economy seems to be a form of adaptation to the world-wide care deficit and interweaves women, from around the post-colonial world where structural adjustment programmes have made good jobs hard to find, with employers who are able to pay privately for care and who are also willing to be part of the underground economy (Sassen 2012).

Unpaid Care Work

Unpaid care work in the home is common in most countries and pivots on the assumption that giving care is natural for women, regardless of pay (in almost all cases, no pay) or working conditions (Folbre 2006a; Tronto 2010). Unpaid work in the community in the form of care for neighbours, extended family and even strangers is generally seen as an understandable extension of women's caring and uncomplaining nature, negating the need for formalized services or pay. This naturalized ethos of feminine care also operates in the formal care economy where, as noted earlier in this section, women tend to expect themselves and each other to care beyond paid hours and often accord this unpaid work with oppositional narratives and meanings (Smith 2007; Charlesworth 2012; Baines and Daly 2015). When unpaid work in the formal sector is taken on as a form of resistance, it rebuilds links between and among people that tend to grow thin in the context of neoliberalism's emphasis on individuality, extreme success and entrepreneurism (Baines and Daly 2015).

However, employers often expect unpaid, additional hours and resources from care workers and, in this case, unpaid care is primarily a form of exploitation that is legitimized through naturalized notions of women's unending and elastic capacity to care anywhere for anyone (Charlesworth 2012). Part-time workers are particularly vulnerable to exploitative expectations of unpaid care work. One part-time care worker reported that she was expected to work four hours per day for pay and four for free (Baines 2004). Failure to do this would have jeopardized her opportunity to obtain increased hours of paid work, or to have a chance of being hired for the rare full-time job that might become available. This kind of care work is compelled volunteerism and has little to do with resistance (Baines 2004), though the work likely contributes to reweaving the thin and broken links between and among people in the under-serviced, austere city.

Those who volunteer from free will also take on unpaid care work and fill gaps in the care economy, contributing to reweaving social ties and relations. However, given that most volunteers have little or no on-the-job training and are notably unreliable (Frumkin 2005), it is difficult to believe that this is a sustainable or quality alternative to well-trained, well-supported, full-time, permanent care workers.

Spanning the home, community, formal and informal economies, unpaid care work can be seen to operate within an imaginary care space within a triangle involving naturalized notions of female caring at one corner, re-knitting the social fabric through self-exploitation at another, and unpaid care as a form of conscious compromise and resistance to austerity and uncaring at the third. Care workers within the various kinds of care economies operate at different points within this imaginary care space based on whether they are spending extra minutes of their own time to have a cup of tea with a home care client; providing tenderness and respect to a frail, elderly person they have been hired 'under-the-table' to care for through the night; organizing public awareness campaigns about the neglected rights of those holding temporary care giver visas; or participating in a picket to keep much needed public services open and to demand fair wages from government. Presumably, the same person could do all these kinds of work and would occupy a dispersed space across the figure, whereas someone operating only as an unpaid care provider in their own home would occupy a smaller space close to naturalized notions of feminine care and a thin connection to re-knitting the social fabric (though they sustain the reproduction of themselves and their family members for the next day). This imaginary care space unites the various forms of unpaid care as being simultaneously different from one another, as well as extensions of similar themes.

Conclusion: What Is and Can Social Work Do?

Care work in the city does not operate in a vacuum. Across the richer nations, it is framed by notably similar national and international policy foci. New Public Management and managerialism reframe paid, formal care work as an endeavour that can not only be Taylorised and rationalized, but also increasingly paid at austere and constrained levels. Immigration policies concerning temporary care giver visas frame in-home and institutional care work for a growing sector of the care workforce, depriving these tax-paying workers from full citizenship rights and workplace protections. Restrictive immigration policy regimes make it very difficult for many women involved in the underground care economy to gain citizenship and, hence, they work without citizenship or labour market protections—vulnerable to deportation and exploitation.

As noted earlier, care workers of all types are bound by the tasks they undertake to patch up people's lives, psyches and bodies so that they can go on to another day and, maybe, make their lives and the lives of those around them better. This link of care provides the basis for inter-care worker solidarity and activism. For though, as noted earlier, care can be, and often is, a solitary, privatized undertaking, it can also be collectivized under models of equity and redistribution, or as part of social reform efforts and movements for social change.

Social workers, as other professionally credentialed and formally educated care workers, have experienced an intensification of their work and a decrease in discretion and autonomy under New Public Management policies. However, social workers remain among the privileged strata of the care work force, able to draw on professional codes of ethics, critical bodies of knowledge and social analysis to explain and understand this changing landscape of working conditions and care. Many social workers also retain community development, policy critique and communication skills that make them highly effective in and highly valued members of social change efforts (Smith 2007; Carniol 2010; Lundy 2011). Social workers often work in unionized workplaces where the resources and knowledge of the labour movement can be called on in aid of social justice causes (Baines 2010; Lavalette 2011).

Folbre (2006b) calls on care workers to form a broad-based coalition of consumers and workers, highlighting their commonalities, building solidarity across differences and emphasizing care's pivotal role in sustaining individuals, families, communities and larger society. Indeed, as feminist and care ethicists argue, though we all tend to give and receive care in various ways throughout our lives, care tends to be seen as something so naturalized that it is not visible (Gray 2010; Tronto 2010). Neither is it recognized as something that we need to politicize and take collective action to strengthen, extend, distribute fairly or address through social justice strategies.

The social location of some care workers, including social workers, provides a larger overview of social pain and suffering in the city, as well as its causes and possible solutions. Care workers with this kind of overview tend to have education and social networks that can build and circulate critical bodies of knowledge, educate diverse publics and influence those with power towards positive change. Moreover, with this broad overview and access to the front lines of care conflicts, social workers can inject realism and complexity to policy critiques and proposed policy changes by adding case histories, real life experiences and by highlighting tensions and dilemmas in the application of policy in everyday practice. As Lake notes, in these grim times, 'it is important to reassert the potential of social action and political practice', given that, as Castell (1983) argues, 'citizens … make cities even if it is one day and one storefront at a time' (p. 196). Finally, as Romero (2012) notes, migrant care workers are positioned very inequitably in the relations of race, class and gender, and are likely to become a new 'group' for social work practice.

As the workers quoted earlier in this section noted, in this neoliberal era of atomized individuality, caring for and about others is an act of resistance itself. Most people never have the opportunity or the skills to change global social policy, or to influence decision makers. Instead, most social change occurs where we live our lives, in small and incremental ways that sustain dignity and build people up to face another day (Aptheker 1989). My research shows that social workers are excellent at resisting workplace and government policies in numerous ways, formal and informal, large-scale and incremental, ranging from encouraging service users to advocate for themselves, even where it involves risk to the worker; bending rules and looking for other ways to obtain for service users everything to which they are entitled and more; taking on many hours of unpaid work in their own agencies and others; organizing service user groups outside their workplaces; building coalitions with social movements and agencies; providing new and innovative services at no charge; and using unions as vehicles for social justice. These practices were, and are, sources of meaning and satisfaction for many social workers and the other care workers with whom they work. As one research participant noted: 'If you haven't got meaning in these jobs, what else have you got?' (Baines 2010: 490).

Acknowledgements The author gratefully acknowledges funding from SSHRC (an MCRI held by P. Armstrong and a CURA held by W. Lewchuk), the work of Carolyn Fram and the contributions of the research participants.

References

Albo, G., & Evans, B. (2011). Permanent austerity: The politics of the Canadian exit strategy from fiscal stimulus. *Alternative Routes. A Journal of Critical Social Research, 10*(22), 7–28.

Aptheker, A. (1989). *Tapestries of life: Women's work, women's consciousness, and the meaning of daily experience.* Boston: University of Massachusetts Press.

Armstrong, P., & Armstrong, H. (2004). Thinking it through: Women, work and caring in the new millennium. In K. Grant, C. Amaratunga, P. Armstrong,

M. Boscoe, A. Pederson, & K. Willson (Eds.), *Caring for/caring about: Women, home care, and unpaid caregiving* (pp. 5–44). Toronto: Garamond.

Armstrong, P., & Armstrong, H. (2006). *Women, privatization and health care reform: The Ontario case*. Ottawa: National Network on Environments and Women's Health.

Armstrong, P., Armstrong, H., & Scott-Dixon, K. (2008). *Critical to care: The invisible women in health services*. Toronto: University of Toronto Press.

Armstrong, P., & Braedley, S. (Eds.). (2013). *Troubling care: Critical perspectives on research and practices*. Toronto: Canadian Scholars' Press.

Aronson, J., & Neysmith, S. (2006). Obscuring the costs of home care: Restructuring at work. *Work, Employment & Society, 20*(1), 27–45.

Aronson, J., & Smith, K. (2011). Identity work and critical social service management: Balancing on a tightrope? *British Journal of Social Work, 41*(2), 432–448.

Baines, D. (2004). Caring for nothing. Work organization and unwaged labour in social services. *Work, Employment and Society, 18*(2), 267–295.

Baines, D. (2010). Neoliberal restructuring/activism, participation and social unionism in the nonprofit social services. *Nonprofit and Voluntary Sector Quarterly, 39*(1), 10–28.

Baines, D. (2016). Moral projects and compromise resistance: Resisting uncaring in nonprofit care work. *Studies in Political Economy, 97*(2), 118–127.

Baines, D. (2011). Resistance as Emotional Labour: The Australian and Canadian Nonprofit Social Services. Industrial Relations Journal. 42(2) March: 139–156.

Baines, D., & Daly, T. (2015). Resisting regulatory rigidities: Lessons from front-line care work. *Studies in Political Economy, 95*(Spring), 137–160.

Baines, D., & McBride, S. (2014). Introduction. In D. Baines & S. McBride (Eds.), *Orchestrating austerity: Impacts and resistance* (pp. 1–18). Halifax: Fernwood Books.

Baines, D., & Van den Broek, D. (2016). Coercive care? Control and coercion in the restructured care workplace. *British Journal of Social Work*. First published online March 22, 2016, doi:10.1093/bjsw/bcw013

Baines, D., Cunningham, I., Lewchuk, W., & Sidhu, N. (under review). How could management let this happen?' Gender, participation, and industrial action in the nonprofit sector. *Social Politics*.

Baines, D., Charlesworth, S., Turner, D., & O'Neill, L. (2014). Lean social care and worker identity: The role of outcomes, supervision and mission. *Critical Social Policy, 34*(4), 433–453.

Bauer, G., & Osterle, A. (2013). Migrant care labour: The commodification and redistribution of care, emotional work. *Social Policy and Society, 12*(3), 461–473.

Beddoe, L. (2010). Surveillance or reflection: Professional supervision in 'The Risk Society'. *British Journal of Social Work, 40*(4), 1279–1296.

Carey, M. (2008). Everything must go? The privatization of state social work. *British Journal of Social Work, 38*(5), 918–935.

Carey, M. (2009). It's a bit like being a robot or working in a factory: Does Braverman help explain the experiences of state social workers in Britain since 1971? *Organization, 16*(4), 505–527.

Carniol, B. (2010). *Case critical: Challenging social services in Canada*. Toronto: Between the Lines.

Castell, M. (1983). *The city and the grassroots: A cross-cultural theory of urban social movements*. London: Edward Arnold.

Charlesworth, S. (2012). Decent working conditions for care workers? The intersections of employment regulation, the funding market and gender norms. *Australian Journal of Labour Law, 25*(2), 107–129.

Clarke, J., & Newman, J. (2012). The alchemy of austerity. *Critical Social Policy.*. doi:10.1177/0261018312444405.

Cohen, M. (2013). Neoliberal crisis/social reproduction/gender implications. *University of New Brunswick Law Journal, 64*, 234–252.

Colley, H. (2012). Not learning in the workplace: Austerity and the shattering of illusion in public service work. *Journal of Workplace Learning, 24*(5), 317–337.

Cunningham, I. (2008). *Employment relations in the voluntary sector*. London: Routledge.

Cunningham, I. (2015). Austerity, personalisation and the degradation of voluntary sector employment conditions. *Competition and Change, 19*(3), 228–245.

Cunningham, I., & James, P. (2009). The outsourcing of social care in Britain: What does it mean for the voluntary sector workers? *Work, Employment and Society, 23*(2), 363–375.

Daly, T., & Szebehely, M. (2012). Unheard voices, unmapped terrain: Care work in long term residential care for older people in Canada and Sweden. *International Journal of Social Welfare, 21*(2), 139–148.

Daly, T., Armstrong, P., & Lowndes, R. (2015). Liminality in Ontario's long-term care homes: Paid companions' care work in the space 'betwixt and between'. *Competition and Change, 19*(3), 246–263.

DaRoit, B., & Weicht, B. (2013). Migrant care work and care, migration and employment regimes: A fuzzy-set analysis. *Journal of European Social Policy, 23*(5), 469–486.

Davies, S. (2011). Outsourcing and the voluntary sector: A review of the evolving policy landscape. In I. Cunningham & P. James (Eds.), *Voluntary organizations and public service delivery* (pp. 15–36). New York: Routledge.

Denton, M., Zeytinoglu, I., Davies, S., & Hunter, D. (2006). The impact of implementing managed competition on home care workers' turnover decisions. *Healthcare Policy, 1*(4), 106–126.

Ehrenreich, B., & Hochschild, A. (2004). Introduction. In B. Ehrenreich & A. Hochschild (Eds.), *Global woman. Nannies, maids and sex workers in the new economy* (pp. 1–14). New York: Henry Holt.

Elgin, C., & Oyvat, C. (2012). Lurking in the cities: Urbanization and the informal economy. *Structural Change and Economic Dynamics, 27*, 36–47.

Evans, B., Richmond, T., & Shields, J. (2005). Structuring neoliberal governance: The nonprofit sector, emerging new modes of control and the marketization of service delivery. *Policy and Society, 24*(1), 73–97.

Ferguson, I., Lavalette, M., & Whitmore, E. (Eds.). (2005). *Globalisation, global justice and social work*. London: Psychology Press.

Folbre, N. (2006a). Measuring care: Gender, empowerment, and the care economy. *Journal of Human Development, 7*(2), 183–199.

Folbre, N. (2006b). Demanding quality: Worker/consumer coalitions and 'high road' strategies in the care sector. *Politics & Society, 34*(1), 11–32.

Frumkin, P. (2005). *On being nonprofit: A conceptual and policy primer*. Cambridge: Harvard University Press.

Grant, K. (2004). *Caring for/caring about: Women, home care, and unpaid caregiving*. Toronto: University of Toronto Press.

Gray, M. (2010). Moral sources and emergent ethical theories in social work. *British Journal of Social Work, 40*, 1794–1811.

Hall, J. (2004). Restriction and control: The perceptions of mental health nurses in a UK acute inpatient setting. *Issues in Mental Health Nursing, 25*(5), 539–552.

Harris, J. (2014). (Against) neoliberal social work. *Critical and Radical Social Work, 2*(1), 7–22.

Harvey, D. (1989). From managerialism to entrepreneurialism: The transformation in urban governance in late capitalism. *Geografiska Annaler Series B. Human Geography, 71*(1), 3–17.

Harvey, D. (2010). *Social justice and the city* (Vol. 1). Athens: University of Georgia Press.

Harvey, D. (2011). *The enigma of capital: And the crises of capitalism*. London: Profile Books.

Lavalette, M. (Ed.). (2011). *Radical social work today: Social work at the crossroads*. London: Policy Press.

Lundy, C. (2011). *Social work and social justice: A structural approach to practice*. Toronto: University of Toronto Press.

McDonald, C. (2006). *Challenging social work: The institutional context of practice*. Basingstoke: Palgrave Macmillan.

McGregor, J. (2007). Joining the BBC (British bottom cleaners): Zimbabwean migrants and the UK care industry. *Journal of Ethnic and Migration Studies, 33*(5), 801–824.

Noble, C., & Irwin, J. (2009). Social work supervision: An exploration of the current challenges in a rapidly changing social, economic and political environment. *Journal of Social Work, 9*(3), 345–358.

Noddings, N. (1984). *Caring: A feminine approach to ethics and moral education*. Berkeley: University of California Press.

OECD (Organisation for Economic Cooperation and Development). (2011). *OECD Health Data 2011*. Online version. OECD. http://www.oecd.org/general/11&ie=UTF-8

Orme, J. (2002). Social work: Gender, care and justice. *British Journal of Social Work, 32*, 799–814.

Peck, J. (2012). Austerity urbanism. *City, 16*(6), 626–655.

Pierson, P. (2002). Coping with permanent austerity: Welfare state restructuring in affluent democracies. In P. Pierson (Ed.), *The new politics of the welfare state* (pp. 369–406). Oxford: Oxford University Press.

Romero, B. (2012). Towards a model of externalisation and denationalisation of care? The role of female migrant care workers for dependent older people in Spain. *European Journal of Social Work, 15*(1), 45–61.

Ross, M. (2011). Social work activism amidst neoliberalism: A big, broad tent of activism. In D. Baines (Ed.), *Doing anti-oppressive practice: Social justice social work* (pp. 251–264). Halifax/Winnipeg: Fernwood Publishing.

Rubery, J., & Urwin, P. (2011). Bringing the employer back in: why social care needs a standard employment relationship. *Human Resource Management Journal, 21*(2), 122–137.

Sassen, S. (2008). Two stops in today's new global geographies: Shaping novel labor supplies and employment regimes. *American Behavioral Scientist, 52*(3), 457–496.

Sassen, S. (2012). *Cities in a world economy* (4th ed.). Newbury Park: Pine Forge Press.

Sharma, N. (2006). *Home economics: Nationalism and the making of 'migrant workers' in Canada*. Toronto: University of Toronto Press.

Shutes, I., & Chiatti, C. (2012). Migrant labour and the marketisation of care for older people: The employment of migrant care workers by families and service providers. *European Journal of Social Policy, 22*(4), 392–405.

Smith, K. (2007). Social work, restructuring and resistance: 'Best practices' gone underground. In D. Baines (Ed.), *Doing anti-oppressive practice. Building transformative, politicized social work* (pp. 145–159). Halifax/Winnipeg: Fernwood Books.

Smith, K. (2011). Occupied spaces: Unmapping standardized assessments in health and social service organizations. In D. Baines (Ed.), *Doing anti-oppressive practice: Social justice social work* (2nd ed., pp. 197–213). Halifax: Fernwood.

Trinci, S. (2006). The contribution of networks to immigrant insertion into the informal economy: Some findings from Tuscany. *International Journal of Sociology and Social Policy, 26*(9/10), 385–396.

Tronto, J. (2010). Creating caring institutions: Politics, plurality and purpose. *Ethics and Social Welfare, 4*(2), 158–171.

Webster, M. (2010). Complexity approach to frontline social work management: Constructing an emergent team leadership design for a managerialist world. *Social Work and Social Sciences, 14*(1), 27–46.

Weinberg, M. (2010). The social construction of social work ethics: Politicizing and broadening the lens. *Journal of Progressive Human Services, 21*, 32–44.

Williams, F. (2012). Converging variations in migrant care work in Europe. *Journal of European Social Policy, 22*(4), 363–376.

Zeytinoglu, I., Denton, M., & Plenderleith, J. (2011). Flexible employment and nurses' intention to leave the profession: The role of support at work. *Health Policy, 99*(2), 149–157.

9

Homelessness in Western Cities

Carole Zufferey

Introduction

Social work responses to homelessness in Western cities are complex. Cities provide opportunities for access to housing, health, education and employment. Worldwide, financial and environmental crises have contributed to rural to urban migration trends, which impacts on urban homelessness. Whilst this chapter focuses on Western cities, it is noted that in newly industrialised countries, environmental problems such as global climate change, drought, soil erosion, desertification and deforestation, as well as population pressures and poverty, have increased numbers of 'environmental refugees' migrating to the city in search of new educational and employment opportunities (Myers 2002). The increasing urbanisation of cities (and ageing populations) can increase pressures on city infrastructures, including housing, health, education and welfare

C. Zufferey (✉)
School of Psychology, Social Work and Social Policy, University of South
Australia, Adelaide, SA, Australia

© The Editor(s) (if applicable) and The Author(s) 2016
C. Williams (ed.), *Social Work and the City*,
DOI 10.1057/978-1-137-51623-7_9

service systems. As cities grow and populations continue to age, urban dynamics have the potential to further exacerbate social inequalities. Social workers respond to homelessness within these changing economic, social and cultural urban conditions.

Contemporary urban policies can create practice tensions for social workers when responding to homelessness. Whilst it must be acknowledged that the visible homeless account for a minority of people who experience homelessness, urban policies and policing responses function spatially to exclude, criminalise and marginalise people who are visibly homeless in the city (Amster 2003, 2008; Donley and Wright 2012). The contemporary neoliberal, urban governance of Western cities focuses on investments, gentrification, deregulation, privatisation, public-private partnerships and property development, which tend to contribute to design patterns that reproduce social inequalities (Kennett 1999; Tonkiss 2013). As Australian author Randolph (2004: 487) notes, the redevelopment of inner-city locations into commercial office spaces and larger and more prestigious buildings reflects the impact of global corporate and technological restructuring on our largest cities. In the modern capitalist city that is increasingly dominated by 'prestigious office locations', sprinkler systems are installed to prevent people sleeping in the doorway (Kennett 1999: 49) and local authorities are designing and building bus stops and park benches that people cannot sleep on. The redevelopment of city places and spaces tends to reinforce middle-class economic aspirations, to the detriment of people on lower incomes who are unable to compete and participate in the 'entrepreneurial' city (Kennett 1999: 49; Amster 2003). These city designs contribute to increasing social inequalities and the polarisation between the rich and poor.

Scholars in the field of the city refer to 'new geographies' of wealth and exclusion, 'shelter deprivation' and cities being constituted by unequal social, economic and political relations, with class, race, ethnicity and gender continuing to be 'key markers of urban inequality' (Stevenson 2013: 3; Tonkiss 2013: 22). As Kennelly and Watt (2011: 768) argue, 'urban spaces are not neutral … they carry the weight of political, social and cultural processes that create distinctive areas of leisure, employment, housing and destitution'. Urban social analysis has long been concerned with the interactions between spaces and social relations, arguing that physical spaces shape social interactions which, in turn, produce and transform urban space (Tonkiss 2003, 2013). Tonkiss (2003, 2013) discusses the 'ethics of indifference' as being the way that differences are lived in the city, which ignores the visibly homeless, people asking for money and, even, acts of violence in public spaces.[1] However, visible homelessness does tend to be constructed by policy makers as a social and spatial problem (Amster 2008) and the surveillance of people who are homeless (on the streets, or in large inner-city shelters) is a 'distinctive feature of the contemporary city' (Doherty et al. 2008: 307).

Henri Lefebvre's (1991) theory of spatiality is relevant to examining homelessness in urban spaces, as it is concerned with the social production of space and the negative consequences of the economic inequalities of capitalism. Lefebvre analyses the *perceived* physical space around us, the *conceived* space of creative imagination and the *lived* space, where social relations take place. Lefebvre (1991: 39) notes that there are particular practices in urban spaces, representations of these spaces and 'representational spaces' that are 'directly *lived* through its associated images and symbols' by the 'users' of that space. Homelessness scholars argue that the social-physical spaces of cities are ultimately bound up with the constitution of privileged (homed) and homeless identities, and people who are homeless are deemed 'out of place' in changing urban contexts (Wright 1997: 6–7). However, this also involves active contestations and conflicts about rights over the use of public space (Tonkiss 2003). People who experience homelessness are active agents who can contest the way they are framed, protest through collective actions and reassert their rights to belong in urban places (Wright 1997). Social work advocates and activists can work with people who experience homelessness to support these resistances.

In Western cities, the policing of homelessness in 'law and order' strategies, to move visible homelessness out of major cities (or particular 'problem' suburbs), is common (Jones 2013). In Europe, social work responses to homelessness are occurring in the context of increasing

---

[1] This comes from an exchange between Laura Gherardi and Fran Tonkiss which forms the preface to the Italian translation of 'The ethics of indifference: Community and solitude in the city', published as 'L'etica dell'indifferanza: comunità e solitudine nella città' (trans. Laura Gherardi) in *Dialoghi Internazionali:città nel mondo* (2010), 13, Autumn, 146–59.

incarceration rates, the over-representation of non-European migrants in overcrowded prisons and the 'hardening of penal policies' at the 'expense of rehabilitation' (Wacquant 2008: 278). Policy and legal responses to homelessness in Western cities involve the selective enforcement of neutral laws against people who are homeless, including the surveillance of loitering, penalising people who sleep and sit in public places, the regulation of 'panhandling' (or begging), limiting food distribution in public places, prohibiting the removing of items from rubbish and recycling bins, and 'clean the streets' sweeps by local authorities (Amster 2003, 2008; Jones 2013: 16). Social workers and policy activists are working with the symbolic and material consequences of these policing practices in urban contexts.

Policy activist organisations such as the European Federation of National Associations Working with the Homeless (FEANTSA) in Belgium and the National Law Centre on Homelessness and Poverty in Washington are key critics of the policing, criminalisation or penalisation of homelessness. The marginalisation of people who are visibly homeless in the city is of particular concern to social workers focusing on human rights and social justice for disadvantaged population groups. People who are homeless in public places are 'othered' and criminalised, but they can also resist the control and surveillance of public authorities (Wright 1997; Amster 2003). Social workers play an important role in facilitating the opportunities that the city provides, as well as challenging approaches that further marginalise and disadvantage people who experience homelessness in urban environments.

Urban Homelessness

Social work is evolving with the diverse and changing landscape of urban homelessness. Homelessness, like social work, is assumed to be an urban issue. Whilst it must be acknowledged that rural homelessness also exists (Cloke et al. 2007), contemporary urban conditions create particular forms of vulnerability. Inner-city public spaces have long provided places for people who experience homelessness, but the scale of urban homelessness has been on the increase worldwide and perceptions of homelessness have changed over time (Forrest 1999; Donley and Wright 2012). In Western cities, 'old' forms of homelessness were perceived to be marginally employed, older, single men, with health and drinking problems (Rossi 1989; Jencks 1994). These men were viewed as a homogenous group who lived in large cities in segregated and inner-city districts, such as 'skid rows' or 'single room occupancy hotels' (Jencks 1994). Homelessness was increasingly perceived to be more heterogeneous, including the 'urban poor', older population groups, younger people, women, children, veterans, families and members of minority groups, dispersed more widely over the urban landscape (Rossi 1989: 61; Blau 1992). Since the implementation of deinstitutionalisation policies in Western cities, it has been argued that there is an increase in people who experience homelessness with psychiatric illnesses, as well as drug and alcohol dependencies (Blau 1992). Furthermore, many inner-city housing precincts were demolished in the 1960s and 1970s when real wages and government benefits were increasing (Jencks 1994: 65). Australian author Randolph (2004: 487) notes that the social and economic restructuring of inner cities has largely seen 'the end of inner cities as places of social disadvantage'. The contemporary challenges facing urban policy makers and social workers relate to the 'increased scale and social division in Australian cities' and 'the suburbanisation of disadvantage' (Randolph 2004: 491). Structural factors such as deinstitutionalisation policies, coupled with the failure of community, social and health care support, as well as the loss of homes through economic hardship and the lack of available affordable housing, have changed the face of homelessness in Western cities.

Gendered Urban Spaces

Homelessness is often responded to by social workers as an urban phenomenon because it is more visible and geographically concentrated in urban areas. When researching literal homelessness in New York, Passaro (2014 [1996]) found that the persistently homeless 'on the streets' are overwhelmingly black men who tend to be excluded from the service system. It is widely argued that women's experiences of homelessness are less visible in urban spaces because they are more likely to experience hidden forms of homelessness, such as living in temporary shelters, 'couch surfing' or staying with friends and family (Murray 2011). As McLoughlin's (2013: 521) research with school-aged home leavers suggests, couch surfing is, in itself, 'an experience and product of dislocation, which (re) inscribes disadvantage' and undermines young people's attempts to gain ontological security. Australian researchers argue that 'couch surfing' challenges prevailing thinking about homelessness as 'rooflessness' and illustrates the 'multiplicity of social practices' through which young people (and women) contend with 'dislocation and struggle for home' (Murray 2011; McLoughlin 2013: 522).

With regard to visible homelessness, Casey et al. (2008) interviewed women in Leeds, London, Sheffield and Norwich, England and challenged literature that has tended to locate homeless women 'on the margins of the urban milieu' (Casey et al. 2008: 913). Women who experience homelessness do occupy urban spaces and public places of 'everyday life', such as public toilets, museums, art galleries, libraries, hospitals, airports, car parks and 'the space surrounding public and private buildings' (Lefebvre 1991; Casey et al. 2008: 903). Women 'actively and strategically use these spaces to their own ends and for their own needs and purposes, extracting and deriving positive benefit from them' (Casey et al. 2008: 905). Women can resist the rules associated with 'occupying public spaces that either directly or tacitly exclude them', by 'engaging in identity work' to not be labelled as 'homeless' (Casey et al. 2008: 899). These strategies by women in Casey et al.'s study included presenting a 'respectable self'; avoiding 'well-known places on the streets' where groups of homeless people congregate and sleep; timekeeping their use of space to avoid being detected; developing relationships with gatekeepers (such as security guards or toilet attendants); keeping up 'interests they had prior to being homeless, such as listening to music, reading and going on the internet' and 'projecting an image of toughness', to avoid 'unwelcome advances of other homeless people', as well as homeless agencies intent on 'rescuing them' (Casey et al. 2008: 909–911). Thus, urban homelessness is negotiated and experienced differently by women.

Women experience homelessness *because* of domestic and family violence, but they are also likely to experience *further* violence whilst visibly homeless in the urban environment (Murray 2011). Women who experience visible homelessness may remain in violent relationships to feel physically safer. Also, homeless young women are more likely than young men to leave home due to sexual abuse (Rosenthal et al. 2006). Watson (2011: 639) interviewed young women in Australia about 'survival sex' and found that young women experiencing homelessness are 'subject to the pressures of individualisation that have been produced by the neoliberal policies of Western capitalist societies', in which they 'are required to find individual solutions to structural problems'. She argues that survival sex occurs within a context of gendered discourses and young women's sense of personal responsibility for managing their own situations (Watson 2011: 639).

Exclusionary Urban Policies

Although urbanisation can involve a process of constantly re-creating possibilities and opportunities over time and space, urban areas can also be hostile places for people who experience homelessness and also other excluded groups (Casey et al. 2008: 914). Stories encountered by social workers in their daily practice are multi-faceted and responses to homelessness vary from locality to locality. Yet, European author Van Eijk (2010) notes that 'urban policies in Western countries have become harsher towards marginalised groups', who are often 'ethnic minority groups' (Van Eijk 2010: 820), constituting representations of who are the privileged and marginalised groups in urban settings. Mehrotra (2010) argues that, globally, social work must increasingly incorporate discussions on migration, diaspora and nationality into their analyses.

Using Rotterdam—the second largest city in the Netherlands—as an example, Van Eijk (2010: 820) argues that economic considerations of the 'neoliberal city' are intertwined with 'ideas about multiculturalism and integration', which focus on 'national unity' and 'demands for social order'. He provides the example of how, in 2005, the Dutch national government implemented a law entitled 'Special Measures for Urban Issues' (nicknamed the 'Rotterdam Act') that 'allows municipal governments to exclude people who depend on social security (apart from social security for the elderly) and cannot financially support themselves and who have not lived in the municipal region in the preceding six years, from the rental housing market in so-called problem areas' (Van Eijk 2010: 823). He argues that 'mixed neighbourhood' policies and strategies focus primarily on 'the integration of ethnic minorities' and that 'all measures to regulate the city population are substantiated by concerns and statistics about the spatial concentration and social segregation of ethnic minorities' (Van Eijk 2010: 824). Paradoxically, these strategies that 'in effect exclude minority groups from certain places' actually aim to include particular groups 'into mainstream society' (Van Eijk 2010: 830). These policies and strategies create new forms of displacement and homelessness that target particular ethnic minority groups, presenting challenges (and opportunities) for the social work profession to contest cultural hegemony (Gramsci 1971), in the spirit of increasing respect and appreciation for diversity.

After the expansions of the European Union (EU) in 2004 and 2007, there is evidence that growing numbers of migrants from within EU countries are presenting to homeless services. Data from railway station programmes piloted by 'L'agence nouvelle des solidarites actives' (ANSA) in Paris (Gares du Nord and L'Est), Brussels (Central Station), Rome (Termini), Berlin (Zoo Station) and Luxembourg (Station) indicate that there has been an increase in European homelessness statistics (ANSA 2011: 71–73) of 'foreigners' or 'undocumented migrants' from new EU countries (including Roma), as well as Latin American, Asian and African countries. Larger cities, such as London, have always attracted significant numbers of migrants, who are then unable to find affordable housing. In her study of homeless migrants, Mostowska (2014: 19) found that, in London, '52 per cent of rough sleepers were migrants, 21 per cent of the homeless in Copenhagen were foreign born and, in Dublin, 19 per cent were non-Irish (with 40 per cent of unknown nationality)'. Migrants are particularly vulnerable to homelessness because of smaller support networks; limited access to legal, housing and employment rights; lack of knowledge of welfare systems; financial and language barriers and dependence on 'sponsor' migration (Mostowska 2014: 19). These issues differ from traditional ideas about the causes of homelessness being related to addictions and psychiatric problems, lack of affordable housing and labour markets conditions

(Fitzpatrick et al. 2012). Increasingly, social workers in urban homeless services are encountering people with diverse support needs that require different skills, knowledge and responses.

Practice Tensions for Social Workers

Social work responses to urban homelessness aligned with social justice and human rights are complex in this contemporary urban environment. Responses to homelessness are provided by governmental and non-governmental services, and all service providers will potentially come across people who experience homelessness. Whilst there has been a increasing trend to use the criminal justice system to respond to people living in urban spaces and public places, social workers are amongst advocates that promote a human rights approach to addressing homelessness (Jones 2013). A 'good city' (Gleeson 2014) can be enhanced by social work's contribution to social action and advocacy that benefits people who experience homelessness.

The increasing complexity of homelessness in contemporary urban contexts challenges social workers to reconsider traditional individualist responses to homelessness. Social work responses to homelessness are constituted by economic, social and political conditions in different countries, as well as organisational contexts within which social workers are employed (Zufferey 2008). How social workers frame homelessness has implications for what interventions are promoted. In Europe, Mostowska (2014) used an interpretive frame analysis to examine social workers' perspectives when working with homeless migrants in European cities. She found that different countries promote different frameworks, such as 'migrant worker' overlaid with an 'exceptional humanitarianism' framework in Copenhagen, compared with an 'undisciplined deviant' frame in Dublin (Mostowska 2014: 18). In this discourse analysis of social work interventions, Mostowska argued that the humanitarian framework, which is less focused on economic efficiency and deviancy, allows social work service providers to express professional values and ethics more aligned with their profession (Mostowska 2014: 19). For example, social workers can construct 'counter-discursive strategies' to promote discourses that are 'less essentialising of ethnic difference' and can point to the positive contributions of migrants (Williams and Graham 2010: 159). As Mostowska (2014: 24) notes, social workers can engage in 'submissive' strategies that are compliant with the state regulations (such as excluding persons from a city shelter with no personal documents and number), as well as 'subversive' strategies that undermine state regulations, which tends to involve informal co-operation between different organisations. She emphasises 'innovative' strategies in Copenhagen that seek more 'structural', long-term solutions for homeless migrants, including funding migrant-specific programmes with private funds, campaigning, advocacy and change-focused research (Mostowska 2014: 25).

Changing urban contexts and homeless populations require holistic social work models of practice, with a wider knowledge base, intercultural skills and increased training in cross-cultural issues (Casey 2014). On the one hand, social workers are implicated in processes that discriminate, individualise, pathologise, essentialise and replicate dominant practices that reinforce social divisions and unequal power relations (Zufferey 2008; Mostowska 2014). On the other hand, the social work profession has a powerful role in publicly questioning the impact of contemporary neoliberal trends on people who experience homelessness, advocating *for* and *with* people experiencing, or 'at risk' of, homelessness (Zufferey 2008: 368). Social work practice informed by human rights and social justice involves a social work 'activism' that occurs in dialogue with service users, not from a position of 'professional elitism' (Yeatman 1998: 33). Although collective action, social inclusion and social cohesion are variously interpreted (Williams and Graham 2010), social work advocacy can involve (re-)interpreting regulations, critical thinking and questioning dominant ideology, guided by social work values and ethics (Mostowska 2014). This way of practising would enhance how social workers are involved in the innovative responses to homelessness currently available to social work in Western cities. The Housing First initiative is one example of a current innovation that aims to intervene more holistically to end chronic, urban homelessness.

Housing First Approaches

In Western cities across the world, innovative policy and practice responses to chronic and visible homelessness have included funding Housing First initiatives. Housing First approaches differ considerably from treatment first approaches that presume chronically homeless individuals cannot maintain their housing until they address their support needs. Treatment first modalities have long been supported by clinical and other professional bodies, who typically viewed housing as outside of their ambit of responsibility, which has included social workers. European authors argue that the Housing First approach requires a 'mind shift' for social workers employed in the field of homelessness because it assumes that people who experience homelessness should be housed as soon as possible and receive immediate intensive support (Benjaminsen 2014: 12). Housing First models promote stable housing as a basic human right and argue that other issues—such as medical, mental health, drug and alcohol, education and employment—can be addressed *whilst* an individual is permanently housed.

The Housing First model was developed by Beyond Shelter Inc. in 1988 in Los Angeles and Pathways to Housing in New York in 1990 (Tsemberis 2010). It is widely promoted as an effective solution to chronic homelessness. The Housing First (or Housing Led) approach, known as the 'Housing First Europe' project, was trialled in ten European cities—Amsterdam, Budapest, Copenhagen, Glasgow, Lisbon, Dublin, Gent, Gothenburg, Helsinki and Vienna—from August 2011 to July 2013 (Benjaminsen 2014). In Canada, the five-year 'At Home/Chez Soi' project was launched in five diverse cities—Vancouver, Winnipeg, Toronto, Montreal and Moncton (2009–2013)—which aimed actively to address the housing needs of people with mental illness who were experiencing homelessness. Following the same principles as the Canadian and American projects, in 2010, the French government launched a Housing First programme in four major cities called 'Un Chez-Soi d'abord' focusing on people with mental illness, or addicted to drugs or alcohol.

There has been some contestation about the efficacy and cost effectiveness of Housing First approaches. In New York, Culhane et al. (2002)

were the first to evaluate the cost effectiveness of permanent supportive housing for people who experience homelessness and have severe
mental illness. Evaluations have found that Housing First substantially
reduces cost in other sectors, such as demand for emergency shelter, frequency and length of hospitalisation, and time in prison (Culhane et al.
2002; McLaughlin 2011). However, the cost reductions generally do not
fully offset the costs of providing Housing First services, except for a
minority of cases of the highest costed chronically homeless individuals.
Nonetheless, these evaluations provided evidence that chronically homeless individuals who receive Housing First interventions can maintain
their housing and have high housing retention rates, which challenges
previously held views. European authors argue that Housing First initiatives enable social workers to promote a proven model for practice
that adheres to 'good practice' techniques and support standards, which
includes obtaining the satisfaction of service users (Bezunartea Barrio
2014: 15). McLaughlin (2011) examined homeless people's service usage
data in the state of Maine, USA, and found that permanent, supported
housing saves money in all categories, with the exception of housing. He
concluded that 'the most humane approach of providing housing is also
the most cost-effective' (McLaughlin 2011: 410).

European authors have argued that, prior to Housing First, social
workers assumed that people who were homeless needed to be made
'housing ready' before they were housed (Benjaminsen 2014: 12). This
approach required people to access treatment prior to being housed and
to move into crisis, temporary and transitional housing (Benjaminsen
and Dyb 2010; Benjaminsen 2014: 12). Housing First approaches
involve a 'change in the balance of power between service providers and
service users' that is often found in institutional settings, such as large
inner-city homeless shelters (Benjaminsen 2014: 12). Social workers participating in Housing First initiatives consider housing as a basic human
right and are required to be familiar with housing policies, civil rights and
immigration legislation that focus on 'guaranteeing the rights' of people
who experience homelessness (Bezunartea Barrio 2014: 15). Consistent
with social work Codes of Ethics globally, social work skills in this field
of homelessness include communication, reflexivity, showing warmth,
empathy, respect, compassion, respecting people's self-determination,

being non-judgemental and developing trusting relationships (British Association of Social Workers 2002; IFWS 2005; National Association of Social Workers 2008; AASW 2010; Bezunartea Barrio 2014: 15). These social work values and ethics guide social workers on how to be involved in community-based developments, social mobilisation and collective action, to respond respectfully to urban homelessness and to advocate against breaches of human rights and the criminalisation of homelessness (Bezunartea Barrio 2014: 15).

In Australia, there has also been a shift in the way homelessness services are now delivered. Advocates argued that more social housing was needed and that Housing First and other models reliant on integrating support with existing mainstream rental housing were unfeasible in Australia because of the tight housing market (Parsell et al. 2013: 17). Australia's response to homelessness included building supportive accommodation facilities such as Common Ground and the Foyer Model for young people experiencing homelessness. The Foyer was originally developed in France to provide for young people moving from rural areas to the city to find work; it was adopted by the UK in the 1990s; first established in Australia in 2003, and was costed and evaluated by Australian researchers (Steen and Mackenzie 2013). Common Ground was founded in Time Square, New York City, in the 1990s by Rosanne Haggerty, with the aim of ending chronic homelessness (Parsell et al. 2013: 3). As Parsell et al. (2013: 8) note, 'the scale and speed with which Common Ground has been adopted across virtually all of Australia, and the level of resources committed from across public and private sectors, is unprecedented'. Common Ground was successfully framed as an innovative idea that encompassed 'permanently ending homelessness', as well as 'fostering socially mixed communities in inner city neighbourhoods' (Parsell et al. 2013: 8). Crucial to the Common Ground model is the engagement with and attraction of funding by 'business and philanthropic sectors' to social housing, which in Australia had been previously 'dominated by the state and traditional welfare paradigms' (Parsell et al. 2013: 8). High-level political advocates and advocacy coalitions—such as the Australian Common Ground Alliance (ACGA)—drove the implementation of the Common Ground international policy transfer, following the New York approach. These key advocates emphasised professional intuition and personal experience, rather than formal evaluations such as randomised control trial (RCTs) research (Parsell et al. 2013: 6).

Alongside Common Ground models were assertive outreach initiatives—such as Street to Home services—that focus on assertively outreaching to 'rough sleepers' with the aim of identifying, prioritising, assessing, referring, supporting and housing vulnerable people who are living 'on the streets'. Typically, 'rough sleepers' in urban locations have been a particular 'target for policy and practice intervention' (Parsell 2011: 330). Parsell (2011: 330–339) outlines differences in outreach models in the Australian context. Traditional models of outreach to 'rough sleepers' provide people with blankets, food and so forth—but not housing. Indigenous approaches focus on 'return to country' strategies that move Aboriginal people out of city locations back to their remote communities of origin. Assertive outreach responses—such as Street to Home initiatives—aim to end homelessness by permanently housing people and providing support to increase housing retention rates. Parsell (2011: 339) argues that assertive outreach interventions are 'consistent' with the principles of social work because they involve respect for individual self-determination, as well as a commitment to social justice and collective advocacy, such as advocating for access to affordable housing.

Lastly, it must be acknowledged that homelessness in the city occurs within social systems that contribute to increasing poverty and homelessness, such as the decline in welfare social safety nets and affordable housing, along with discrimination and violence (Noble 2015). Therefore, it remains important for social workers to advocate for systemic and social change to prevent homelessness and to intervene early to assist people who are at risk of experiencing homelessness, or are actually in that situation. Prevention, systems reform and early intervention approaches are central to social work advocacy and intervention. There are a number of prevention strategies that aim to combat homelessness; these tend to focus on city localities (Cloke et al. 2007; Sandberg, 2013). Social work responses to homelessness require simultaneous measures at different levels, which include innovative social policy initiatives and targeted action aimed at preventing, reducing and ending homelessness. The primary prevention of homelessness includes national housing plans that either provide increased social housing, or facilitate access to social housing for people who are homeless. Secondary prevention may involve reducing numbers of evictions, or intervening to prevent homelessness for people who are leaving prisons, mental health facilities, or hospitals. Tertiary prevention includes the reduction in the number of people who are chronically homeless, such as through Housing First initiatives and by improving the current service networks by providing access to health care and employment, as well as housing (Evangelista 2013: 162–163). Social work responses to urban homelessness therefore include advocating for the prevention of homelessness, challenging policies and practices that breach human rights and social justice, and intervening to house people with complex needs who are chronically homeless.

Conclusion

This chapter examined contemporary urban conditions that constitute urban homelessness and social work in Western cities. Responses have tended to focus on the deficiencies of homeless people, rather than the constraints that marginalised and poor people face in maintaining and/or accessing affordable housing. The Housing First initiatives have shown that access to housing is central to resolving homelessness. Social workers can assist to re-orientate homelessness programmes to focus on these broader structural constraints. Social work responses to visible homelessness have always been associated with the city and urban locations. Social workers can advocate for and contribute to a 'good city' that improves and ameliorates the situation of people who experience homelessness. Social workers have the potential to be 'submissive' to state regulations that respond to homelessness through the surveillance and policing of people who are visibly homeless, which can potentially breach human rights and increase social inequalities (Zufferey 2008; Mostowska 2014). However, social workers can also resist and be 'subversive' towards disrespectful urban policies, by undermining state regulations and practices that do not benefit people who experience homelessness (Zufferey 2008; Mostowska 2014). This chapter reinforces the advocacy and social change mandate of the social work profession that would resist and subvert disrespectful responses to homelessness, and promotes 'innovative' initiatives that seek more 'structural', long-term solutions to homelessness (Mostowska 2014).

Acknowledgements   I would like to thank Guy Johnson and Juliet Watson for their insightful comments and helpful suggestions for improving this chapter.

References

AASW (Australian Association of Social Workers). (2010). Code of ethics. Retrieved from http://www.aasw.asn.au/practitioner-resources/code-of-ethics

Amster, R. (2003). Patterns of exclusion: Sanitizing space, criminalizing homelessness. *Social Justice, 30*(1), 195–221.

Amster, R. (2008). *Lost in space: The criminalization, globalization, and urban ecology of homelessness.* New York: LFB Scholarly Publishing.

ANSA (L'agence nouvelle des solidarites actives). (2011). *HOPE in stations: Homeless people in European train stations. Preliminary scientific analysis.* Paris: ANSA.

Benjaminsen, L. (2014). 'Mindshift' and social work methods in a large-scale housing first programme in Denmark. In FEANTSA Magazine *Social work in services with homeless people in a changing European social and political context* (pp. 12–13). Brussels: European Federation of National Organisations Working with the Homeless (AISBL).

Benjaminsen, L., & Dyb, E. (2010). Homelessness strategies and innovations. In E. O'Sullivan, V. Busch-Geertsema, D. Quilgars, & N. Pleace (Eds.), *Homelessness research in Europe* (pp. 123–142). Brussels: FEANTSA.

Bezunartea Barrio, P. (2014). Social workers: Challenges and contributions to housing first support programmes. In FEANTSA Magazine *Social work in services with homeless people in a changing European social and political context* (pp. 14–15). Brussels: European Federation of National Organisations Working with the Homeless (AISBL).

Blau, J. (1992). *The visible poor. Homelessness in the United States.* New York: Oxford University Press.

British Association of Social Workers. (2002). The code of ethics for social work. Retrieved from http://cdn.basw.co.uk/membership/coe.pdf

Casey, B. (2014). Education and training provision for homeless sector workers: Contexts, benefits and challenges. In FEANTSA Magazine *social work in services with homeless people in a changing European social and political context* (pp. 6–9). Brussels: European Federation of National Organisations Working with the Homeless (AISBL).

Casey, R., Goudie, R., & Reeve, K. (2008). Homeless women in public spaces: Strategies of resistance. *Housing Studies, 23*(6), 899–916.

Cloke, P., Johnsen, S., & May, J. (2007). The periphery of care: Emergency services for homeless people in rural areas. *Journal of Rural Studies, 23,* 387–401.

Culhane, D. P., Metraux, S., & Hadley, T. (2002). Public service reductions associated with placement of homeless persons with severe mental illness in supportive housing. *Housing Policy Debate, 13*(1), 107–163.

Doherty, J., Busch-Geertsema, V., Karpuskiene, V., Korhonen, J., O'Sullivan, E., Sahlin, I., Tosi, A., Petrillo, A., & Wygnańska, J. (2008). Homelessness and exclusion: Regulating public space in European cities. *Surveillance & Society, 5*(3), 290–314.

Donley, A. M., & Wright, J. D. (2012). Safer outside: A qualitative exploration of homeless people's resistance to homeless shelters. *Journal of Forensic Psychology Practice, 12*(4), 288–306.

Evangelista, G. F. (2013). Prevention, homelessness strategies and housing rights in Europe. In S. Jones (Ed.), *Mean streets. A report on the criminalisation of homelessness in Europe* (pp. 159–168). Belgium: European Federation of National Organisations Working with the Homeless. Brussels: FEANTSA.

Fitzpatrick, S., Johnsen, S., & Bramley, G. (2012). Multiple exclusion: Homelessness amongst migrants in the UK. *European Journal of Homelessness, 6*(1), 31–57.

Forrest, R. (1999). The new landscape of precariousness. In P. Kennett & A. Marsh (Eds.), *Homelessness: Exploring the new terrain* (pp. 17–36). Bristol: Polity Press.

Gleeson, B. (2014). *The urban condition.* Abingdon/New York: Routledge.

Gramsci, A. (1971). *Selections from the prison notebooks of Antonio Gramsci* (Q. Hoare & G. N. Smith, Trans.). New York: International Publishers.

IFSW (International Federation of Social Workers). (2005). Ethics in social work: Statement of principles. Retrieved from http://ifsw.org/policies/code-of-ethics/

Jencks, C. (1994). *The homeless.* Cambridge, MA: Harvard University Press.

Jones, S. (Ed.). (2013). *Mean streets. A report on the criminalisation of homelessness in Europe.* Belgium: European Federation of National Organisations Working with the Homeless (FEANTSA), Housing Rights Watch, European Federation of National Associations Working with the Homeless (AISBL).

Kennelly, J., & Watt, P. (2011). Sanitizing public space in Olympic host cities: The spatial experiences of marginalized youth in 2010 Vancouver and 2012 London. *Sociology, 45*(5), 765–781.

Kennett, P. (1999). Homelessness, citizenship and social exclusion. In P. Kennett & A. Marsh (Eds.), *Homelessness: Exploring the new terrain* (pp. 37–60). Bristol: Polity Press.

Lefebvre, H. (1991). *The production of space*. Malden: Blackwell.

McLaughlin, T. C. (2011). Using common themes: Cost-effectiveness of permanent supported housing for people with mental illness. *Research on Social Work Practice, 21*(4), 404–411.

McLoughlin, P. (2013). Couch surfing on the margins: The reliance on temporary living arrangements as a form of homelessness amongst school-aged home leavers. *Journal of Youth Studies, 16*(4), 521–545.

Mehrotra, G. (2010). Toward a continuum of intersectionality theorizing for feminist social work scholarship. *Affilia, 25*(4), 417–430.

Mostowska, M. (2014). 'We shouldn't but we do …': Framing the strategies for helping homeless EU migrants in Copenhagen and Dublin. *British Journal of Social Work, 44*(suppl 1), i18–i34. First published online 12 May 12 2014. doi:10.1093/bjsw/bcu043.

Murray, S. (2011). Violence against homeless women: Safety and social policy. *Australian Social Work, 64*(3), 346–361.

Myers, N. (2002). Environmental refugees: A growing phenomenon of the 21st century. *Philosophical Transactions of the Royal Society of London B: Biological Sciences, 357*(1420), 609–613.

National Association of Social Workers. (2008). Code of ethics. Retrieved from http://www.socialworkers.org/pubs/code/code.asp

Noble, A. (2015). *Beyond housing first: A holistic response to family homelessness in Canada*. Toronto: Raising the Roof (www.raisingtheroof.org).

Parsell, C. (2011). Responding to people sleeping rough: Dilemmas and opportunities for social work. *Australian Social Work, 64*(3), 330–345.

Parsell, C., Fitzpatrick, S., & Busch-Geertsema, V. (2013). Common ground in Australia: An object lesson in evidence hierarchies and policy transfer. *Housing Studies*. doi:10.1080/02673037.2013.824558.

Passaro, J. (2014 [1996]). *The unequal homeless men on the streets, women in their Place*. London: Routledge.

Randolph, B. (2004). The changing Australian city: New patterns, new policies and new research needs. *Urban Policy and Research, 22*(4), 481–493.

Rosenthal, D., Mallett, S., & Myers, P. (2006). Why do homeless people leave home? *Australian and New Zealand Journal of Public Health, 30*(3), 281–285.

Rossi, P. (1989). *Without shelter. Homelessness in the 1980s.* New York: Priority Press Publications.

Sandberg, L. (2013). Backward, dumb, and violent hillbillies? Rural geographies and intersectional studies on intimate partner violence. *Affilia: Journal of Women and Social Work, 28*(4), 350–365.

Steen, A., & Mackenzie, D. (2013). *Financial analysis of foyer and foyer-like youth housing models.* Melbourne: Swinburne Institute for Social Research: Swinburne University and Commonwealth of Australia.

Stevenson, D. (2013). *The city.* Cambridge, UK: Polity Press.

Tonkiss, F. (2003). The ethics of indifference. Community and solitude in the city. *International Journal of Cultural Studies, 6*(3), 297–311.

Tonkiss, F. (2013). *Cities by design. The social life of urban form.* Cambridge, UK: Polity Press.

Tsemberis, S. (2010). *Housing first. The Pathways model to end homelessness for people with mental illness and addiction.* Center City: Hazelden.

Van Eijk, G. (2010). Exclusionary policies are not just about the 'neoliberal city': A critique of theories of urban revanchism and the case of Rotterdam. *International Journal of Urban and Regional Research, 34*(4), 820–834.

Wacquant, L. (2008). *Urban outcasts. A comparative sociology of advanced marginality.* Cambridge, UK: Polity Press.

Watson, J. (2011). Understanding survival sex: Young women, homelessness and intimate relationships. *Journal of Youth Studies, 14*(6), 639–655.

Williams, C., & Graham, M. (2010). Travelling hopefully: Race/ethnic relations and social work: A transnational dialogue. *European Journal of Social Work, 13*(2), 155–161.

Wright, T. (1997). *Out of place: Homeless mobilizations, subcities, and contested landscapes.* Albany: State University of New York Press.

Yeatman, A. (Ed.). (1998). *Activism and the policy process.* Sydney: Allen & Unwin.

Zufferey, C. (2008). Responses to homelessness in Australian cities: Social worker perspectives. *Australian Social Work, 61*(4), 357–371.

10

Living on the Edge: New Forms of Poverty and Disadvantage on the Urban Fringe

Sonia Martin and Robin Goodman

Introduction

The spatial distribution of areas of relative wealth and poverty within cities varies and all cities display some kind of differentiation of prosperity and experience. These are often well-entrenched and well-acknowledged; however, rapidly growing cities in the 21st Century are showing a dynamism that may challenge long-held understandings of locations of disadvantage. Like cities around the world, Australian cities have always exhibited disparate patterns of wealth and disadvantage and, historically, for much of the 20th Century and prior to the 1960s–70s, low-income earners typically resided in the inner city while the majority lived in sprawling suburban

S. Martin (✉)
School of Global, Urban and Social Studies, RMIT University,
Melbourne, VIC, Australia

R. Goodman
School of Global, Urban and Social Studies, RMIT University, Melbourne,
VIC, Australia

© The Editor(s) (if applicable) and The Author(s) 2016
C. Williams (ed.), *Social Work and the City*,
DOI 10.1057/978-1-137-51623-7_10

comfort. Economic, social and demographic changes in recent decades, however, have seen major shifts in these established patterns with traditional working-class areas becoming elite gentrified neighbourhoods with sky-rocketing property prices. As the cities have continued to expand outwards, a significant issue of housing affordability has pushed low-income families to the urban fringe. There is growing concern that the physical distance from central cities is creating new forms of exclusion and disadvantage.

These new patterns of spatial differentiation have particular implications for how disadvantage is identified and understood, how social policy can respond, and the new forms of human service intervention these spatial forms of disadvantage may warrant. For social workers, who have a long history of working with disadvantaged communities, these changes also present new opportunities and challenges. In order to respond to this changing context, greater awareness of the importance of place, its characteristics, its advantages and limitations is needed. A more spatially aware approach to practice may be enhanced by greater collaboration with urban and regional planners in the allocation of resources and a stronger focus on advocacy for better infrastructure and service provision. Such an approach is especially pertinent, as the public and community welfare sectors are increasingly operating within a climate of retraction that constrains workers' capacity to work in more innovative and creative ways in public and third sector human service organisations.

These issues are explored in three parts. In the first part of the chapter, we examine the spatial distribution of disadvantage in Australia, drawing on the recent work of Burke and Hulse (2015) to discuss three inter-related forms of spatial disadvantage. In the second part, we explore the ways in which the three forms come together to create particular challenges and opportunities for human service provision in outer-urban areas. This discussion is extended in the third part, which focuses more specifically on social work and argues that greater consideration of the ways in which urban spaces shape disadvantage is needed for the profession to better respond to new and emerging forms of spatial disadvantage. While the focus of the discussion is on Australia, the findings have theoretical, policy and practice relevance to other countries seeking to respond to spatial disadvantage in a context of changing urban forms. Many of the changes in patterns of wealth and disadvantage experienced in Australia's largest cities will be shared by other cities, particularly in Europe, which are accommodating growth by outward expansion, while their inner cities gentrify.

Shifting Terrain: The Profile of Disadvantage in Urban Australia

The vast majority of Australia's almost 24 million inhabitants live in the city and surrounding metropolitan areas. In 2011, almost 80% of Australians lived in the major cities, with nearly 70% residing within the eight capital cities (ABS 2015a). Of the capital cities, Melbourne is the fastest growing, increasing its population by 9% in the five years 2008–2013, compared with a growth rate in Sydney, Australia's largest city, of just under 8% for the same period (ABS 2015a).

Over time, the pattern of wealth and disadvantage in Australia has altered and the depth of inequalities has become more marked. In 2013–14, Australia's Gini coefficient—which is a measure of inequality ranging from 0 where income or wealth is evenly distributed to 1 where it is held by one person—was 0.333 compared with 0.302 in 1994–95 (ABS 2015c). The picture of inequality is largely one of wealth accumulation. In 2011–12, the wealthiest 20% of households in Australia accounted for 61% of total household net worth, compared with the 20% of households with the lowest net worth, who accounted for only 1% (ABS 2015c).

Inevitably, these distributions of income and wealth are spatially pronounced. While the provision of key services—such as schools and policing by state rather than local government in Australian cities, and the expansion of the welfare and health systems over the last century—has moderated spatialised class divisions, patterns of advantage and disadvantage nonetheless existed and were well-known, visible and fairly entrenched. These variations created areas of working-class pride or stigma (depending on your viewpoint), and a clear indication of places to which welfare and other services could be directed. The older patterns of comparative advantage have been overlaid with new distributions determined primarily by proximity to centres of employment and services, mainly in central cities. While some areas may be clearly identified as long-standing places of disadvantage, other areas have undergone significant changes and are not as easily identifiable as either advantaged or disadvantaged. These changing patterns may be attributable to a range of factors, including a massive move in employment; manufacturing (which had been largely suburbanised) has declined or disappeared, and the advanced service sectors which prefer central locations have grown (Kelly et al. 2014; DIRD 2015: 65–70). The Australian Government's annual State of Australian Cities Report for 2014–15 (DIRD 2015: 48) noted this trend, stating that the 'outward movement of disadvantage and population is occurring concurrently with an inward concentration of higher-order jobs, placing many residents far from the opportunities of the inner city'.

Today's knowledge-intensive economy is specialised, globally connected and dependent on a workforce of highly skilled employees. Location in central business districts (CBDs) and inner suburban areas gives these businesses the best access to this workforce. A recent Grattan Institute report confirms that central cities are the powerhouses of the Australian economy. This presents a challenge for policy, however, as 'too many workers live too far away to fulfil our cities' economic potential' (Kelly et al. 2014: 1). There are very few jobs on the urban fringe, a consequence of constructing residential communities with little space for anything else.

Gentrification of the inner cities is also an important contributing factor to spatial differentiation as demand for inner city housing, which previously was the domain for the poor and working class, pushes up property prices and pushes those without the capacity to pay further out (Atkinson et al. 2011). Beginning in the 1970s, old working-class housing was refurbished and, from the late 1980s, a new wave of middle-class settlement in and around the CBD occurred (Mullins 2000, in Murphy et al. 2011: 53). Additionally, changes in lifestyle preferences—the favouring of areas better endowed with shops, restaurants, social and recreational opportunities, and better served by public transport—have added to these trends. Australians in full-time employment work increasingly long hours, and it is partly the phenomenon of these time-poor workers, along with generational cultural change, that has fuelled the popularity of 'café culture'. All of these trends have increased the value of central locations to the point at which most inner and middle suburbs have serious housing affordability problems. While, clearly, some people choose to live in outer suburban or rural communities for lifestyle or other reasons, for many people housing affordability constrains choice and effectively forces them to reside in areas away from services and facilities, which has a direct negative impact on them and their family's welfare and well-being:

> Australia's cities are now increasingly characterised by the significant spatial divide between areas of highly productive jobs and the areas of populations based services ... urban fringe areas are becoming more distant from many of the established employment, education and health opportunities. (DIRD 2015: 41)

This view of changing spatial patterns been supported by a number of recent studies including that of Burke and Hulse (2015: 2) who find that 'spatial disadvantage in Australian cities is now increasingly an outer-suburban problem'. The authors make a useful distinction between differing ways in which areas might be considered to be disadvantaged. They suggest that there are three distinct forms of spatial disadvantage identified in the literature. Firstly, there is the *concentration of poverty*, which is identified predominantly by concentrations in a location of low-income households. Secondly, there is *disadvantage of resource access*, which can be identified as an area relatively deficient in resources such as employment, education, services and public transport. Thirdly, there are areas that have a *spatial concentration of social problems*, such as crime, substance abuse and domestic violence (Burke and Hulse 2015: 3).

An area could exhibit all of these characteristics, but it may not. An area that is disadvantaged by poor resourcing might have lower housing costs due to its lower market appeal, thereby attracting greater numbers of lower-income households. But whether a concentration of low-income households leads to a concentration of social problems depends upon a variety of factors including the extent of change within an area, and the resources and opportunities available to households, over time. As Burke and Hulse (2015) point out, Australian cities have actually shown a higher degree of dynamism and change than their counterparts in the UK and USA. This is, in part, explained by the fact that, while they had concentrations of poverty and some concentrations of social problems, they were not disadvantaged in terms of access to resources:

> From the 1950s to the 1970s Australian households, including the very poorest in the inner cities, had resource advantages which today's outer-urban poor may not have. The best hospitals, some of the best schools, good libraries, most university campuses and excellent public transport were on the doorstep of or located in so-called disadvantaged inner areas, and the nature of federal/state funding meant that this was not eroded over time. These areas were concentrations of low-income people but certainly were not areas of resource disadvantage! (Burke and Hulse 2015: 12)

The three types of spatial disadvantage provide a useful frame for further investigating the new forms of poverty emerging on the urban fringe, and we apply these to the discussion that follows.

Concentrations of Poverty

The picture of inequality in Australia is reflected in estimates of relative poverty. Cross-nationally, of the 31 developed nations identified by the OECD in its 2012 estimates, Australia ranked 24th highest with 14% of its population in relative poverty. While lower than the United States (17.9%) it was higher than the United Kingdom (10.5%), and much higher than the Scandinavian countries (OECD 2015). There is marked variability within Australia, with Tasmania showing the highest levels, at 15.1% in 2011–12, as well as significant differences in household types with single parent families showing the highest rates at 19.3% (Phillips et al. 2013). In Melbourne, Victoria, demographic patterns are most clearly displayed in a series of maps compiled for the government using Australian Bureau of Statistics census data referred to as the Social Atlas (DTPLI 2015). It shows a clear and repeated pattern of relative concentrations of higher-income, tertiary-educated, professionally employed households in the inner and middle-ring suburbs, with a few exceptions, and lower-income households, recent immigrants and those with lower levels of education primarily concentrated in outer urban areas.

A major determinant of the income profile of residents of an area is the cost of housing. In Australia, the vast majority of housing is supplied by the private sector with public housing available only to the sections of the population most in need. The majority of people own, or are purchasing, their own home (67%), or rent in the private rental market (26%) (ABS 2011). The largest Australian cities have been experiencing a housing affordability crisis as average house prices have been rising at a much greater rate than average incomes for several decades. Property price increases have been by far the most extreme in Sydney, which saw an annual increase of 18.9% for the year to June 2015, while the figure for Melbourne for the same period was 7.8% (ABS 2015b). In Melbourne, the median house price more than doubled from A$190,000 to A$500,000 between 2000 and 2011 (or by 263%). Over the same period, the average wage increased by only 64%, (A$42,500 in 2000 to A$66,500) (DTPLI 2013). The differential rises in wages and property prices can be partly attributed to taxation policies that encourage investment in property by offering tax deductions for costs associated with rental property. As house prices have increased, purchasing a home has become increasingly difficult for many on low to middle incomes (Yates and Berry 2011), with high housing costs in the inner and middle areas pushing many towards the fringe. The cost of housing is not only creating differentiated markets across the metropolitan area, but also movement between them is becoming more difficult as the gaps between expensive and cheaper areas increase. As Hulse and Pinnegar (2015: 22) have noted, there is now 'reduced mobility between housing markets within our metropolitan areas, and disadvantage increasingly enshrined and embedded as a function of distance and location'.

A recent analysis, prepared as part of the latest Victorian state government metropolitan plan (DTPLI 2014), shows the income needed to afford housing in different parts of Melbourne. The authors find that 'In 1994, a household on an average income could purchase a dwelling within 10 kilometres of the CBD [which] moved to 24 kilometres in 2000 and 40 kilometres by 2009' (DTPLI 2014: 65). Their analysis clearly illustrates the differential impact of rising property prices and incomes on affordability, and shows that only the outer areas of Melbourne are affordable to those on moderate to low incomes. A similar pattern of affordability is evident for those renting with affordable rental accommodation also concentrated in outer urban areas. In 2011–12, average housing costs were 44% higher in capital cities than outside capital cities (ABS 2013) and, in 2013, only 10% of rental properties were affordable to those in receipt of Centrelink payments (DTPLI 2014). As shown in Fig. 10.1, living on the urban fringe does not necessarily mean households will avoid financial stress.

The type of property and its suitability for different household types is also a significant factor in the choices available to those on low incomes. Another analysis, considering housing options for single women, showed that only one suburb—Melton, some 37 kilometres from the CBD—had two-bedroom rental properties for less than one third of the average female income (Perkins 2015). The Council to Homeless Persons submission to the Family Violence Royal Commission on domestic violence showed that the only affordable locations for single women were outer suburbs predominantly on the urban fringe (CHP 2015). While public housing in Australia is more affordable than private rentals, with those renting from state and territory housing authorities paying 19% of their average income on housing costs in 2011–2012 (ABS 2013), it is not

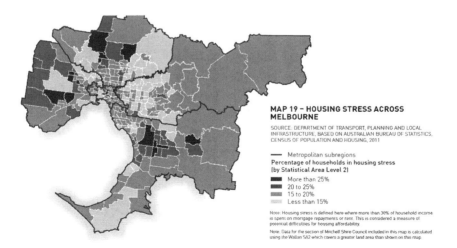

MAP 19 – HOUSING STRESS ACROSS MELBOURNE

SOURCE: DEPARTMENT OF TRANSPORT, PLANNING AND LOCAL INFRASTRUCTURE, BASED ON AUSTRALIAN BUREAU OF STATISTICS, CENSUS OF POPULATION AND HOUSING, 2011

—— Metropolitan subregions
Percentage of households in housing stress (by Statistical Area Level 2)

■ More than 25%
▨ 20 to 25%
▨ 15 to 20%
▨ Less than 15%

Note: Housing stress is defined here where more than 30% of household income is spent on mortgage repayments or rent. This is considered a measure of potential difficulties for housing affordability.

Note: Data for the section of Mitchell Shire Council included in this map is calculated using the Wallan SA2 which covers a greater land area than shown on this map.

Fig. 10.1 Housing stress across Melbourne (*Source:* Department of Transport, Planning and Local Infrastructure 2014, p. 65)

widely available and waiting lists are extensive, with some having been on the list for more than ten years. In Melbourne, for example, there were nearly 206,000 applicants on the waiting list for government-funded social housing in mid-2014, and 46% of public rental housing applicants classified as in greatest need spent more than two years on a waiting list (AIHW 2015). Housing choices are being increasingly constrained and there is a growing number of Australians who are being locked out of home ownership and into relatively less secure and desirable accommodation, and still others who are finding it increasingly difficult to find any suitable accommodation options whether in state housing or private rental and find themselves homeless and/or reliant upon families, friends and charities.

Some people make deliberate decisions to relocate from inner city areas to more affordable outer areas knowing they are reducing their prospects of finding employment but feeling they have little choice. This is captured in the account of a middle-aged woman, collected as part of a large study into the lived experience of welfare, who explained high rent prices were 'pushing' her further out from the city centre and away from services and employment (Murphy et al. 2011: 53–54). The same study illustrated the anguish some mothers faced relocating to more affordable areas and away from their own networks and those of their children. Capturing the insecurity felt by many of the single-mother participants, Edna commented, 'moving your children around and disconnecting your children from their school, from their friends, is devastating', while Josephine conveyed the angst of ensuring her 'children are properly housed' (Murphy et al. 2011: 58).

Disadvantage of Resource Access

Places that provide access to fewer resources—such as employment, education, services and public transport—are locations that disadvantage their residents, identified by Burke and Hulse as the second characteristic of spatial disadvantage.

Arguably the most important of resources to which people need access is employment. While it might be the goal of many planning strategies to encourage a distribution of jobs and employment opportunities across the metropolitan area of cities, in reality this is often beyond the control of governments. Good planning can ensure that infrastructure which could be needed by industry is in place, and that sufficient land is available for industrial or commercial businesses to start up, the centralising preferences of many high-tech and advanced industries seem hard to sway. Spiller (2014: 364) analysed the number of jobs within a 30-minute drive or a 45-minute public transport ride from an inner suburb and a fringe suburb in Melbourne. He found that a resident of the fringe suburb could reach just 16% of total metropolitan jobs by car, compared with 41% for residents of the inner suburb and— more staggeringly—that only 0.2% of total metropolitan jobs could be reached by public transport from the fringe suburb compared with 33% for the inner resident. Spiller noted that access to jobs is a proxy for access to services, as, for example, jobs in the health sector at a location meant the provision of health services. He concluded that, due to the great expansion of suburbs away from the city centre and its jobs, 'the suburban fringe generation of today has relatively few choices compared with their counterparts of 20 or 40 years ago' (2014: 365). This is confirmed by Kelly et al. (2014: 24), who showed that access to jobs falls away rapidly with distance from the CBD and in 'in some outer suburban growth areas of Melbourne just 10% of Melbourne's jobs can be reached within a 45 minute drive'.

Governments can, however, ensure that transport provision is such that residents have greater access to jobs beyond those in their immediate neighbourhood. Cheshire et al. (2014: 49) note the compounding effects of economic, service and transport deficits in their recent report on place disadvantage in Australia, commenting that 'in places in which local economic opportunities are scarce or inaccessible, transport connectivity to more "healthy" economies is critical for the capacity of residents to access opportunities for education, training and employment'.

A Parliamentary Inquiry by the Victorian state government in 2012 into Liveability Options in Outer Suburban Melbourne found that inadequate public transport infrastructure was the issue on which it received the most evidence (OSISDC 2012: 280). The experience of commuting was captured in a study of life in ten different Australian suburbs (Williams et al. 2009: 15). For many people interviewed long hours commuting was time taken away from more important pursuits such as spending time with their families, as well as being expensive in real terms (Williams et al. 2009: 15). Women, in particular, reported that the necessity to work far from their homes and children placed them under stress, and that working close to where their children were located during the day was important. As a consequence, the women were more likely to settle for less desirable or poorly paid jobs closer to home that enabled them to reduce the need for travel. For those unable to find work locally, the authors found that 'Many workers (particularly women) reduce their days at work, cut back their employment or find they must 'downshift' in terms of careers, skills and promotional opportunities when they find the commuting cost of quality jobs is just too high in both time and money' (Williams et al. 2009: 16). Somewhat ironically, the savings made in purchasing a cheaper house on the urban fringe might soon be reduced or eliminated by having to take reduced wages or pay greater fuel costs.

A compelling analysis of the combined effects of mortgage stress and high transport costs was undertaken by Dodson and Sipe (2007), who proposed a Vulnerability Assessment for Mortgage, Petrol and Inflation Risks and Expenses (VAMPIRE) index. The authors found that people living on the fringes of Australian cities are facing increased challenges due to higher transport costs and lower incomes, creating greater areas of vulnerability to future cost rises. In the large capital cities of Brisbane, Sydney and Melbourne, it is generally those households that are located in socioeconomically disadvantaged and car-dependent outer-suburban locations that will be most vulnerable to current high and potential future rising petrol prices. By comparison, those localities in central and inner areas will be relatively less socioeconomically disadvantaged as a result of rising fuel prices given the location of employment, particularly for high waged sectors, which is concentrated in the CBD of most Australian cities (Dodson and Sipe 2007: 57). This finding of vulnerability to the price impacts of travel costs was confirmed by Delbosc and Currie (2011: 1137) who found that, despite high levels of car ownership—94% on the urban fringe compared with 79% for in the inner suburbs—residents in fringe areas were significantly more likely to say they could not do some of the activities they wished to do because of transport problems (Delbosc and Currie 2011: 1136). Most of these missed opportunities were 'social and leisure activities including a small but significant number of missed opportunities for work. This may have a downstream influence on well-being or social exclusion' (Delbosc and Currie 2011: 1136).

Social Problems

The third characteristic of spatial disadvantage described by Burke and Hulse (2015: 3) is 'the areas that have a disproportionate incidence of problems that society sees as unacceptable'. Here, disadvantage includes crime, drug addiction, domestic and other violence, unemployment, vandalism and anti-social behaviour. In Australia, research has focused primarily on concentrations of income poverty, rather than concentrations of social problems. This is, in part, because the spatial visibility of social problems is not as apparent as it is in some areas within the United States—such as the housing projects in Chicago, or parts of some European cities—and where discussions and debates about urban ghettoes and 'an underclass' are more prolific. It may also be because spatial areas within Australia are much more dynamic and areas that were once sites of concentrated poverty are no longer because they have become gentrified (Burke and Hulse 2015: 6).

A recent study by Vinson and Rawsthorne (2015) is the most comprehensive examination of locational disadvantage across Australia that draws on a variety of, albeit limited, data sources. One of the challenges of undertaking research into spatial trends in Australia is the limited availability of geographically referenced social data, especially when compared with the social data sets available in other countries including the United States. While the picture of neighbourhood disadvantage within specific localities remains incomplete, what the authors' have achieved is significant. Notably, their study revealed concentrations of cumulative and persistent indicators of disadvantage in areas across Australia, including unemployment, long-term unemployment, criminal convictions, domestic violence, confirmed child maltreatment and low-income (Vinson and Rawsthorne 2015). They concluded that disadvantaged localities feature prominently in rural areas and on the fringes of metropolitan areas, but their analysis does not explicitly differentiate outer-urban areas—new and established—from the other geographic areas.

Family violence is a significant social problem that is receiving considerable attention, not just in Australia, but also in other developed countries. The World Health Organization (WHO) has as one of its areas of concern a reduction in violence against women (WHO 2015) and a recent review of family violence law in Australia recommends it be defined as 'violent or threatening behaviour or any other form of behaviour that coerces or controls a family member or causes that family member to be fearful' (Australian Law Reform Commission 2010). There is a groundswell of activity in Australia including a national parliamentary inquiry (2014) and Victorian royal commission (2015), public demonstrations and television campaigns aimed at increasing community awareness and improving responses to incidents.

Family violence is not confined to specific geographical areas and, while it is present in affluent areas, it is much more pronounced in lower socioeconomic areas. Higher rates in the outer suburban and rural areas are apparent, and indigenous women are more likely to experience violence, and more serious violence, than non-indigenous women (Vinson and Rawsthorne 2015: 38–39), even though the available data is limited and subject to under-reporting. As Whitzman (2014) points out, unlike inner-urban areas and capital cities, outer suburbs concentrate three types of risk. Women who are pregnant or with young children are most at risk of violence and often find it difficult to escape violence; housing stress exacerbates family tensions and a lack of affordable housing means women have limited alternative housing options; and, outer suburbs generally lack the social support services needed to address family violence (Whitzman 2014). Good urban planning in outer urban areas, Whitzman argues, includes wraparound services that involve schools, legal aid, specialised court services and counselling, emergency housing and assistance, rather than simply water, sewers, roads and rubbish collection.

There is evidence that other forms of violence and social disorder are concentrated in particular geographic locations. Adult and juvenile offending, for example, is spatially concentrated in Victoria, with 25.4% of those remanded coming from just 2.2% of 726 postcodes in 2008–

2010, while 25% of prison admissions in 2003 came from just 2.1% of the 647 postcodes (Vinson and Rawsthorne 2015: 60).

Discussions and debates about 'neighbourhood effects', predominantly arising from the United States, draw attention to concentrations of social problems in particular locales, and their visibility and influence on residents and the local community. In the Australian literature, there is acknowledgement of the cumulative effects of a range of indicators on well-being and the ways in which one form of disadvantage can reinforce the impact of one or more other sources (for example, Vinson and Rawsthorne 2015: 10), but there are reasons to be concerned about identifying specific localities as sites of disadvantage as it influences the perceptions of the people who live there. Kelaher et al. (2010), for example, explored the stigmatising effects of poor neighbourhoods on the identity of residents and their health. While Arthurson (2013), in her work on social housing and social mix, commented on the anticipated benefits of social mix in Australian policy that may lower area-based stigma and create more inclusive communities, while emphasising neighbourhood-based problems rather than 'neighbourhood effects'.

Combining the Attributes: A New Area of Concern for Human Services

Not all areas that are considered disadvantaged within cities will show signs of each of the three characteristics. It is the combination that is of particular relevance here, and the causal links between one attribute and another. As we identified earlier, Burke and Hulse (2015) have argued that areas of spatial disadvantage in Australian cities have not been as entrenched and severe as some of their US and UK counterparts; in part, because they were not disadvantaged in terms of access to resources. So, poorer areas which had concentrations of poverty did not necessarily also have entrenched social problems because access to resources enabled people to move out of poverty more easily.

There are real reasons to be concerned, however, that this fortunate situation could be changing. All the evidence we have presented so far suggests that the provision of vital infrastructure, resources and services is critically lacking in the existing outer suburbs, as well as the new suburbs being constructed on the fringes of Australian cities. This suggests that the planning for these suburbs has been sadly lacking, and that the economic and social implications of poor planning need far more attention.

A report by the Grattan Institute (Kelly et al. 2012), *Social Cities*, argues that social needs are not being adequately addressed in the planning of Australian cities. It suggests that neighbourhood cohesion and social connections have diminished in recent decades, a trend that is worsening as more people live on their own (Kelly et al. 2012). Cities, the report argues, should be better planned and built to increase connectedness by enabling greater interaction through an efficient urban transport system and more walkable communities, with improved mobility and reduced time spent on commuting. Not enough attention is given to designing and providing for places of human interaction. 'We need to give greater weight to social connection in the way we build and organise our cities', including paying greater attention to accessibility and the creation and maintenance of public spaces and community centres (Kelly et al. 2012: 49).

The community or 'third' sector continues to play an important role in meeting the needs of individuals and families in regions across the country. One recent initiative undertaken by a large not-for-profit organisation, the Brotherhood of St Laurence, aims to tackle the less visible forms of disadvantage in one new housing development on the fringe of Melbourne. The organisation provides services through the Jindi Family and Community Centre, which provides maternal and child health care, community rooms, a kindergarten and long-hours child care. Part of the workers' role is to listen to the community and to respond to the stories of isolation and stress, and, for some, loneliness and depression, and to provide appropriate support (Green 2015). While the service may appear simply an add-on to the planned council-funded services, it is important to note that the organisation's presence was part of a deliberate strategy to respond to the changing face of suburban disadvantage in Melbourne (Green 2015). It is an initiative that is complementary to other place-based work being carried out by the organisation, but it is a developing area of practice for the agency and other similar third sector organisations. The differential visibility of disadvantage within urban areas and a fragmented or absent sense of disadvantage in outer urban areas, means that the most appropriate location of services is no longer as obvious to human service organisations as it once was. There is, thus, substantial scope for governments and human service organisations to respond in more innovative ways.

Yet the capacity of the community sector to actively engage in seeking innovative solutions to social problems is increasingly being constrained. Warning of the implications of recent changes, Nicholson (2014) and Smyth (2014) argue that the increasing marketisation of social services undermines the community development functions of the community welfare sector as agencies increasingly operate as 'business rivals' more involved in delivering services for government than they have historically. The Shergold report (2013), the product of a Victorian government commissioned project into community and human service sector reform, is criticised for its 'near exclusive focus on the role of the [community] sector as a contracted service provider for government, to the neglect of its other functions' (Smyth 2014: 7). The community sector, in Shergold's view, includes for-profits alongside not-for-profit organisations in a sector he calls 'public economy', and should become more 'businesslike' and 'entrepreneurial' (Smyth 2014: 7). Commenting on the 'over-extension of the market economy into the social sphere', Smyth continues:

> In this framework, voluntary organisations do not seek to complement government action alongside the market as in the 'welfare state' or 'social investment state'. Rather the framework seeks to dispense as far as possible with the role of government as provider of social services on the basis of citizenship entitlements, while promoting in its place privatised services in a market economy on the basis of 'user pays'…. Market failure and excessive inequality are simply wished away. (Smyth 2014: 9)

Given the level of government commitment to the market sphere and to private enterprise, it seems unlikely that the profile of outer-urban disadvantage is likely to change anytime soon, and there is a real risk of further entrenching spatialised inequalitites. All of these factors have implications for meeting the service needs of disadvantaged communities in outer metropolitan areas and for how human service workers, including social workers, respond. It is this latter group to which we now turn our attention.

Rethinking 'Urban Social Work'

Social workers have long been involved in the provision of services and support to disadvantaged communities and the individuals and families that inhabit disadvantaged areas, and their capacity to respond to this new environment is informed by their organisational context of practice and the nature of their role. Social workers occupy a range of positions across public, private and third sector organisations and the various positions they hold may or may not be specifically named as 'social work' roles. Those employed in community organisations, such as the Brotherhood of St Laurence mentioned above, or in local government may have more scope to engage directly in issues relating to spatial disadvantage than those social workers who do not. Arguably, however, the issues we have raised about the extent and nature of outer-urban disadvantage have implications for all social work practitioners and for the ways in which they understand and carry out their work.

There is a considerable body of social work literature that explicitly acknowledges the ways in which geographic location shapes disadvantage, but this is largely confined to a focus on rural and regional social work. As noted by Shaw (2011: 11), social work research 'has had little to say about engagement of social work and urban life'. Similarly, Geldof (2011) reflects on the increasing ethnic diversity in Europe and explores the distinct challenges these changes present for developing an urban social work. He argues that social work in urban areas differs from that in less urbanised areas on the basis of larger urban scales, which means that social workers may not be familiar with clients and their networks, enhanced concentrations of social problems that may reinforce the disadvantage of an area's inhabitants, and the existence of more complex networks with which workers are required to cooperate (Geldof 2011: 30). Rather than suggesting Australian social work has little concern with place, it is likely to reflect social work's normalised view of social work as urban. Limited specific attention to the spatial dimensions of practice—aside, perhaps, from that in rural and regional areas—suggests that social work may be blind to the specific spatial attributes and differential needs of urban areas, how these might be changing and the opportunities for different forms of practice.

The challenge for social work is how to adapt existing practices to new and emerging spatial needs in a manner that reflects the social justice mandate of the profession. Both the International Federation of Social Workers (IFSW) and the Australian Association of Social Workers (AASW) make explicit professional commitments to the pursuit of human rights and social justice as fundamental principles of practice (AASW 2010; IFSW 2015). But the capacity of the profession to pursue these ideals comes with a number of core challenges, including the often conflicting roles of controlling or managing social problems, and meeting organisational objectives of efficiency and cost effectiveness. Worker experiences of these tensions will vary according to organisational context and the nature of their role but, by and large, there is no easy resolution to these difficulties and they are issues with which many workers continue to grapple. Moreover, as capacity of the profession to pursue its social justice mandate is being increasingly constrained by neoliberal policy priorities, there is a real risk that the change mandate of the profession will continue to be eroded in spite of its intentions.

We propose a form of 'urban social work' that takes into account these two main challenges: how to better respond to the new spatial forms, and how to respond in a manner commensurate with the professions social justice mandate. We suggest that an approach to practice that draws practitioner consciousness to the contemporary needs of urban areas and facilitates greater awareness of the built environment and the importance of working collaboratively with urban planners in the allocation of resources be developed. Good planning and good social work practice pay attention to three inter-related factors: concentrations of poverty as reflected in the income profiles and housing costs of particular geographic areas; differential access to resources, which means that workers advocate for adequate infrastructure to support access to jobs and services; and, the nature and extent of social problems within particular urban areas. It is the ways in which these three factors coalesce that leads to entrenched disadvantage within particular geographic areas, as noted by Burke and Hulse (2015). The challenge for social work is to respond in ways that acknowledge these factors alongside their capacity to act in a context of market forces and resource constraints for social services.

Closer collaboration between the two professions of social work and urban planning would present a stronger voice advocating that greater attention needs to be paid to the social and economic implications of deficiencies in the built environment. Strategies for collaboration must include greater individual and community consultation in the development and implementation phases of new housing estates and master-planned communities. The strategies are commensurate with community development practices that aim to 'engage with communities in ways that empower communities to *take collective responsibility* for their own development' (Kenny 2006: 10, in Bay 2012: 24). But, in order to do this, adequate resourcing needs to be put in place beforehand and the problem in new urban areas is often that they are simply too far away and too disconnected to be able to provide the level of services needed. While many master-planned estates offer better amenities within them than earlier basic subdivision that characterised the development of many Australian suburbs, the focus on internal design may have distracted planners from more fundamentally important needs. Social workers can remind them of the importance of connectedness to jobs, transport, education facilities, as well as various health and social services.

Conclusion

Planning and social work share a commitment to equity, yet this often comes second—if at all—to pragmatic and cost concerns in the planning process. Urban development in countries such as Australia is dominated by the needs of the private sector who undertake it and who predominantly find the provision of new houses on greenfield sites easier and less costly to build than infill development in existing areas. Governments also play an important role and one that extends beyond the provision of appropriate levels of infrastructure, including transport and access to jobs, as well as social services for new suburbs. There has been a history of state governments acting simply as a 'rubber stamp' for developers, with significant social impacts that undermine their social and economic responsibilities to citizens and their well-being. While ensuring adequate resourcing and infrastructure is in place and taking a more active stance in the development and planning phases may be politically undesirable and expensive, the long-term economic and social consequences of creating sites of entrenched disadvantage are even more significant. The effects on individuals and communities in outer-suburban areas will continue to be considerable, while Australia's profile of inequality will become increasingly segregated on the basis of geography. Challenging the standard practice of the private sector for principles of equity and fairness is difficult, and compounded by a context of encroaching marketisation of human services that serves to constrain social work advocacy, yet it is not beyond the power of either profession. In fact, it is part of the fundamental values at the historic heart of both and a point on which they might find common purpose.

References

AASW (Australian Association of Social Workers). (2010). *Code of ethics.* Canberra: AASW.

ABS. (2011). Census of population and housing. http://www.abs.gov.au/websitedbs/censushome.nsf/home/data?opendocument#from-banner=LN. Accessed 2 Sept 2015.

ABS. (2013). Housing occupancy and costs, 2011–2012, 4130.0.

ABS. (2015a). Population clock, 3235.0. http://www.abs.gov.au/ausstats/abs@.nsf/0/1647509ef7e25faaca2568a900154b63?OpenDocument. Accessed 31 Aug 2015.

ABS. (2015b). Residential property price indexes: Eight capital cities, 6416.0. http://www.abs.gov.au/ausstats/abs@.nsf/mf/6416.0. Accessed 7 Oct 2015.

ABS. (2015c). Household income and wealth Australia, 2013–14, 6523.0. http://www.abs.gov.au/ausstats/abs@.nsf/Lookup/by%20Subject/6523.0-2013-14-Main%20Features-Income%20and%20Wealth%20Distribution-6. Accessed 11 Sept 2015.

AIHW (Australian Institute of Health and Welfare). (2015). Demand for housing assistance grows: More seeking rent assistance and social housing waiting lists remain long. http://www.aihw.gov.au/media-release-detail/?id=60129551198. Accessed 1 Sept 2015.

Arthurson, K. (2013). Neighbourhood effects and social cohesion: Exploring the evidence in Australian urban renewal policies. In D. Manley, M. Van Ham, N. Bailey, L. Simpson, & D. Maclennan (Eds.), *Neighbourhood effects or neighbourhood based problems? A policy context.* Dordrecht: Springer Science and Business.

Atkinson, R., Wulff, M., Reynolds, M., & Spinney, A. (2011). *Gentrification and displacement: The household impacts of neighbourhood change* (Rep. No. 160). Australian Housing and Urban Research Institute.

Australian Law Reform Commission. (2010). *Family violence: A national legal response* (ALRC Report 114 (5.167)). Canberra: Australian Government.

Bay, U. (2012). Making a living in diverse rural and remote communities. In J. Maidment & U. Bay (Eds.), *Social work in rural Australia: Enabling practice*. Crows Nest: Allen & Unwin.

Burke, T., & Hulse, K. (2015). Spatial disadvantage: Why is Australia different? *AHURI Report.* ISBN: 978-1-922075-70-3. Melbourne: Australian Housing and Urban Research Institute.

Burke, T., Stone, J., Glackin, S., & Scheurer, J. (2014). *Transport disadvantage and low-income rental housing* (Positioning paper 157). Melbourne: Australian Housing and Urban Research Institute.

Cheshire, L., Pawson, H., Easthope, H., & Stone, W. (2014). *Living with place disadvantage: Community, practice and policy* (*AHURI final report* No. 228). Melbourne: Australian Housing and Urban Research Institute.

CHP (Council to Homeless Persons). (2015, March). Submission to the Family Violence Royal Commission. http://chp.org.au/policy/submissions/. Accessed 11 Oct 2015.

Delbosc, A., & Currie, G. (2011). The spatial context of transport disadvantage, social exclusion and well-being. *Journal of Transport Geography, 19,* 1130–1137.

DIRD (Department of Infrastructure and Regional Development). (2015). *State of Australian cities 2014–15, Progress in Australia's regions*. Canberra: Commonwealth of Australia.

Dodson, J., & Sipe, N. (2007). Oil vulnerability in the Australian city: Assessing socioeconomic risks from higher urban fuel prices. *Urban Studies, 44*(1), 37–62.

DTPLI (Department of Transport, Planning and Local Infrastructure). (2013). Metropolitan planning strategy—Fact sheets: Sources of data. http://www.planmelbourne.vic.gov.au/__data/assets/pdf_file/0012/130332/330_60_5-Sources-of-Data-11052012.pdf. Accessed 12 Sept 2015.

DTPLI (Department of Transport, Planning and Local Infrastructure). (2014). *Plan Melbourne: Metropolitan planning strategy*. Melbourne: Victorian Government.

DTPLI (Department of Transport, Planning and Local Infrastructure). (2015). Social atlas of Melbourne Geelong and regional cities. http://www.dtpli.vic.gov.au/data-and-research/population/census-2011/social-atlas. Accessed 11 Oct 2015.

Geldof, D. (2011). New challenges for urban social work and urban social work research. *European Journal of Social Work, 14*(1), 27–39.

Green, S. (2015, August 29). Fraying on the fringe: Dealing with disadvantage in Mernda. *The Age Newspaper.* http://www.theage.com.au/victoria/fraying-on-the-fringe-dealing-with-disadvantage-in-mernda-20150825-gj6zrf.html. Accessed 1 Sept 2015.

Hansen, R. (2012). A tale of two Melbournes? The disparities of place and how to bridge the divide, *Sambell Oration to the Brotherhood of St Laurence*, 27 November 2012. Melbourne: Brotherhood of St Laurence.

Hulse, K., & Pinnegar, S. (2015, January). Housing markets and socio-spatial disadvantage: An Australian perspective. *AHURI Report.* http://www.ahuri.edu.au/publications/download/ahuri_myrp704_rp6h. Accessed 1 Sept 2015.

IFSW (International Federation of Social Workers). (2015). Statement of ethical principles. http://ifsw.org/policies/statement-of-ethical-principles/. Accessed 2 Sept 2015.

Kelaher, M., Warr, D. J., Feldman, P., & Tacticos, T. (2010). Living in 'Birdsville': Exploring the impact of neighbourhood stigma on health. *Health and Place, 16*, 381–388.

Kelly, J., Breadon, P., Davis, C., Hunter, A., Mares, P., Mullerworth, D., & Weidmann, D. (2012). *Social cities.* Melbourne: Grattan Institute.

Kelly, J., Donegan, P., Chisholm, C., & Oberklaid, M. (2014). *Mapping Australia's economy: Cities as engines of prosperity.* Melbourne: Grattan Institute.

Murphy, J., Murray, S., Chalmers, J., Martin, S., & Marston, G. (2011). *Half a citizen: Life on welfare in Australia.* Crows Nest: Allen & Unwin.

Nicholson, T. (2014). The future of the community welfare sector, Speech, 27 May 2014. Fitzroy: Brotherhood of St Laurence.

OECD. (2015). Poverty rate (indicator). http://www.oecd-ilibrary.org/content/indicator/0fe1315d-en. Accessed 11 Sept 2015.

OSISDC (Outer Suburban/Interface Services and Development Committee). (2012). *Inquiry into liveability options in outer suburban Melbourne.* Melbourne: Parliament of Victoria.

Parliament of Australia. (2014). Domestic violence in Australia, Senate Finance and Public Administration References Committee. http://www.aph.gov.au/Parliamentary_Business/Committees/Senate/Finance_and_Public_Administration/Domestic_Violence. Accessed 18 Sept 2015.

Perkins, M. (2015, April 29). Women fleeing violence only able to afford one suburb in Melbourne: Melton. *The Age Newspaper,* Melbourne.

Phillips, B., Miranti, R., Vidyattama, Y., & Cassells, R. (2013). *Poverty, social exclusion and disadvantage in Australia.* Canberra: NATSEM.

Royal Commission into Family Violence. (2015). http://www.rcfv.com.au/. Accessed 18 Sept 2015.

Shaw, I. (2011) Social work research—an urban desert?, European Journal of Social Work, 14:1, 11-26.

Shergold, P. (2013). *Service sector reform: A roadmap for community and services reform*. Melbourne: Victorian Department of Premier and Cabinet and Victorian Council of Social Services.

Smyth, P. (2014). The lady vanishes: Australia's disappearing voluntary sector, Presentation, Brotherhood of St Laurence, 14 August. Fitzroy: Brotherhood of St Laurence.

Spiller, M. (2014). Social justice and the centralisation of governance in the Australian metropolis: A case study of Melbourne. *Urban Policy and Research, 32*(3), 361–380.

Vinson, T., & Rawsthorne, M. (2015). *Dropping off the edge 2015: Persistent communal disadvantage in Australia*. Australia: Jesuit Social Services and Catholic Social Services.

Whitzman, C. (2014). Urban planning offers path out of domestic violence, *Opinion, The Drum*, posted 23 April 2014. http://www.abc.net.au/news/2014-04-23/whitzman-urban-planning-and-a-path-out-of-domestic-violence/5406644. Accessed 29 Aug 2015.

WHO (World Health Organization). (2015). Violence and injury prevention. http://www.who.int/violence_injury_prevention/violence/sexual/en/. Accessed 11 Sept 2015.

Williams, P., Pocock, B., & Bridge, K. (2009). *Linked up lives: Putting together work, home and community in ten Australian suburbs*. Adelaide: Centre for Work and Life, University of South Australia.

Yates, J., & Berry, M. (2011). Housing and mortgage markets in turbulent times: Is Australia different? *Housing Studies, 26*(7–8), 1133–1156.

11

Educating for Urban Social Work

Susie Costello and Julian Raxworthy

Introduction

With predictions of The Urban Age bringing 75% of the world's populations into cities by 2050 (Gleeson 2014), governments, businesses, academics and professionals will confront unprecedented 'wicked issues' of rapid urban growth, poverty, food insecurity and biodiversity loss on a global scale. Academics have a role in preparing graduates to work collaboratively in multi-stakeholder partnerships to consider and shape the consequences of rapid urban growth on vulnerable people. Yet, stakeholders from different disciplinary origins often see things differently

S. Costello (✉)
School of Global Urban and Social Studies, RMIT University, Melbourne, VIC, Australia

J. Raxworthy
University of Cape Town, Cape Town, South Africa

© The Editor(s) (if applicable) and The Author(s) 2016
C. Williams (ed.), *Social Work and the City*,
DOI 10.1057/978-1-137-51623-7_11

259

'engendering value conflicts and struggles over the definition of and approach to the problem' (Dentoni and Bitzer 2015: 69). This chapter argues that collaboration between social workers and colleagues from the built environment is necessary in the face of the wicked problems of the city. Social work's Global Agenda themes of social justice, sustainability and inclusiveness (Jones and Truel 2012) urge social workers to give people a voice in the urban-living decisions that will affect them.

This chapter, highlights first some commonalities and differences between social work, urban planning and landscape architecture in contributing to social processes of city making and design. Drawing on experiences in one Australian city, Melbourne, it reports ideas generated in a focus group discussion between urban planning and social work academics co-located within the same school. A case study involving social work and landscape architecture students working together on a project on a public housing estate identified challenges for interdisciplinary student planning projects. The chapter concludes with suggestions for interdisciplinary education for social workers and students of the built environment.

Synergies Between Social Work and Urban Planning and Landscape Architecture Disciplines

A brief overview of social work, urban planning and landscape architecture disciplines' professional bodies outlines the different and overlapping knowledge and skills for these programs.

The International Federation of Social Workers (IFSW) defines social work as:

> a practice-based profession and an academic discipline that promotes social change and development, social cohesion, and the empowerment and liberation of people. Principles of social justice, human rights, collective responsibility and respect for diversities are central to social work (IFSW 2014: n.p.).

Social work:

engages people and structures to address life challenges and enhance well-being (IFSW 2014: n.p.)

and is:

underpinned by theories of social work, social sciences, humanities and indigenous knowledge (IFSW 2014: n.p.).

The Australian Association of Social Workers (AASW) accredits social work degrees to teach principles, knowledge and practices of direct practice plus macro approaches of:

partnerships, communities and groups; advocacy; community work; social action to address both personal difficulties and systemic issues, research, social policy development, administration, management, consultancy, education, training, supervision and evaluation to further human wellbeing and social development (AASW 2010: 9).

The Planning Institute of Australia (PIA) defines planning as a profession:

specifically concerned with shaping cities, towns and regions by managing land use, development, infrastructure and services [and by developing and implementing] plans and policies for the controlled use of urban and rural land … [planners] advise on economic, environmental, and social needs of land areas (PIA 2011: 17).

Techniques of planning include urban design and economic, social, environmental and transport planning (PIA 2011: 12), all of which have resonance with social work's macro aspects. Knowledge and skills required for social planning include:

knowledge of the main sources of information about communities, including census and survey data, basic demographic statistics, analysis and presentation and … principles and issues of social impact analysis. Skills include the production and implementation of social and cultural plans, the capacity to undertake basic primary and secondary data gathering and analysis, … assess the equity, health and social inclusion aspects of urban and regional plans and practices and … planning for social infrastructure and remediation of socio-spatial disparities (PIA 2011: 20).

Planning graduates are expected to be able to operate:

in a manner that respects cultural diversity, the need for equity in outcomes, with skills in working with 'hard to reach' populations in a diverse and globally oriented society (PIA 2011: 9–12).

The Australian Institute of Landscape Architects (AILA) describes their discipline as working alongside government and allied professions:

to improve the design, planning and management of the natural and built environment. [Landscape architects] combine theoretical and practical skills to balance environmental and human needs [in areas from regional planning and urban design right through to the design of streetscapes and small pocket parks. Landscape architects' education includes] fields such as design, drawing, construction, ecology, environment, geology, botany, urban theory, urban planning, land management and, like urban planning and social work, ethics, aboriginal culture and cultural resources... Landscape architects examine, resolve and articulate better ways to live in our complex, fast-changing world. They advance our cities and safeguard our natural environments (AILA 2015: n.p.).

Landscape architecture and urban planning students' practical classes take the form of studios where 'students visit sites, hand-draw, create models, use computer programs, and learn how to create spaces that respond to their social and environmental surroundings'. In design studios, students 'form ideas, collaborate with established design professionals and meet fellow students who will be future co-workers and collaborators' (AILA 2015: n.p.).

The three disciplines share professional standards and academic requirements for complex critical, strategic thinking and analysis for planning for human wellbeing. Underpinning each of these professions is a strong ethical value base of social inclusion, equity, community planning for remediation of social disparities and respect for diversity, culture and indigenous knowledge. Yet, we have not moved far from the situation that Sadan noted in 1997 (p. 177), that:

> almost no dialogue exists among the various professions engaged in community planning … community work, urban planning, macrosocial work, architecture, urban geography, community psychology, community psychiatry.

Interdisciplinary education can address a range of skills, from the interpersonal skills and dialogue needed in community development, to technical, design, economic and policy making skills of planning, architecture and social work.

Social work stands to gain considerably from such an interdisciplinary leap. For example, skills in social surveys, demographic mapping and impact assessment can assist social workers to document the living conditions of diverse vulnerable groups in order to advocate for social change. Hillier (2007) suggested that social workers should learn skills such as how to use geographic information systems (GIS), computer hardware and software used by urban planners and government departments to capture, integrate, map and analyse physical, built environmental spatial data. Using GIS, social workers can conduct community needs and assets, and map social trends to improve policy, practice and service delivery.

Similarly, Holland et al. (2011) propose a number of mixed methods for social workers to explore the inter-relationship between neighbourhoods and child and adult wellbeing, including the use of computer based mapping systems (GIS) to map the 'non-measurable properties of place, human experience, social hierarchies, power relations, and theoretical relationships that are of concern to critical geography' (Pavlovskaya 2006: 2015, in Holland et al. 2011). They describe mobile interviews that enable participants to take researchers through neighbourhoods on foot, to deepen their understanding of place as a physical environment and relationships. The walkways can be tracked on the mobile phone and have been used to build understandings of how to safeguard children in specific neighbourhoods (Holland et al. 2011).

Australian social work academic Tony Vinson and colleague Rawthorne have met Hillier's challenge and mapped the geographical distribution of disadvantage throughout Australia. Their data identifying Australian postcode communities with high social needs and concentrated disadvantage are critical resource materials for government, service providers, communities and scholars, social planners and social workers. Yet, planning is always a social political activity and interpretation of data depends on the worldview of the persons interpreting such data (Sadan 1997). A campaign in Melbourne used Vinson and Rawthorne's (2015) data as a basis to propose increased supervision, control and punishment for people from postcodes where criminal activities and prison admissions are high, rather than using the data correlates of poverty, unemployment, low family income, lack of internet access, low educational attainment, child maltreatment and domestic violence to plan for increased education, employment and support services in those postcode areas (Willingham 2015). A social work commentary could provide an alternative voice to this interpretation of data.

Studying the rationale of different theories that influence strategies of intervention is common territory of programs within the College of Design and Social Context at RMIT University in Melbourne, Australia. The college includes landscape architecture, social work and urban planning programs yet, despite 15 years of co-location, the disciplines have done little to realise the benefits of collaboration in education and research.

In a step towards increased collaboration between urban planning and social work, professors in the disciplines of social work and urban planning initiated a focus group discussion between their academics. The discussion focused on a set of questions about the disciplines' common histories and missions, academic locations and consideration of what prevents interdisciplinary collaboration and learning, each of which will be discussed.

The Focus Group

First, the focus group with social work and urban planning academics discussed common histories and missions in both disciplines' aspirations to 'improve' social conditions and the search for utopian model cities. The curricula in both academic programs include the history of the settlement movement, land, welfare and housing reforms, the aetiology and improvement of slum conditions, subsidised rent accommodation, the development of social housing and urban poverty (Holst 2006). Jane Addams (1860–1935), the social worker who inspired critical social work's origins, can be described as a social planner. Working in the USA in the late 1800s, Addams lobbied for basic infrastructure, sanitation, water, basic health care and housing to improve conditions for people migrating to the city. She argued that, rather than giving individual alms, social justice and social change can transform the plight of the poor.

A key planning text by Fincher and Iveson (2008) proclaims similar missions of justice and remediation in cities through three logics of social planning: redistribution to redress disadvantage, recognition to define the attributes of groups of people so their needs can be met and encounter planning for interaction and sociality. Where highways and public transport go and where development projects and parks are built reinforce the spatial differences of urban populations. As described by Vinson and Rawsthorne (2015), 'spatial sorting' (Lee et al. 2015b: 10) segregates groups of people by income and ethnoracial identity across postcodes in metropolitan areas, cities, suburbs, small towns, neighbourhoods and housing units; for example, by class and race. Fincher and Iveson (2008) reveal planners' synergies with social workers in considering the needs of diverse people to reduce inequality between people and places.

Second, as referred to elsewhere in this book, both disciplines engage in research to tackle social problems in the city. Social worker and planner team Castelino and Whitzman (2008) mapped and correlated higher incidences and impacts of domestic violence with sites of isolation and the lack of transport, services and police presence in the outer fringes of the city. Porter and Barry's (2015) case studies on indigenous communities in Australia and Canada remind us that urban development and nation-building have displaced and 'sought to eradicate Indigenous ownership presence and connection to cities' (p. 24). Holland et al. (2011) use spatially oriented social work research to explore the interactions between neighbourhoods and adult and child wellbeing in Chile, the USA and Wales. Further examples of collaborative social planning research appear elsewhere in this book.

Third, the focus group wondered what prevents greater collaboration between urban planning disciplines. The first constraint identified is professionals' lack of understanding of the scope of their own and others' professional roles. For example, the built environment focus of social planners in local government can mean they overlook the needs and concerns of citizens and not actively involve them in decision making processes that affect their wellbeing and quality of life (Hornby 2012). A planning academic in the focus group cited a case where planners approved an application for a religious building next to an established building of a different religion, which resulted in inter-religious community hostilities. Community consultation may have averted antagonistic community responses, or smoothed the way for reconciliation between the congregations, but consultation was not part of the brief. It may not even have been considered by the planners.

Atkinson et al. (2015) found that planners are restricted in their goals for interdisciplinary collaboration by the limit of their brief to physical issues. Urban planning academics in the focus group commented that council-employed planners do not think of social workers to conduct community consultation; they tend to choose community development workers. Even social work academics Hoatson and Grace (2002) called on community development workers, rather than social workers, to facilitate participatory processes for the review of public housing redevelopment. Social work academics in the focus groups agreed that planners can be seen as 'permit stampers' for developers, a misperception that planners are also concerned about. Whilst one aspect of planners' work is to scrutinise developers' building proposals through local councils and civil administrative tribunals, their roles are far broader, as described earlier. As this text shows, social workers' need greater understanding of material, visual and environmental aspects of the built environment.

The second constraint to interdisciplinary collaboration identified in the focus group was   the lack of social planning skills taught in social work education. This is not a new idea. In the 1970s, Cafferty and Krieg (1979) urged social work academics to equip students to be able to identify the impacts certain types of land development might have on vulnerable social groups. They berated social work's lack of training in social impact analysis and in the planning stages of land development projects that have social consequences. Cafferty and Krieg argued that social workers should be able to collect and interpret baseline information in order to increase planners' sensitivity to the social aspects of the physical parameters of clients' lives. An example of where a contextual planning perspective could have made a difference occurred when Melbourne's Federation Square opened at the end of 2002 without catering for access needs of people who use wheelchairs or infant strollers. This oversight is being addressed some 12 years later, involving rebuilding to accommodate a belated Disability Action Plan (Federation Square 2014).

Finally, the focus group acknowledged that it is not easy to forge links if your paths do not cross, so location within the academy is significant in positioning their program identity. In Australia, most social work programs are located within allied health sciences faculties, with a focus on clinical practice, rather than broader systemic issues of poverty, housing or politics. Similarly, most urban planning programs are located with physical and spatial design schools such as architecture, engineering or geography, rather than within social sciences. Despite the synergies between the two disciplines, an internet search for universities offering joint degrees in planning and social work reveal few options. In the USA, Columbia University in New York, the Universities of Detroit and Iowa, and the University of Southern California (USC 2015) offer specialities in Community Organization, Planning and Administration in their Masters of Social Work. The University of Michigan describes their Urban Planning course in social work as preparing students to work for social changes at the community level, developing skills in organising groups for social action, planning and developing community-based services and involving people in the planning process (Taubman 2015). The University of Michigan social work researchers (Holland et al. 2011) focus on the relationships of neighbourhoods to risks of substance use, parenting and child outcomes among racial minority populations.

In Europe, the School of Social Work in the Northwest Switzerland University of Applied Sciences and Arts runs an Institute for Social Planning and Urban Development (UASANS 2015). The Department of Sociology and Social Work at Aalborg University in Denmark runs a Master of Social Work degree course in urban development and settlement strategies (Alborg 2015). Flinders University's Bachelor of Social Work and Social Planning degree appears to be the only joint planning and social work degree in Australia.

The six participants in the focus group agreed that broader social perspectives in their curricula are needed for students to contextualise social problems in relation to place, space, community connections to land and the geography of the city. Despite overlapping domains, insufficient dialogue occurs between academics and students concerning the complex issues of the urban environment. Joint university educational programs for urban planners and social workers are not common, and most social work and urban planning students neither learn about each other's disciplines, nor realise their natural synergies. The following case study describes a project that offered an opportunity for students to learn about each other's disciplines.

The Case Study

This case study describes a project in which the authors supervised students from social work (Costello) and landscape architecture (Raxworthy) in a housing consultation and design project. The project was modelled on a successful interdisciplinary student project conducted at Waterloo housing estate in Sydney. Australia, led by social work academic and demographic mapper Tony Vinson (1997). The estate in Victoria comprises four 20 story towers, providing 800 two or three bedroom apartments (Roberts 2012). Rather than employ consultants from the private sector, the state government Office of Housing (OoH) established a partnership between the university and a community agency on the estate. The task for four social work students on a three-month field education placement was to consult with residents about their needs for redesigning the landscape of the estate, then pass on these views to 20 landscape architect students who would use the ideas to design landscape models in response. The OoH would then implement the plans, in ongoing consultation with landscape architect staff from the university.

Preparation

To orientate students who had not previously been on a public high-rise housing estate, the landscape architect academic facilitated a bus trip to visit estates around the city. This trip was an early defining moment of difference. On arrival at the first estate, landscape architecture students jumped off the bus with cameras, ready to photograph the estate landscape. Social work students, well-briefed in respectful and egalitarian ways of working with people, strongly challenged their taking photographs 'in people's homes without consent'. The social work academic's absence meant that the resultant questions about the rights of public housing residents compared with residents in private rental accommodation, and boundaries on an unfenced public housing estate were insufficiently examined as an interdisciplinary exercise. Griggs (2012) identifies such exploratory conversations as necessary to avert interdisciplinary wariness.

The project was coordinated by a Steering Committee comprising OoH bureaucrats, representatives from local welfare agencies, elected tenant representatives, other residents and interpreters, RMIT University supervising staff and social work students. The landscape architect students met weekly for a design studio, which meant that they were not on site when the Steering Committee meetings were held. A lack of clarity about the roles and responsibilities of the different parties made it difficult to know whether the purpose was to document residents' needs (social work students' agenda), design some possible plans (landscape architect students' agenda), or to improve the appearance of the landscape on the estate (state government's agenda). The unclear agenda was compounded by the academic agenda, where students were enrolled in university courses requiring an assessable outcome (Raxworthy and Costello 2012).

In a gesture to reduce students' outsider status and enhance their opportunity to understand the experience of living on the estate, the OoH made an apartment available on the housing estate as a student office during the day. The four social work students were to spend each day there, preparing for consultations with residents. Their task supervisor from the community agency worked off-site, and planned to meet with them once a week. She set them the task of furnishing the apartment themselves on a limited budget, as would residents. While this seemed like a good idea theoretically, it proved difficult to obtain the furniture and impeded the start of the project. Students experienced the accommodation as isolating and unsafe. Their occupancy upset some residents, who expressed concerns that students were using what could be someone's living space (Mansfield et al. 2001). The landscape architecture students had a different task and less presence on the estate. They used the apartment space for their design studio for two hours each week with their tutor present at all times, spending the rest of their time in computer laboratories on campus, mapping the estate, then designing physical responses to the social work students' summary of residents' suggestions.

Process of Consultation

Three impediments made the consultation process difficult: lack of safety on the estate, debates about the methods to be used, and lack of clarity about the different consultation roles of the landscape architecture and social work students.

The main impediment to obtaining residents' views regarding landscape improvements was the violence on the estate. Social work students very quickly became aware that residents' needs for safety and security were far greater than their needs for beautifying the landscape. Spending each day on the estate, social work students heard residents' stories of deprivation and danger, and were exposed to similar experiences of violence. Two students walked into a crime scene where a cleaner had been stabbed. Others witnessed men threatening each other with knives and guns over a drug deal outside their apartment office. Police responses to these incidents were slow and ineffective, and students were frightened and reluctant to remain on the estate. Their reporting of these events tended to be dismissed not only by representatives from local agencies who had developed immunity to reports of violence, but also by their academic supervisors.

The second impediment was the differences of opinion about methods of consultation, the only forum for resolution of which was Steering Committee meetings. To gain maximum resident participation, Steering Committee members wanted the social work students to access residents' views via door-knocking. Fresh from a semester on community development, advocacy and respectful consultative processes, social work students opposed door-knocking out of consideration for residents' privacy. Having spent time on the estate setting up their office apartment, social work students knew that territoriality was a significant issue, particularly for those involved in the drug trade, and that walking the floors would almost certainly make them targets for robbery and assault. They convinced the Steering Committee against door-knocking and, instead, developed, translated and posted flyers in five community languages at the base of each tower, inviting residents to a series of community barbeques on the estate where they would have opportunities to offer opinions to the landscape architect and social work students about the design project.

Overall, the students heard from 98 residents from diverse backgrounds and age groups, as well as local workers, and maintenance and security staff. Residents attributed the dangers to the freedom that drug traders had on the estate and they wanted the following changes: safe play areas for children, well-lit safe pathways and reduced bushes in order to see potential attackers. They requested 24-hour security presence to stop drug users injecting or dealing in the laundries, or coming onto the estate, and to stop vandalism, theft and abuse in the car park and estate grounds. They asked for diversity in the security guards' ethnicity so that residents from different language backgrounds could converse with them. Residents asked for improved rubbish removal, complaining about blood and saliva in stairwells and lifts, rubbish, broken glass and syringes in the grounds, vandalised barbeque and recreation areas, and poorly maintained buildings, lifts, gardens and grassed areas. They identified the need for a shop and spaces to fix their cars. A need for access to interpreters and translations was identified by residents who appreciated the translations provided for the community consultations.

The social work students became increasingly sceptical about the design aspect of the consultation project, which they conveyed to the landscape architect students. Discipline-specific jargon added to the difficulties of communication and, without a forum in which to explain terms of space, edge, form, or the place of empathy, voice and representation, students went about their businesses separately, thus missing the opportunity for interdisciplinary learning. Hillier (2007) ascribes one of social workers' roles in community planning as mediators, translating technical jargon into terms understandable to colleagues, clients and funders.

With a deadline to present models in order to pass their subject, the landscape architecture students continued with their designs. Some landscape students involved themselves in the consultations with residents and their designs responded to residents' ideas; for example, one design included car pits in the car parks; another, a supermarket in the base of one of the towers, as requested by a resident. Other plans were purely exercises in design, such as the idea of enclosing the estate with a moat to emphasis boundaries between public and private space, and designs for attractive but non-functional pathways and bench patterns. To the landscape architecture lecturer, these types of schemes represented theoretical tests of opposite scenarios in order to compare and contrast across the studio. Perhaps the student who designed a lake in the space between the towers had researched the potential for peace and restoration the presence of water can have, despite the potential hazards for small children, for example (Lee et al. 2015a). Designs that focused on solutions to residents' safety concerns involved lighting plans, changes in surfaces of playgrounds and meeting areas to reduce risk (such as replacing loose bark with a flat surface to avoid hidden syringes), reduction of vegetation and increased glassed sections for improved visual safety (Raxworthy and Costello 2012).

Outcomes of the Housing Design Project

The consultation and design project, and the landscape architects' final assessment for their subject culminated in an interactive design exhibition, held in a marquee on the housing estate, with interpreters, balloons and a barbeque. Landscape architect students presented, explained and heard feedback about their designs, displayed as balsa wood and cardboard models, drawings and plans (Mansfield et al. 2001). For the social work students, however, an incident on the day of the exhibition had a significant impact on the project. One of the social work students was held up at knifepoint and robbed on the estate on the way to the exhibition. The university terminated the social work fieldwork placement immediately. Police responded quickly to this report of violence and remained present on the estate for the following few days. During this time, residents reported a drop in the level of crime and violence, and a sense of increased safety. Social work students completed their placement on campus, writing and distributing their report (Mansfield et al. 2001) to the Steering Committee members and other interested parties.

A month later, the OoH organised a further exhibition to coincide with a visit to the estate by the state government Director of Housing. Despite the hot summer evening, the community hall was crowded with 60–70 residents and children. The models were displayed but the landscape architects students were not there to explain them, as the semester had finished. Social work students attended and gave some explanations of the plans and models. The process of consultations had made residents aware of their common complaints and about their rights to safety, and they were ready to challenge the OoH to do something about the violence, inadequacy of security, cleaning and maintenance needs on the estate.

Having read the social work students' report documenting residents' views of crime and violence on the estate, the Director of Housing responded to their concerns with a commitment to review the security, cleaning and maintenance contracts, inviting residents to apply for the positions. An immediate outcome was to fund neighbourhood action groups and tenants' associations. Security was increased to 24 hours per day seven days a week, and security staff were placed in the foyers of each tower to monitor access into the buildings (Dean 2001). The landscape architecture students' work was used as the basis for a separate consultancy for a new masterplan for the estate undertaken by the landscape architecture staff working on the project, as well as an additional consultancy for a centre at the base of the towers, which was later implemented by different consultants.

Two years later, another social work placement reported an increased sense of safety with Housing Services Officers in tower foyers and restricted access systems in all buildings. A new security company had trained staff to break down some of the barriers between people on the estate. Some of these worked as concierges in the foyers of the towers asking visitors to sign in and talking with people as they passed through. A new policy emerged to hire a percentage of tenants as cleaners and maintenance workers. The reduced numbers of syringes collected by cleaning staff indicated a reduction in the drug use and trade, and a greater perception of safety. In terms of landscape, many of the landscape students' suggestions featured in renovations undertaken by the OoH, such as one-stop shops at the base of buildings, the trimming or clearing of thick, low bushes so that visibility was greater across the estate and new signs prohibiting non-residents from entering without invitation. Lighting was improved and increased.

The project could be said to have achieved the goals of consultation and designs that met residents' needs; yet, it was not until the students were harmed that residents' reports of daily experiences of violence were taken seriously by decision makers and appropriate responses made. Then, the fact that the social work students had listened to and documented residents' fears and suggestions facilitated residents' ability to express their fears and demands to decision makers in a way that was heard. Whilst personally affected by their experiences of violence on the estate, social work students felt that, professionally, their consultation had represented residents' view and achieved a safer outcome for residents. Likewise, the landscape architecture students designed models in response to resident consultation, and fulfilled the requirements of the subject.

Social work students reported learning how to design and implement a community consultation, speak publicly, navigate power relations within a steering community, work as a (social work) team and the importance of critical thinking, context analysis and advocacy to speak out for people affected by violence and danger. What was missing was interdisciplinary learning and collaboration between the landscape architecture students and social work students. A more clearly articulated reflection process between both groups before, during and at the end of the project may have allowed interdisciplinary differences to be articulated and mutually understood.

Discussion of Interdisciplinary Learning from Case Study

The housing design project had great potential for interdisciplinary student learning and exchange about social planning. Its failure in achieving that highlights three key themes to consider for interdisciplinary student projects: the need for preparation and background information, clarifying the goals and roles of all parties, strategies for managing interdisciplinary differences and the nature of community consultation.

First, any student project should prepare students and academics by establishing clear goals and tasks and researching the issues and unaddressed recommendations of prior reports. The project was set up hastily to comply with the OoH timelines. Briefings occurred between senior academics at university, senior bureaucrats at the OoH and the CEO of the community agency in a fragmented way that neither included the social work or landscape architect academics supervising the student project, nor the students. Previous research conclusions about the housing estate that could have formed a beginning point for the project (OoH 2003) were not taken sufficiently into account at the outset. Second, since academic requirements may not align with government or community agendas in community-university partnerships, joint projects need the goals and the mutual and exclusive roles of each party clarified before the project commences, with clear processes for refining details as the project proceeds. It is important to know who holds financial and directional responsibility and the decision making processes before commencing projects. Students should be involved in developing shared understandings of ethical approaches to practice, means of communication, university and community timelines, and behavioural expectations in the community, in order to develop professional practices. From the design perspective, social work students need to understand the role of seemingly subjective activities such as drawing and designing as types of design thinking, which produce rationale outcomes despite using artistic processes.

Third, involving students from different disciplines in mixed team projects is likely to present misalignments and conflicts due to differing discipline philosophies and loyalty but, van Ewijk (2011) suggests, curiosity, respect and collaboration can make the differences productive. Academic leaders have a responsibility to structure opportunities for interdisciplinary dialogue (Griggs 2012). Such conversations were difficult to arrange due to the different physical arrangements and timing of the students' time on the site, resonating with Atkinson et al.'s (2015: 11) findings that being physically separated makes interdisciplinary communication difficult. A central aspect of interdisciplinary projects is leadership, to facilitate learning between researchers, professionals, students and community actors. Projects require a leader who can conceptualise the process and aims of the team, take the lead and come to decisions in critical situations. Leaders from different disciplines have different areas of expertise; there is not always a clear hierarchical structure (van Ewijk 2011). The lack of clear leadership in the housing design project hampered its potential for interdisciplinary exchange and learning.

Social work students saw their task more as advocating for residents' needs for safety than conveying their landscape needs. Landscape architecture students engaged well on the occasions they met residents and focused on design response to residents' request for landscape changes, resulting in plans for the supermarket, car pits and safer surfaces in the children's playground. This represents a difference in how the disciplines go about achieving aims that they agree on in principle. For designers, an issue needs a physical solution for the contribution of the discipline to be valued and effective. Dialogue between the disciplines was needed to make sense of different perspectives. The opportunity to debate the effectiveness of design as an intervention in a context of danger was missed. Hoatson and Grace (2002) claim that, while safety can be enhanced by minimising large open spaces and introducing pathways, stronger, more practical measures such as policing and strict management practices are needed. Yet, urban green spaces have been noted as reducing crime and vandalism, alleviating stress and anxiety, and improving people's wellbeing through exercise and physical activity (Lee et al. 2015a). Social work writer and activist Jackson (2011, 2012) advocates for inner-city dwellers to grow and swap food and to forage from fruit trees and edible weeds for sustainable living.

Fourth, redevelopment of public housing estates entails collaborative consultation. To do this properly is difficult and it takes time to engage and listen to stakeholders, hence the choice of the two groups of students. Mixed community research projects should include residents because researchers are then forced to listen more actively and explain the issues to them (van Ewijk 2011: 51). Although tenants were the most affected by the redevelopment, they comprised a small proportion of the membership of the Steering Committee and had less access to money, decision makers and organisational experience. Ongoing support and facilitation of diverse tenants' participation are minimum requirements to enable them to be equal players in the partnership process and improves their commitment and cooperation. The social work students' advocacy for interpreters for non-English speakers in the Steering Committee meetings is an example of this. For effective outcomes, says van Ewijk, community consultation should work with residents as equal partners, involve them in defining and analysing problems, listen to the problems they identify and invite their suggestions for solution, as did the Minister for Housing at the end of the housing research project.

These findings resonate with international scientific findings promoted in *Nature* which says: 'The best interdisciplinary science comes from the realization that there are pressing questions or problems that cannot be adequately addressed by people from just one discipline' (*Nature* Editorial 2015: 290).

Conclusion: Implications for Education Between Social Work and Urban Planning

This chapter has explored the advantages of interdisciplinary learning and practice between students of social work and the built environment. Social workers and professionals in built environment disciplines already work in collaborative ways to promote social, environmental and community aspects of spatial planning, but students are not made fully aware of the interdisciplinary potential. Students from social work could benefit from expanded learning more about practical aspects of urban planning—such as how to use geographic information systems computer mapping programs for demographic data collection and analysis, and how to conduct impact assessments and consultations about the built environment. Built environment students, already aware of the social history of planning and the city, could benefit from opportunities to engage with affected communities regarding the impact of planning and design on their lives in collaboration with social workers. Such exchanges rely on academics creating collaborative learning opportunities such as interdisciplinary dialogue in joint classes in organisational studies, conflict resolution and community development, availability of interdisciplinary electives, and creating role-play scenario-based projects about community consultations and engagement with difficult people and joint projects, particularly in local government and other forums of the built environment.

Interdisciplinary community projects run as studios or field education placements need to be well-planned and managed with collegiate clarity between academic leaders about the project objectives, including the benefits to affected people. They need leadership from academic staff to facilitate dialogue between themselves and students to exchange their philosophies, goals, theories and discipline-specific jargon. Student roles and expectations, timelines and processes for learning from each other, and ways of communicating dilemmas and resolving differences must be established at the outset. The advent of The Urban Age heightens the urgency for academic staff in urban planning, social work and other built environment disciplines to come together to create interdisciplinary learning opportunities.

References

AASW. (2010). Australian Association of Social Workers code of ethics. https://www.aasw.asn.au/document/item/1201

AILA. (2016). Australian Institute of Landscape Architects www.aila.org.au

Alborg. (2015). Alborg University. http://www.en.match.aau.dk/about-aau-matchmaking/Internal+matchmakers+and+department+profiles/Sociology+and+Social+Work/

Atkinson, J., Churilov, M., Leslie, G., McPhee, S., Noall, H., Peek, P., & Tyssen, L. (2015). Collaborative practice in Victoria local government. Report compiled from research conducted by students in the Contemporary Local Government course POLI 1034 at RMIT University, Melbourne.

Cafferty, P., & Krieg, R. (1979). Social work roles in assessing urban development. *National Association of Social Workers, 24*(3), 225–231.

Castelino, T., & Whitzman, C. (2008). The rhetoric of family violence prevention in Victoria, Australia. *Journal of Family Studies, 14*(2–3), 310–321.

Dean, A. (2001, October 3) High-rise safety fears. *The Melbourne Times,* p 3.

Dentoni, D., & Bitzer, V. (2015). The role(s) of universities in dealing with global wicked problems through multi-stakeholder initiatives. *Journal of Cleaner Production, 106,* 68–78.

Federation Square Pty Ltd Disability Action Plan. (2014). https://s3-ap-southeast-2.amazonaws.com/assets-fedsquare/uploads/2015/02/Federation-Square-Disability-Action-Plan1.pdf

Fincher, R., & Iveson, K. (2008). *Planning and diversity in the city: Redistribution, recognition and encounter.* Basingstoke: Palgrave MacMillan.

Gleeson, B. (2014). *The urban condition.* Abingdon: Taylor & Francis.

Griggs, D. (2012). Solving the world's wicked sustainability problems. Monash Sustainability Institute, Monash University Clayton. http://monash.edu/news/show/solving-the-worlds-wicked-sustainability-problems

Hillier, A. (2007). Why social work needs mapping. *Journal of Social Work Education, 43*(2), 205–222.

Hoatson, L., & Grace, M. (2002). Public housing redevelopment: Opportunity for community regeneration? *Urban Policy and Research, 20*(4), 429–441.

Holland, S., Burgess, S., Grogan-Kaylor, A., & Delva, J. (2011). Understanding neighbourhoods, communities and environments: New approaches for social work research. *British Journal of Social Work, 41*, 689–707.

Holst, H. (2006). Slums and land. *Parity, 19*(10), 6–7.

Hornby, F. (2012). *Australian local government and community development: From colonial times to the 21st century.* North Melbourne: Australian Scholarly Publishing.

IFSW (International Federation of Social Workers). (2014). http://ifsw.org/policies/definition-of-social-work

Jackson, S. (2011). One good turn(ip) deserves another. *Earth Garden*, March–May, 34–36.

Jackson, S. (2012). Spades and the city. *The Big Issue, 17*, 20–21.

Jones, D., & Truel, R. (2012). The global agenda for social work and social development: A place to link together and be effective in a globalised world. *International Social Work, 55*(4), 454–472.

Lee, A., Jordan, H., & Horsley, J. (2015a). Value of urban green spaces in promoting healthy living and wellbeing: Prospects for planning. *Risk Management and Healthcare Policy, 8*, 131–137.

Lee, B., Matthews, S., Iceland, J., & Firebaugh, G. (2015b, July). Residential inequality: Orientation and overview. *The Annals of the American Academy, AAPSS, 660*, 8–16.

Mansfield, P., McCombe, N., Panek, S., & Walker, B. (2001). *The Atherton gardens design project consultation report, unpublished student report.* Melbourne: RMIT University.

Nature Editorial. (2015). Mind meld: Interdisciplinary science must break down barriers between fields to build common ground. *Nature, 525*(7569), 289–290.

OoH (2003) Conversation with Office of Housing employee, November 2003.

PIA (Planning Institute of Australia). (2011). Accreditation policy for the recognition of Australian planning qualifications for the urban and regional planning chapter. Adopted by PIA National Council 18 November 2010 (with amendments added - effective 25th August 2011). Kingston: ACT.

Porter, L., & Barry, J. (2015). Bounded recognition: Urban planning and the textual mediation of indigenous rights in Canada and Australia. *Critical Policy Studies, 9*(1), 22–40. doi:10.1080/19460171.2014.912960.

Raxworthy, J., & Costello, S. (2012). The real unreal: Lessons from the Atherton gardens design project. In M. Dodd, F. Harrisson, & E. R. Charlesworth (Eds.), *Live projects: Designing with people* (pp. 38–50). Melbourne: RMIT University Press.

Roberts. (2012). Social impact assessment: Background report—Fitzroy. Melbourne: Roberts Evaluation Pty Ltd. http://www.dhs.vic.gov.au/__data/assets/pdf_file/0007/753199/Roberts-Social-Impact-Assessment-Fitzroy-Final-Report-2012.pdf

Sadan, E. (1997). Empowerment and community planning. Translated from Hebrew by Richard Flantz. http://www.mpow.org/elisheva_sadan_empowerment.pdf

Taubman. (2015). Taubman College, Michigan. http://taubmancollege.umich.edu/urbanplanning

Turnbull, M. (2015). Changes to the Ministry. Transcript of the Prime Minister: The Hon Malcolm Turnbull MP. http://www.malcolmturnbull.com.au/media/Ministry

UASANS (University of Applied Sciences and Arts). (2015). Northwestern Switzerland, School of Social Work. http://www.fhnw.ch/socialwork/iss

University of Southern California. (2015) Master of Planning/Master of Social Work.https://msw.usc.edu/academic/concentrations/community-organization-planning-and-administration

van Ewijk, H. (2011). Collaboration in community research. *European Journal of Social Work, 14*(1), 41–52.

Vinson, T. (1997). Report on the Waterloo Community Development Project, School of Social Work, University of New South Wales.

Vinson, T., & Rawsthorne, M. (2015). *Dropping off the edge: Persistent communal disadvantage in Australia*. Richmond: Jesuit Social Services, Catholic Social Services.

Willingham, R. (2015). Prisons failing to make the state safe: Ombudsman. *The Age*, 18 September. http://www.theage.com.au/victoria/half-young-offenders-in-victoria-returning-to-jail-within-two-years-new-report-20150917-gjommz.html

Conclusion: Urban Themes in Twenty-First Century Social Work

Charlotte Williams

In concluding the book, it seems fitting to restate the argument that the need to provide pertinent answers and sustainable responses to the most troubling issues of our time lies within our reach. The impacts of globalisation and associated processes of urbanisation have far-reaching consequences that cannot be left to neglect, drift and mismanagement. Cities can promote or mitigate sustainable development; they can exacerbate or ameliorate poverty and inequality, segregation and exclusion, environmental degradation and, thereby, affect human wellbeing as a whole. The city is, at one and the same time, local and enmeshed in these global processes—and these global conditions are acutely experienced and influenced in the places and spaces of cities. The way in which cities are planned, managed and developed will have critical impact as,

C. Williams
School of Global, Urban and Social Studies,
RMIT University,
GPO Box 2476, Melbourne,
VIC 3001, Australia

© The Editor(s) (if applicable) and The Author(s) 2016
C. Williams (ed.), *Social Work and the City*,
DOI 10.1057/978-1-137-51623-7

by 2050, urban dwellers double in number to encompass nearly three quarters of the world's population. The UN-Habitat 2012 Manifesto for Cities accordingly argues, 'the battle for a more sustainable future will be won or lost in cities' (UN-Habitat 2014: 6)

It may be all too easy to regard effecting change to the future of cities as simply the preserve of the planners, architects, engineers and policy-makers in city hall—or, indeed, the prerogative of private developers. It would be simply wrong to imagine that matters of the use of public space, public resources and public service delivery are out of our hands. Prioritising an urban agenda is critical to extending the historic mission and values of social work. The commitment to social justice, extending care and social support, and bolstering social sustainability can be made tangible and measurable on this scale. This text has put forward the proposition that we are key stakeholders in this process of change, working with and on behalf of the most vulnerable and marginalised communities in any city anywhere to maximise their involvement and voice, to assist in meeting their needs and to minimise the impacts of hostile urban policies. We have ownership over and a unique access to these matters in ways other professional groupings do not. To this end, social workers must be co-producers in crafting what UN-Habitat call 'a new urban paradigm for the city we need' (2014: 8).

In presenting *the city* as a new point of departure for contemporary social work, the re-visiting and re-visioning that has been the enterprise of this book extends the focus of our disciplinary concerns and sharpens the lens of our professional remit. Part of the re-working has been to proffer the city as a creative platform for forging change and to eschew the negative scripts of the city that have dominated much of social work discourse. This is not an empty celebration of city-living. Cities undoubtedly have deleterious effects on human wellbeing, but they are also the seat of change. Opportunity and freedoms accompany risk and insecurities in the metropolis in equal measure. In the diversity-proximity nexus, solidarities as well as exclusivities are generated (Tonkiss 2013). Care, co-operation, reciprocity and exchange are central and everyday elements of city-living as much as are isolation, neglect and discrimination. People make and people lose their livelihoods in cities. The *urban condition* reflects these dualisms and so should our response.

If the evolution of the profession were shackled to the capitalist city in reactive and compensatory roles—or what I called the 'street cleaner model'—then a reconsideration of the various ways in which the city has come to be explained opens up new ways of envisioning the social work role. Through the Marxist lens, we understood the geography of inequalities and the skewed class-based distribution of power on spatial scale. Yet, Marxist urban researchers depicted a rather static city based on capitalist accumulation, wealth and poverty, gentrification and degradation, consumption and waste. These understandings of the capitalist city remain central but their limitations in explaining the complexities and serendipities of contemporary city life and the multiple perspectives that can be gleaned through lived experiences and human agency are evident. In understanding cities as lived and relational spaces in Lefebvre style, it is possible to take into account the structural considerations of inequality and disadvantage whilst engaging with multi-dimensional and multiple spaces for social action and change.

Making explicit the city as a sphere of action in which pragmatically to exploit political leverage and to capture and crystallise change efforts in collaboration with significant others has been one objective of this text. By the by, with others, I have posited the implications of this re-positioning of social work as productive route to forging a credible and legitimised social work identity. It is not too far a call to suggest professional social workers as being poised to emerge as practice leaders in creating productive collaborations of practice involving the vast collective that is human service workers, care and support workers, community and youth workers, and users of services in both the formal and informal welfare economies of the city. Care and social support are vital urban resources and fundamental to economic development. Demonstrating civic leadership in forging urban innovations in meeting needs is within our remit. There is a need to change values, to insert ethical considerations into decision-making at every level and across the relevant professions and disciplines. Social work is well-placed to promote shared values for an ethical leadership in the city. The caveat lies in the ability to shift from a defensive narrative of resistance and move to a confident and informed narrative of change built on a keen attention to contemporary trends and astute insight into the dynamics and possibilities of the neo-liberal city we have.

The moment is opportune. A number of important developments signal the timeliness of this shift of focus. At international level, the UN-Habitat programme has launched the Habitat III World Urban Campaign: Better City, Better Life and established the Urban Thinkers Campus to take forward a number of activities, events and debates aimed at coordinating and shaping the future of urban spaces in the twenty-first century. The campaign is working with national governments, encouraging them to launch their own national urban campaigns in consultation with civil society, private sector agencies and local authorities. An outcome of this programme will be the establishment of a New Urban Paradigm aimed at generating solutions to the most critical urban issues (UN-Habitat 2016). Governments everywhere are accordingly gearing up for the urban agenda.

Closer to home, regional and local authorities are developing local frameworks and initiatives with communities and neighbourhoods as active participants in metropolitan decision-making. The default setting of new governance now aims to engage with local citizens and NGOs to tackle problems with local knowledges in which capacity at local level is built and new experts by experience emerge, rather than relying on the imposition of top-down centralised solutions. A considerable momentum exists to incorporate social dimensions into planning for sustainability. Now, more than ever before, urban planners are engaging with different disciplinary orientations; as Fincher and Iveson argue (2008: 216), 'the provision of social services has been placed firmly within the scope of planning', and governments are concerned with the interstices of social sustainability. The space for collaboration, co-production, co-design and experimentation is ripe for exploitation and for asserting alternative perspectives to the mainstream and conventional approaches. New allies await.

Moreover, a revolution is happening by stealth as part of a wider process of reclaiming control over social welfare and wellbeing. Groups and various forms of community motivated by an ethic of care and shared social responsibility are active in communal spaces, both virtual and actual, reclaiming the unused and the disused land spaces of cities. In the informalities of the city, alternative provisionings are being generated, and new ways of meeting need and new orthodoxies of care are being forged on what Tonkiss calls the 'surfaces of common life' (2013: 161). This common life, the new localisms and the infra-states generated are 'one to watch'. These movements and emergent developments require support, encouragement, evaluation and wider articulation as part of a critical urban social work practice.

In putting forward the idea of social work as engaged in a *co-operative city by design* model, I do not seek to hark back to the building of utopias, blueprints or urban ideals. The urban planners, architects, landscape architects and those in city hall have long acknowledged the discrepancy between vision and implementation, planned action and outcomes, and the ways in which the best-laid plans become derailed in power shifts, policy developments, contestation and contingency (Stevenson 2013). It will never be easy to capture the surprises and the unplanned and emergent developments of such a multi-scalar, multi-actor arena. But what this concept may signal is purposefulness, collaboration, innovation and intent on the part of public professionals to produce or craft something 'better', more equitable and more sustainable than we have now. It locates social work as a normative activity, not simply a technical one, immersed not detached, as ethical and engaged citizens of the city and as actors within it. It implies a holistic model of change which incorporates the overlapping, complex and intertwined nature of social problems and the need for cross-disciplinary and cross-professional responses. It argues for the combination of knowledges and expertise, exploiting the localised and experiential, rather than reliant on distant and centralised expertise. It points to the generation of practice and academic knowledge through research, education and advocacy.

The potential of our intervention at city level is clear and the assertion of our social work values never more keenly expressed. Perhaps a lesson of this text is a stronger focus in social work education on the skills and opportunities for inter-disciplinary collaboration in teaching and learning; skills in influencing policy and in generating policy alternatives; skills in engaging user perspectives and capacities; a sophisticated multi-cultural literacy; and, above all, being able to read and know the city and its dynamic. It will be up to educators to muster the enthusiasm of students, engaging them in innovative, cross-disciplinary projects that generate real and beneficial outcomes as part of their learning experiences. The rewards of cross-disciplinary exploration are immense, as this book demonstrates.

The plea to practitioners is towards the presumption of leadership in a concerted and co-ordinated collaboration at city level and towards articulating the place of social work in shaping the future city. Bolstering the substantive dimensions of urban citizenship and the *right to the city* for all, in Lefebvre's sense, requires multi-level action underpinned by a strong value base. This notion of urban citizenship takes us well beyond the ways in which citizenship has conventionally been understood. Its referents are not a national boundary or the legal status of nation-state denied to so many urban dwellers but, rather, a reference to the enactments, felt membership, habitation, access, participation and agency within the common life of the city.

As for research, there are endless possibilities that social work can contribute to an urban research agenda, as outlined in Chap. 4. High on the policy list will be a focus on diversity and the nature of superdiverse neighbourhoods; on care and caring, and the capacities of communities to provide care; work on social cohesion, sustainability and work on youth and the city. New forms of community expression and new configurations of need beyond category will need to be captured; the nature of the links between rural and urban living explored in relation to access to services; and the role of technology in access to information and services as the digital divide increasingly becomes a marker and cause of poverty and inequality. Research on social enterprises and their beneficial effects, ethnographies of need in place and strengths-based community evaluations are but a few from my ever growing list of ideas. Urban studies such as these, engaging a range of disciplines, have an important role to play in providing a robust evidence base for policy and practice.

There is a final point to be made here about *Social Work and the City* in addition to the points made above about impact, leverage, timeliness and opportunity, and social work values. It is about the importance of vision: envisioning the type of *the future we want—the city we need*, to use UN-Habitat phraseology (2014). In times of rapid change, business as usual or muddling through is not enough. Change compels us to move beyond conventional wisdoms and our comfort zone in working out new ways forward and looking towards new destinations (Albrechts

2010). There are new ways to think about what resources are available, how they are used and how they are distributed. There are new concepts and methods to develop and considerations of how these translate into practice arenas to be worked through. Transformation and change rely on visions, possible futures and generating an alternative conceptual lens. They rely on sound analysis of what is and creativity in suggesting what might be. Such visions have the power to counter complacency, to provide actors with views of the future that can be shared, to motivate towards change and to provide a clear sense of direction. Generating such a vision is a collective process. This book has sought to advance social work's place in crafting the vision of a just, equitable and sustainable city for all.

I conclude by thanking my collaborators in this endeavour.

References

Albrechts, L. (2010). More of the same is not enough! How could strategic spatial planning be instrumental in dealing with the challenges ahead? *Environment and Planning B: Planning and Design, 37,* 1115–1127.

Fincher, R., & Iveson, K. (2008). *Planning and diversity in the city: Redistribution, recognition and encounter.* Basingstoke: Palgrave Macmillan.

Stevenson, D. (2013). *The city.* Cambridge: Cambridge Polity Press.

Tonkiss, F. (2013). *Cities by design: The social life of urban form.* Cambridge: Polity Press.

UN-Habitat. (2014). The future we want, the city we need. http://unhabitat.org/the-future-we-want-the-city-we-need/. Accessed 11 Jan 2016.

UN-Habitat. (2016). Urban thinkers campus. http://unhabitat.org/urban-thinkers/. Accessed 11 Jan 2016.

Index

A

ableism, 124, 175, 177, 182, 184, 189, 190
Addams, Jane, 54, 265
age-friendly approach, 152, 153, 158, 160–2, 163–6
ageing, 153–5, 160, 162
agile working arrangements, 26
alienation, 7, 28
alternative moral landscape, 122
ambivalence, 17, 132
Amin, A., 57, 77
anomie, 7, 28
anthropological approach, 76
anti-racist, 138
area-based initiatives, 61, 63, 84
area effects, 59, 104–6
Aronson, J., 160, 201
Arthurson, K., 248

At Home/Chez Soi project, 225
Atkinson, J., 59, 266, 275–6
Atkinson, R., 105, 106
austerity, 9, 17, 44, 81, 112, 124, 165, 196, 197
Australia, 74, 75, 121, 159, 175, 227, 235–40, 262–4
    concentrations of poverty, 240–3
    concern for human services, 248–50
    disadvantage of resource access, 243–6
    social problems, 246–8
    urban social work, 251–3
Australian Association of Social Workers (AASW), 252, 261
Australian Bureau of Statistics, 240

Note: Page number followed by 'n' refers to footnotes.

© The Editor(s) (if applicable) and The Author(s) 2016
C. Williams (ed.), *Social Work and the City*,
DOI 10.1057/978-1-137-51623-7

Australian Common Ground
        Alliance (ACGA), 227
Australian Institute of Landscape
        Architects (AILA), 262

B

Baines, Donna, 124
banlieues, 128, 144
Barnardos, 48
Barry, J., 265
Bartlett, R., 164
Bauböck, R., 134
Becker, G., 157
Begun, A.L., 116
Belgian Ageing Studies, 157
Beyond Shelter Inc., 225
Bigby, C., 181, 184
Blacks, Freed, 50
Boccagni, Paolo, 137, 138
Booth, Charles, 100
Brenner, N, 21–2
Brueggermann, W.G., 80, 92–3
Bryant, L., 112
Buffel, T., 158
Burgess, Ernest, 30
Burke, T., 236, 239, 240, 243, 246,
        248, 252

C

café culture, 238
Cafferty, P., 266, 267
Canada, 10, 84, 225, 265
Canadian disability, 175
Canadian social work, 183
care, 6–8, 56, 59–60, 85, 88–9, 160,
        194–6, 200, 282, 283
    in the formal economy, 198–203

in the informal economy, 203–5
social work, 207–9
unpaid care work, 205–7
care deficit, 193
Casey, B., 220
Castelino, T., 265
Castells, Manuel, 208
    The Urban Question, 31
central business districts (CBDs),
        238, 241, 242, 244, 245
Charity Organisation Society (COS),
        48, 49, 99–101, 103
Chenoweth, Lesley, 184
Cheshire, L., 244
Chicago School, 30, 31, 53, 100,
        101, 106, 128, 143
Child First, 84
Christensen, P., 79
cities, 15, 17, 281–3
    as community, 54–5
    engaging with the urban—
        theoretical trajectories,
        36–8
    as environment, 55–6
    historical intersections, 46–51
    as machine, 52–3
    new urban ascendancy, 18–23
    opportunities of, 23–7
    orientation, themes and
        approaches, 5–9
    as system, 53–4
    theorising, 27–36
citizenship, 8, 25, 51, 65, 123,
        162–5, 174, 204, 286
city space, 19, 32, 35, 58, 77, 80
civil society, 57, 63–6, 89
codes of ethics, 208, 226
College of Design and Social
        Context, 264

Colonial Poor Laws, 50
Columbia University in New York, 267
Common Ground, 227, 228
commonplace diversity, 131, 144
community, 8, 19, 20, 35, 44, 54–5,
        61, 84, 92–3, 105–7, 113,
        116, 156, 180, 200, 266
Community First in Wales, 63
Community Organization, 267
computer hardware, 263
Conradson, D., 107
Convention on the Rights of Persons
        with Disabilities (CRPD),
        176, 183
co-operative city by design model,
        57, 285
Costello, Susie, 125
couch surfing, 220
Coulton, C., 103, 107
Council to Homeless Persons, 242
counter-discursive strategies, 223–4
Crul, Maurice, 144, 145
Culhane, D.P., 225–6
cultural sensitivity, 139–40
Cunningham, I., 201–2

D
Daly, T., 204
D'Cruz, H., 72
Delgado, M., 55, 76, 77, 108
Department of Sociology and
        Social Work at Aalborg
        University, 267
Dickens, Charles, 47
digital technology, 26
Director of Housing, 273
disability, 173–5

activism, 186–8
social and cultural constructions
        of, 175–7
social work and, 181–6
spatial exclusions and inclusions,
        178–81
Disability Action Plan, 267
disablement, 174, 178
diswelfares, 52
divercities, 15, 122
diversification of diversity, 123, 130,
        139, 144
diversity, 1, 16, 17, 20, 29, 30, 111,
        123, 130, 133–6
Dodson, J., 245
Dominelli, Lena, 145
        Green Social Work, 22
Durkheim, Emile, 28

E
East End of London, 100
Engels, Freidrich, 28
        *The Conditions of the Working
        Class in England* (1892), 28
entrepreneurial city, 65, 128, 216, 250
environmental sustainability, 4, 8,
        15, 38, 55, 64, 111
ethical care, 199
ethic of indifference, 19
ethnic minority groups, 221–2
European cities, 129, 131, 132, 143,
        144, 225, 246
European Federation of National
        Associations Working
        with the Homeless
        (FEANTSA), 218
European Union (EU), 222

Evers, A., 64, 88, 89
Expulsions, 133

F

Fabian policy research tradition, 99
family violence, 220, 247
Family Violence Royal Commission, 242
Federation Square, 267
Ferguson, Harry, 114
Field Educators, 74
Fincher, R., 36, 77, 79, 90, 265, 284
Flinders University, 267
focus group, 73, 74, 77–80, 87, 264–8
Folbre, N., 208
Forde, C., 87–8
Foresight Future of Cities Program, 121
formal economy, 198–203
Foyer Model, 227
France, 128, 130, 227
Frawley, P., 181, 184

G

Galcanova, L., 156
Geldof, D., 123, 166, 251
gentrification, 26, 32, 128, 144, 238, 283
geographic information systems (GIS), 112, 115, 263
geographies of care, 59, 107
Gini coefficient, 237
Gleeson, Brendan, 178
Global Agenda for Social Work, 3, 260

Global Network of Age Friendly Cities (GNAFC), 162
global north, 22, 159
good city, 8, 36, 223, 229
Goodman, R., 124, 125
Grace, M., 266, 276
Graham, M., 134
Grand Prix, 78
Grattan Institute, 238, 249
Gray, M., 199
Greenfield, E.A., 161
grey economy, 194, 196, 203, 204
Griggs, D., 269

H

Haggerty, Rosanne, 227
hamstrung, 81
harmonious cities, 154
Harvey, David
    Social Justice and the City, 31
heroic agency, 3
heterogeneity, 21, 110, 153, 176
hidden dysfunction, 75
high-profile domestic violence, 87
Hillier, A.E., 112, 263, 271
Hill, Octavia, 48, 54
Hoatson, L., 266, 276
Holland, Sally, 113, 263, 265
homelessness in Western cities, 124, 125, 215, 217, 218
    exclusionary urban policies, 221–3
    gendered urban spaces, 219–21
    Housing First approaches, 225–9
    urban homelessness, 218–19
Hornby, F., 266
Horschelmann, K., 58, 79

hostile architectural responses, 79
housing design project, 272–4
Housing First approaches, 125, 224–9
Housing Services Officers, 273
Hull House, 48, 128
Hulse, K., 236, 239–41, 243, 246,
    248, 252
human rights, 15, 66, 91, 125, 174,
    176, 218, 223, 227, 251

I

illegal care, 203, 204
immigration policies, 202, 207
indignado movement, 16
informal economy, 203–5
Inheriting the City, 129
inner-city public spaces, 218, 219
Institute for Social Planning and
    Urban Development, 267
integration, 8, 20, 64, 134–6, 222
inter-culturalisation, 134–5, 139–40
inter-disciplinary approach, 107,
    125, 133, 278
International Federation of Social
    Work (IFSW), 159, 183,
    252, 260–1
intersectional approach, 186
inter-sectionality, 137, 139–40
Ioakimidis, V., 165
Isaacs, B., 152
Iveson, K., 36, 77, 79, 90, 265, 284

J

Jack, Gordon, 104
Jeyasingham, Dharman, 26,
    108, 109

Jindi Family and Community
    Centre, 249, 251
John A. Hartford Foundation, 159

K

Kathryn Church, 174
Katz, B., 151–2
Kelaher, M., 59, 248
Kelly, J., 244
Kennelly, J., 216
Kintrea, K., 59, 105, 106
Koch, R, 35
Krieg, R., 266–7
Kucera, Christina, 72

L

Lala Ashenberg Straussner, S., 54
landscape architecture, 260–4,
    272, 276
landscapes of care, 76, 94
Latham, A., 35
Lavalette, M., 6
League for Social Reconstruction, 195
League of Coloured Peoples, 48
Lebeaux, C.N., 188–9
Lefebvre, Henri, 32–3, 78, 79,
    108, 217
The Urban Revolution, 31
Liberal government, 121
lifetime neighbourhoods, 154
Lightfoot, E., 105
liquid migration, 141
liquid social work, 114
Liveability Options in Outer
    Suburban Melbourne, 244
Lloyd, L.H., 165

local governance, 62–6
Loughran, H., 116
Lynch, D., 87–8

M

majority-minority cities, 129, 130,
144, 145
Manchester, 28, 158, 162
marginalisation, 159, 218
Martin, S., 124, 125
Marxist analysis, 28, 31, 32, 34, 53,
283
Marx, Karl, 28, 47
mass disasters, 21, 22
Master of Social Work, 267
master servant relationship, 83
Mayhew, Robert, 47
McCann, M.E., 116
McKenzie, Lisa, 112
McKenzie, S., 61, 62
McLaughlin, T.C., 219, 226
mega-cities, 23
Mehrotra, G., 221
Melbourne, 12, 22, 73, 75, 84,
125, 237, 240–5, 249,
260, 267
Melbourne Cup, 78
Merriman, P., 115
metropolis, 2, 52, 103, 104,
194, 282
Meyer, C., 27, 52
migration, 4, 18, 20, 44, 110, 127,
129, 130, 133–6
Minister for Cities, 121, 260
minority ethnic groups, 127, 157
mixed community, 276
mixed neighbourhood policies, 222

Mostowska, M., 223, 224
Mowbray, M., 63, 64, 85–6
multi-culturalism, 134, 285
multi-dimensional approach, 34, 80,
164, 283
Mumford, Lewis, 153

N

National Institute for Care and
Clinical Excellence
(NICE), 163
nationality, 131, 134, 221
National Law Centre on
Homelessness and Poverty
in Washington, 218
Naturally Occurring Retirement
Communities (NORCs), 161
Neely, B., 58
neighbourhood effects, 248
neighbourhood exclusion, 156
neoliberal city, 221
neo-liberalism, 81, 195, 196, 206
New Public Management, 64, 198,
205, 207
new transnational urbanism, 20
new urban ascendancy, 18–23
New Urban Paradigm, 284
New York City, 72, 161,
189, 227
New York Times, 72
Neysmith, S., 201
Nicholson, T., 250
non-governmental organisations
(NGOs), 6, 284
non-traditional settings, 77, 108
North America, 30, 159
Northern California, 157

Northwest Switzerland University of Applied Sciences and Arts, 267
NSPCC, 48

O

O'Brien, M., 79
O'Connor, D., 164
Office of Housing (OoH), 268, 269, 273–5
Organisation for Economic Cooperation and Development (OECD), 153, 193, 240

P

Pain, R., 158
Parker, S., 189
Park, Robert, 30, 128
Parliamentary Inquiry, 244, 247
participation re-development, 92
Passaro, J., 219
Pearson, G., 47
personalisation, 160, 193
person in environment (PIE), 55
philanthropy, 48
Phillips, Kolko, 54
Phillipson, C., 123
physical inaccessibility, 178
piecemeal social engineering, 99
Pierson, P., 197
Pinnegar, S., 241
place-making concept, 84, 85
place-shaping concept, 84
Plan Melbourne, 73

Planning Institute of Australia (PIA), 261–2
policy activist organisations, 218
political correctness, 134
popular social work, 6
Porter, L., 265
poverty, 4, 17, 19, 49, 102, 105, 110, 124, 125, 157, 239, 264, 286
pragmatic policy-oriented research, 100
Prince, J., 124
Protestant Christianity, 29
public services, 44, 59, 199, 282

Q

Qualitative Geographical Information Systems (QGIS), 112

R

Randolph, B., 216, 219
Rawsthorne, M., 246, 263–5
Raxworthy, Julian, 125
Ray, M., 123
resource access, 239, 243–6
rhythms of city life, 33
Richmond, Mary, 103
rights-based approach, 163, 182, 190
right to the city, 33, 34, 78, 79, 286
RMIT University, 73, 74, 264, 269
Rogowski, S., 44
Romero, B., 208
Rotterdam, 127, 221
rough sleepers, 222, 228
Rowles, G., 156–7
Rubery, 202

S

Samura, M., 58
Sassen, Saskia, 133, 204
Saunders, Doug, 143
Scharf, T., 156, 157
Schmid, C., 21–2
School of Global, Urban and Social
    Studies, 264
School of Social Work, 267
Schrooten, M., 110
Scotch, Richard, 178
self-exploitation, 200, 206
service user, 26, 45, 83, 107, 113,
    114, 196n3, 199, 201, 226
Settlement movement, 48, 99–101,
    103
Shaw, I., 99, 100, 109, 251
Sheldon, S., 152
Shergold, P., 250
Simmel, Georg, 28, 29
Sipe, N., 245
Smith, A., 160
Smith, S., 61, 85
Smyth, P., 250
social activism, 203
Social Atlas, 240
social care, 59, 88, 158, 159
Social Cities, 249
social exclusion, 80, 131, 155–8
social inclusion, 63, 152, 155–8, 224
social issues, 5, 21, 25, 50,
    100–2, 122
social justice, 7, 31, 57, 91, 92, 97,
    159, 282
social movement, 32, 51, 66, 80,
    187, 194, 195
social policy, 11, 24, 48, 63, 155,
    187, 228

social sustainability, 8, 57, 61–2, 92,
    94, 282, 284
social work, 1, 2, 5, 6, 9, 71, 94–5,
    188–90
    age-friendly practice and
        citizenship, 163–5
    care, 88–9, 207–9
    changing attitudes towards older
        people, 162–3
    city as community, 54–5
    city as environment, 55–6
    city as machine, 52–3
    city as system, 53–4
    constraints, challenges and
        opportunities, 81–4
    consultation process, 270–2
    developing an age-friendly
        practice, 160–2
    and disability, 181–6
    disability activism, 186–8
    education, implications for,
        277–8
    engaging with the urban—
        theoretical trajectories, 36–8
    evolution and development of, 43
    experiences of inclusion and
        exclusion, 155–8
    focus group, 264–8
    historical intersections, 46–51
    housing design project, outcomes
        of, 272–4
    interdisciplinary learning, 274–7
    leadership and innovation in city,
        89–91
    local governance and civil society,
        63–6
    new urban ascendancy, 18–23
    opportunities of the city, 23–7

place and space, 57–60
place-based considerations, 84–6
planning cities for ages, 165–7
power, social justice and city,
    78–81
practice issues, 86–8
practice tensions for, 223–4
preparation, 268–70
principles, 93–4
re-examination and a
    re-positioning of, 45
refreshed urban practices, 91–3
research, 98
    building place and space,
        103–9
    collaborations and
        partnerships, 115–16
    new possibilities, 109–15
    traditions and social work,
        98–102
rethinking, 251–3
revisiting urban practice, 73–4
scale, 60–1
social and cultural constructions
    of disability, 175–7
social sustainability, 61–2
social work with older people,
    159–60
spatial exclusions and inclusions,
    178–81
and superdiversity, 136–9
synergies, 260–4
theorising the city, 27–36
urban environments, 159–60
visualising urban spaces, 74–8
socio-economic redistribution, 187
Soydan, H., 99
spatiality theory, 58, 108, 217

spatial segregation, 143, 144
Special Measures for Urban Issues, 221
Spiller, M., 244
sporadic riots, 128
Stainton, T., 182, 183, 188
Steering Committee, 269–71, 273,
    276, 277
Stevenson, D., 33
street cleaner model, 52, 57
Street to Home services, 228
subversive strategies, 224
superdiversity
    beyond methodological
        nationalism, 131–3
    inter-cultural competences,
        cultural sensitivity and
        inter-sectionality, 139–40
    migration and diversity, policy
        responses, 133–6
    as organisational challenge, 140
    scenarios, 144–6
    social work and, 136–9
    transmigrants as new challenge,
        141–3
    urban context, 128–31, 143–4
    and urban policies, 140–1
*Superdiversity in the Heart of
    Europe*, 129
supra-local actors, 25, 90
Sure Start, 84
survival sex, 221
Sydney, 237, 241, 245, 268
Sykorova, D., 156

T

Taylorist scientific model, 200
temporary foreign workers, 130, 135

temporary visa care workers, 202, 203
Thrift, N., 57, 77
Titmuss, R., 52
Tonkiss, Fran, 18–19, 36, 46, 65, 92, 217, 285
Townsend, P., 152
Toynbee Hall, 48, 128
transmigrants, 105, 110, 123, 141–3
Turnbull, Malcolm, 260

U

UN 2012: Better Urban Future, 24
unemployment, 19, 47, 145, 181, 189
UN-Habitat, 282, 284, 286
United Kingdom, 39, 102, 128, 152, 175, 240
United Nations, 24
United Nations Convention on the Rights of Persons with Disabilities (CRPD), 176, 189
Universities of Detroit and Iowa, 267
University of Michigan, 267
University of Southern California, 267
unpaid care work, 205–7
Unwin, 202
urban age, 2, 16, 56, 151–2, 259
    city, opportunities of, 23–7
    engaging with the urban— theoretical trajectories, 36–8
    new urban ascendancy, 18–23
    theorising the city, 27–36
urban areas, 157
urban Australia, 237–40
    concentrations of poverty, 240–3
    concern for human services, 248–50
    disadvantage of resource access, 243–6
    social problems, 246–8
    urban social work, 251–3
urban context, 37, 143–4, 155
urban crisis, 7, 9, 17, 31, 52
urban environments
    age-friendly practice and citizenship, 163–5
    age-friendly practice, developing an, 160–2
    changing attitudes towards older people, 162–3
    experiences of inclusion and exclusion, 155–8
    social work with older people, 159–60
urban informality, 65
urbanisation, 2, 29, 34, 153–5, 173, 221
urban life, 29, 37, 132, 174, 179, 189
urbanology, 37, 117
urban planning, 12, 36, 125, 252, 260–4, 266, 267, 277–8
urban policies, 32, 110, 124, 125, 140–1, 153, 216, 221–3
urban social work, 71, 94–5
    care, 88–9
    city as community, 54–5
    city as environment, 55–6
    city as machine, 52–3
    city as system, 53–4
    constraints, challenges and opportunities, 81–4
    consultation process, 270–2

education, implications for, 277–8
focus group, 264–8
housing design project, outcomes
    of, 272–4
interdisciplinary learning, 274–7
leadership and innovation in city,
    89–91
place-based considerations, 84–6
power, social justice and city,
    78–81
practice issues, 86–8
preparation, 268–70
principles, 93–4
refreshed urban practices, 91–3
rethinking, 251–3
revisiting urban practice, 73–4
synergies, 260–4
visualising urban spaces, 74–8
urban sociology, 31, 99, 106
urban studies, 27, 30, 31, 35, 36, 286
Urban Thinkers Campus, 284
USA, 31, 50, 99, 100, 102, 129, 159,
    239, 246, 248, 265, 267

V

van Blerk, L., 58, 79
van Eijk, J., 221
van Ewijk, H., 8, 24, 57, 123, 275
vertical communities, 75
Vertovec, Steven, 129, 130
Vick, A., 185
Victorian London, 50
Vinson, Tony, 246, 263–5, 268
Vulnerability Assessment for
    Mortgage, Petrol and
    Inflation Risks and Expenses
    (VAMPIRE), 245

W

Wacquant, Loïc, 144
Watt, P., 216
Webb, S., 49, 82
Weber, Max, 28, 29
Webster, M., 199–200
welfare hubs, 59, 76
welfare state activities, 179–80
wellbeing, 3, 8, 15, 19, 22, 25, 55,
    57, 104, 112, 163, 262
Wessendorf, Susanne, 144
Western cities, 215, 217, 218
    exclusionary urban policies,
        221–3
    gendered urban spaces,
        219–21
    Housing First approaches,
        225–9
    urban homelessness, 218–19
Whitzman, C., 247, 265
wicked issues, 21, 110, 259
Wilensky, H.L., 188–9
Williams, Charlotte, 134
Williams, Monte, 72
Wirth, Louis, 29
World Health Organisation (WHO),
    152, 153, 158, 247

Y

Young, I.M., 184

Z

Zapf, M.K., 55, 103
Zimbalist, S.E., 102
zones of transition, 157
Zufferey, C., 124